CONCEPTUALIZING CRUELTY TO CHILDREN IN NINETEENTH-CENTURY ENGLAND

Ashgate Studies in Childhood, 1700 to the Present

Series Editor: Claudia Nelson, Texas A&M University

This series recognizes and supports innovative work on the child and on literature for children and adolescents that informs teaching and engages with current and emerging debates in the field. Proposals are welcome for interdisciplinary and comparative studies by humanities scholars working in a variety of fields, including literature; book history, periodicals history, and prior culture and the sociology of texts; theater, film, musicology, and performance studies; history, including the history of education; gender studies; art history and visual culture; cultural studies; and religion.

Also in this series:

Conceptualizing Cruelty to Children in Nineteenth-Century England

Literature, Representation, and the NSPCC

MONICA FLEGEL
Lakehead University, Canada

ASHGATE

Published by
Ashgate Publishing Limited
Wey Court East
Union Road
Farnham
Surrey, GU9 7PT
England

Ashgate Publishing Company
Suite 420
101 Cherry Street
Burlington
VT 05401-4405
USA

www.ashgate.com

British Library Cataloguing in Publication Data
Flegel, Monica
Conceptualizing cruelty to children in nineteenth-century England : literature, representation, and the NSPCC
    1. Child abuse – England – Public opinion 2. Child abuse in literature 3. English literature – 19th century – History and criticism 4. Social work with children – England – History – 19th century 5. Public opinion – England – History – 19th century
    I. Title
    362.7'6'0942'09034

Library of Congress Cataloging-in-Publication Data
Flegel, Monica.
  Conceptualizing cruelty to children in nineteenth-century England : literature, representation, and the NSPCC / by Monica Flegel.
    p. cm.
  Includes bibliographical references.
  ISBN 978-0-7546-6456-7 (alk. paper) — ISBN 978-0-7546-9311-6 (ebook) 1. English fiction—19th century—History and criticism. 2. Children in literature. 3. Child abuse in literature. 4. Children—Great Britain—Social conditions. 5. National Society for the Prevention of Cruelty to Children. 6. Literature and society—England—History—19th century. I. Title.

  PR878.C5F54 2009
  820.9'3526945—dc22

2008044427

ISBN: 978-0-7546-6456-7

Mixed Sources
Product group from well-managed
forests and other controlled sources
www.fsc.org Cert no. SA-COC-1565
© 1996 Forest Stewardship Council

Printed and bound in Great Britain by
MPG Books Ltd, Bodmin, Cornwall.

Contents

Acknowledgments

There are many to thank for the support I have received during the course of writing this book. First and foremost, I am grateful for the support of the National Society for the Prevention of Cruelty to Children (NSPCC), and in particular for the assistance provided by Nicholas Malton, the archivist at the NSPCC Library and Information Service in London. I would also like to thank the Institute for Historical Research and the Mellon Foundation for making that research possible, and the Social Sciences and Humanities Council of Canada, the Province of Alberta, and the University of Alberta for the financial support they provided during the course of this project.

Numerous friends and colleagues have read, discussed, and evaluated this manuscript at many points in its history. First and foremost, I would like to thank Peter Sinnema for his kindness, his difficult questions, and his insightful critiques—much of what is best in this manuscript comes from his guidance. I am also grateful for the assistance of Susan Hamilton, whose patience and wisdom continue to inspire me, and of Raymond Jones, whose eye for detail caught many an error. I was very lucky to enjoy the benefits of a fabulous writing group: my love and thanks to Gabrielle Zezulka-Mailloux, Karen Clark, Laura Davis, and Kelly Laycock for their friendship, and for the work they put into reading numerous drafts of this project. My gratitude as well to Laura Berry and to Lydia Murdoch, who provided advice and asked questions that forced me to make this a better manuscript, and whose own work provided the model against which I judge my own.

I would like to thank my friends, family, and colleagues, who provided me with emotional support, advice, and encouragement during the course of this project, and Vickie and Symba, who gave all the support it was in their power to give.

Finally, I would like to thank the staff, and the families and children of the Saskatoon Crisis Nursery, for it was my experiences working there that led me to this topic.

Introduction

In *The Queen's Reign for Children* (1897), William Clarke Hall writes that, prior to the passage of the "Children's Charter" in 1889, "there was no such offence known to English Law as the mere ill-treatment, no such offence as the mere neglect of a child. The Society resolved to create these offences."[1] Hall refers here to the National Society for the Prevention of Cruelty to Children (NSPCC), and to that organization's role in developing and disseminating the concept of what is now known as child abuse. While cruelty to children undoubtedly existed before the advent of this law, Hall's statement reminds us that it only emerged as a distinct legal concept in England in the late nineteenth century. Previously, as Hall argues in *The Law Relating to Children* (1905), it was true "that in some cases 'ill-treatment' might constitute a common assault, that 'neglect' might be an offence under the Poor Law Amendment Act, 1868, if it were to supply food, and if it caused *serious* injury to the child's health, and that 'abandonment' was an offence if the child was under two years of age, and if its life had been endangered"; he concludes by noting, however, "that such provisions were inadequate is now obvious."[2] Hall's assertion that the "creation" of the crime of cruelty to children emerged from a need for a single, unifying definition that would adequately address child suffering in England speaks to a transition in the conceptualization of child endangerment in which the NSPCC was deeply invested. That is, while assaults against and mistreatment of children prior to the "creation" of child abuse could be and were prosecuted under the same laws that protected adults, the passage of the "Children's Charter" lent to such acts of violence a new significance: not just cases of assault, but also of "mere ill-treatment" and "mere neglect" became reconfigured, under the new law, as acts of "cruelty to children."

In terms of the Society's narratives, the emergence of "cruelty to children" as a new type of crime depended upon and gave rise to both a need for NSPCC inspectors who could uncover and police it, and to NSPCC propaganda and casework, which described, classified, and circumscribed what cruelty to children was, who committed it, and how it could be stopped. The social casework method—by which inspectors constructed detailed documents for each instance of cruelty investigated—played a large part in identifying areas of concern, which the Society then presented to the government as proof of the need for new and greater legislation protecting children. Moreover, such casework was reworked for publication within the Society's journal, *The Child's Guardian*, where case

---

[1] William Clarke Hall, *The Queen's Reign for Children* (London: T. Fisher Unwin, 1897), 159–60.

[2] Hall, *The Law Relating to Children* (London: Stevens and Sons, Limited, 1905), 27.

studies of cruelty to children were used to "pain the imagination and grieve the hearts" of its readers, in order to "annihilate the bliss of ignorance of any but their own happy homes, putting them into some English child's place, to watch the ways of their parents, and see the effects on little minds and limbs which cannot much longer bear them."[3] These case studies sought to demonstrate to the English public the necessity of intervention on behalf of abused children, as well as the singular effectiveness of the NSPCC in providing such protection. The story of the emergence of child protection and the NSPCC that emerges here is therefore one of centralization: of a single crime that seeks to encapsulate a broad number of dangers facing children; of a unified, national organization that sought to take on the task of identifying and ameliorating that crime; and of a specialized, professional discourse—casework—developed for the purpose of intervention and protection.

Although children who faced harm, cruelty, or neglect were definitively classified as abused children in part through the NSPCC's work at the end of the century, prior to that, child endangerment was constructed and understood in a variety of ways. The endangered child could be represented as a slave of British industry, as a victim of emotional neglect, as a companion of abused animals, as a savage street urchin, or a dangerous criminal offender. Furthermore, while the endangered child was, as Laura Berry observes in *The Child, the State, and the Victorian Novel*, "frequently and often sensationally represented as an innocent imperiled by cruelties," these cruelties "were as likely to be administered at the hand of a relative as by an administrative arm of the state."[4] Prior to the passage of the "Children's Charter," therefore, cruelty to children could be understood as something other than the abuse of a child by a parent or guardian: it could be understood as a labor issue, as an education issue, as a health issue.

In charting the territory of this new crime, the NSPCC built upon pre-existing narratives of child suffering—narratives that prevailed within a variety of genres and discourses throughout the nineteenth century. Rather than being restricted to the legal or the social-scientific realm, the endangered child in nineteenth-century discourse "cross[ed] generic boundaries with relative ease. A nineteenth-century reader was as likely to find an impassioned argument against child labor in Elizabeth Barrett Browning's poetry ("The Cry of the Children") as in a parliamentary blue book."[5] However, as Berry argues in the conclusion of her text, "about the time when child welfare and social work began to emerge as categories with recognizable and defining limits—the narratives of childhood distress that so dominated nineteenth-century fictional writing began to disappear."[6] This "relative disappearance," according to Berry, coincided with the invention of the

---

[3]   Benjamin Waugh, "Our New Year," *The Child's Guardian* 2.1 (January 1888), 1.

[4]   Laura Berry, *The Child, the State, and the Victorian Novel* (Charlottesville: University of Virginia Press, 1999), 2.

[5]   Ibid., 3.

[6]   Ibid., 164.

"case history," and from this coincidence she argues that "it is hard to dismiss the conclusion that, with the appearance of the formal apparatus of child welfare, the creative and complex use of the figure of the child victim was no longer so readily available."[7] Instead, as I would further argue, the more complex figure of the endangered child was, in part, replaced by the abused child—a figure whose place was ensconced within nascent child-protection discourse.

What the emergence of the NSPCC and the new crime of cruelty to children represent is the moment when the rise of new professions and genres—such as child protection and social casework—became the authoritative voices in the field of social intervention. This is not to suggest that these voices were uncontested, or that the desire of organizations like the NSPCC to produce unifying definitions of the problem of cruelty to children were entirely successful. However, the rise of professional discourse and its accompanying narratives of social ills and their solution signaled, in many ways, an end to a broader discussion of social issues that included literary interventions as legitimate and *authoritative* interventions— much to the impoverishment, I will argue, of social discourse. And though I will be focusing here on the subject of cruelty to children in particular, the transition I identify speaks to an alteration in the wide variety of social "work" performed by genre in the early to mid-Victorian period. That is, the development of institutional professions and practices not only saw the codification of particular kinds of suffering and the emergence of casework as an authoritative genre—it also coincided with the development of schools of thought that suggested that an obvious investment in and engagement with political and social issues had no place in the realm of art. Literary works were certainly still written on social problems after the invention of the modern welfare state, but it is undeniable that such texts were no longer as authoritative—as were, for example, the "social problem" novels of the mid-Victorian period—in the definition of social ills and their cure.

This transition, far from being restricted to the realm of the merely discursive, had material effects upon the subjects of that discourse—in this case, upon the lives of children. The prevalence of the suffering child in a wide variety of Victorian texts and genres occurred, in part, because the child itself was a figure still very much under construction, and efforts to define just what that child was were aided by discussions of what it could or should do, what could or should be done to it, how one could or should react to it. As a result of its encapsulation in narratives of child-protection at the end of the century, however, the meaning of the abused child and of childhood itself became relatively fixed and determined. What an abused child meant was what the new cultural assumption of child protection said it meant, and what could be done for it was determined by that assumption.

The abused child of legal and social casework was (and is) not, however, an entirely stable entity. Because the new rationality of child protection was mapped upon the existing terrain of narratives of child suffering and endangerment—

---

[7]   Ibid., 165.

narratives that were often, as I have stated, contradictory—fissures can be found within that rationality that threaten its single, unifying narrative. It is the work of this project to exploit those fissures—to trace the persistence of, and divergence from, pre-existing stories and representations of child endangerment in order to reveal the irresolvable contradictions located within a rationality of childhood and of child endangerment that persists to this day.

In my analysis of the displacement of narratives of child endangerment with the narrative of child protection, I wish to consider the consequences of this shift for both parents and children in England. The NSPCC's primary depiction of the abused child as helpless, defenseless, and innocent, for example—a depiction largely inspired, I will suggest, by literary representations of childhood—certainly served to make the child a worthy subject of social intervention, but it also limited what a child could do and what a child could be. Furthermore, while mid-Victorian literary and social representations of endangered childhood placed the blame for a child's endangerment in a variety of sectors—the individual, the social, the commercial—thus imagining a broader sense of responsibility for providing "childhood" to all children, the late-Victorian emergence of the abused child places such responsibility firmly in the domain of the individual. In so doing, organizations like the NSPCC participated in what Lydia Murdoch identifies as a common child-saving narrative of the late nineteenth century, in which "By scripting the evolution of poor children in melodramatic terms of rescue and reformation, philanthropists produced narratives that focused on individual and family pathologies rather than on the broader structural causes of poverty."[8]

This book will therefore concern itself with the issues of class, genre, and the relationship between the two. In a study of this type, the writer has to balance between offering a broader analysis of wide-ranging narratives and a close attention to detail that respects generic, period, and paradigmatic difference. In an attempt to provide this balance here, the first two chapters provide a broad historical framework that outlines the development of child protection, the role played by genre in the delineation of social concerns, and the construction of the child, while the latter chapters focus on close readings of key texts. Furthermore, while narratives of child endangerment in the nineteenth century were certainly found in discourses across the spectrum—medical, scientific, legal, and the emergent field of psychoanalysis, to name only a few—I focus primarily on the two genres (still broadly defined) that I believe contributed most significantly to narratives of child protection found in the writings of the NSPCC: the literary and the social-scientific. Finally, because I am interested in the ways in which debates about endangered childhood in the nineteenth century surface and resurface in these genres before becoming subsumed in the overarching narrative of child protection, I will be focusing in my chapters on four broad themes: the child and

---

[8]   Lydia Murdoch, *Imagined Orphans: Poor Families, Child Welfare, and Contested Citizenship in London* (New Brunswick, New Jersey, and London: Rutgers University Press, 2006), 14.

the animal, the child performer, the child as victim of commerce, and the child criminal.

All of these chapters benefit from historical and literary studies that have gone a long way towards elucidating endangered childhood in nineteenth-century England: notably, George K. Behlmer's landmark study of the NSPCC, *Child Abuse and Moral Reform in England, 1870–1908* (1982), Hugh Cunningham's excellent analysis of representations of poor children in *The Children of the Poor: Representations of Childhood since the Seventeenth Century* (1991), and Laura Berry's insightful examination of the relationship between literary and social texts in the construction of "endangered childhood" in the nineteenth century, *The Child, the State, and the Victorian Novel* (1999). More recently, texts such as Lydia Murdoch's *Imagined Orphans: Poor Families, Child Welfare, and Contested Citizenship in London* (2006) and Dennis Denisoff's collection, *The Nineteenth-Century Child and Consumer Culture* (2008) attest to the increased interest in the importance of the child and childhood in Victorian studies. In 2004, Sally Shuttleworth noted that

> Scholars in the humanities over the last thirty years have added first gender, then race, as factors to be considered alongside class in all forms of historical and textual analysis. With the benefit of hindsight we can look back in mild embarrassment to key works in our fields that seemed oblivious to the importance of empire in the Victorian era, or to the workings of gender ideology. Is it now time to add age, and more specifically childhood, to the triumvirate of class, gender and race?[9]

My own work seeks to build upon previous scholarship in order to make the argument that childhood is in fact a crucial concept for understanding the Victorian period. Through an examination of the child, and specifically, the endangered child, I hope to illuminate the fears, hopes, and desires that were continually caught up in the figure of the child in the nineteenth century, many of which persist today.

But more importantly, I believe my focus on the NSPCC adds significantly to current scholarship on Victorian childhood. While work has been done on the NSPCC from a historical standpoint, there has been no work, to my knowledge, on the NSPCC's discourse from a literary studies point of view, nor do many of the works noted above devote the kind of attention to the literature of the organization that I provide here. The NSPCC was very far from being the only society devoted to saving the endangered child in the nineteenth century, though it was certainly the primary organization concerned with cruelty to children. Furthermore, as I will outline in the first chapter, the NSPCC provides an interesting example of an organization that straddled the worlds of private charity, on the one hand, and governmental organization, on the other. Throughout the late nineteenth

---

9   Sally Shuttleworth, "Victorian Childhood," Roundtable: Victorian Children and Childhood, *Journal of Victorian Culture* (Spring 2004), 107.

century the Society stressed its role as a private charity, asserting that such work as it undertook on behalf of abused children could not be undertaken by mere government agencies. However, the Society was also intimately involved in the passage of new laws, it employed a complex organizational structure that eschewed the local in favor of the national, and it openly begged for governmental assistance in its work on behalf of the nation's children, and as such, provided the model for government interventions of the twentieth century. As a result, the NSPCC can be seen as exemplary of the kinds of discursive transitions I am tracing here, from the individual interventions of authors to the institutional interventions of organized societies. Analyzing the NSPCC's rhetoric, in particular, provides me with an opportunity to engage with the complex interactions between the personal and the institutional so central to the genre of the case study. For much of this study, the London SPCC's (later, the NSPCC) rhetoric is represented solely by Benjamin Waugh, the first director of the organization. Though it might be problematic to associate his own fiery and often vitriolic language with the institution itself, it is nevertheless the case that for much of the late nineteenth century, Benjamin Waugh *was* the voice of the NSPCC. Focusing on the extent to which Waugh's own language, and the narratives he employs, derive from earlier literary representations of the endangered child serves to demonstrate the extent to which those representations were both crucial to the concept of the abused child we have inherited from the nineteenth century, while also distanced from the larger textual and social narratives that first shaped them and, I would argue, gave them greater complexity.

The first chapter provides a historical overview of the NSPCC's emergence, placing its discourse within the context of nineteenth-century literary and social-scientific interventions into social problems. These various genres—statistics, case studies, journalism, and literature—were, I argue, mutually constitutive, with literary texts drawing upon the "findings" of statistical studies and journalism for their narratives of suffering subjects, and with social-scientific texts drawing upon the techniques and narratives of literature in order to create a connection between suffering subject and concerned audience. I argue that the NSPCC's own case studies, particularly in its early years, also draw upon the "humanitarian narrative" Thomas Laqueur identifies as central to these various discourses and their treatment of social problems and their amelioration. However, the development of the NSPCC into a professional organization, with its own inspectorate and methods, saw a concomitant transformation in the NSPCC's discourse away from narratives that relied upon "sympathy ready-made" to narratives that relied upon the Society's singular authority. Finally, I move into an examination of the endangered child as a particular object of social concern, one first largely constructed in the realm of the literary but eventually encapsulated within the genre of social casework.

Chapter 2 examines how the question of "what a child is" was addressed in the nineteenth century through the depiction of the relationship between children and animals. It is my contention that both the child and the animal were defined through their role as either victims or perpetrators of violence. In an examination of a variety of texts, including philosophical writings by John Locke and Jean-Jacques Rousseau, selected poems by Samuel Taylor Coleridge and William Blake, sections from novels by Wilkie Collins and Charles Dickens, and articles written by Waugh, I argue that it is only through an understanding of how the child was conceived of as both similar to, yet separate from, the animal, that we can begin to understand the process by which the child as a feeling, vulnerable subject came into dominance in the mid- to late nineteenth century. I then examine the ways in which residual linkages between animals and children served to support both the NSPCC's cooperation and competition with the Royal Society for the Prevention of Cruelty to Animals (RSPCA), a relationship that greatly influenced the NSPCC's construction of the abused child and of the crime of child abuse.

Chapter 3 inquires into the figure of the child performer in nineteenth-century discourse. If narratives that linked the animal and the child served to define what a child was, then narratives of child performance helped to define what a child could do. Texts such as Caroline Norton's *A Voice from the Factories* (1836), Charles Dickens's *Nicholas Nickleby* (1838–1839) and *Hard Times* (1854), Henry Mayhew's *London Labor and the London Poor* (1851–1852), O. F. Walton's *A Peep Behind the Scenes* (1877), and Ellen Barlee's *Pantomime Waifs* (1884) all concern themselves with the problem of the child's body in action and on display. Discourses of child performance sought to negotiate between child labor and child play, and as such, forcefully demonstrate the transition that occurred in the nineteenth century between residual and emergent conceptions of childhood. However, representations of child performance also focus upon the role of the adult audience, and as such, serve to elucidate the construction of adult responsibility towards suffering and endangered childhood. Finally, I argue that the problems surrounding the inclusion of the performing child under the rubric of "cruelty to children" were the result of the various contradictions inherent in the many narratives surrounding the figure of the child performer.

In my fourth chapter, I examine narratives that explore the relationship between the endangerment and abuse of children and financial gain. Such narratives, I argue, seek to negotiate between what were perceived to be England's two defining virtues: its commerce and its happy homes. Beginning with an analysis of anti–child labor literature, such as Frances Trollope's *The Life and History of Michael Armstrong, the Factory Boy* (1840) and Charlotte Elizabeth Tonna's *Helen Fleetwood* (1839–1840), I will suggest that such texts work to transform a political and social issue—the condition of labor in factories—into a domestic problem, in which the destruction of affective family relationships is depicted as the true tragedy of child labor. By comparison, texts such as Dickens' *Nicholas Nickleby* and *Dombey and Son* (1848) demonstrate the ways in which the middle-class home was represented as capable of achieving a balance between the needs of commerce and the requirements of domestic ideology. Finally, I will focus on the NSPCC's involvement in the child life insurance debate of the 1890s. In its attacks upon this practice, I suggest, the NSPCC argues that the lower- and working-class home should be permeable not by the demands of commerce, but by the influence and instruction of its own inspectors.

Chapter 5 analyzes juvenile delinquency as a test case for the limitations of "cruelty to children." Of the many representations of the endangered child prevalent throughout the nineteenth century, the child who committed crimes was the one who proved, in many ways, most difficult to enclose within the NSPCC's narrative constructions of child protection. As such, the juvenile delinquent remains to this day a figure of great complexity—one who continually challenges both narratives about the nature of childhood and about social concern on behalf of that child. In an examination of texts such as Dickens's *Oliver Twist* (1837–1839), Mary Carpenter's *Reformatory Schools* (1851) and *Juvenile Delinquents* (1853), and articles from *The Child's Guardian*, I argue that the delinquent child disrupts binary oppositions between child and adult, between child independence and child dependence, and between the child as salvageable and the child as lost—and that, in so doing, reveals the extent to which constructions of the victimized child appeal to us not on behalf of the child's own suffering, but on behalf of what we would like that child to represent.

Finally, my conclusion moves into the early twentieth century in order to examine the figure of the NSPCC inspector. The NSPCC was adamant that its work served to preserve homes, rather than simply to prosecute offenders, and the figure of the Inspector worked, I argue, as a means of balancing the personal and the institutional. Configuring the Inspector as an avuncular friend of the family, the NSPCC sought to put a personal face to the Society, one who could persuade parents to behave according to the law through force of personality as well as through legal retribution. Ending my analysis with this figure allows me to demonstrate the extent to which, in the case of abused children at least, the Society successfully represented institutional (even by a private charity) intervention as the sole appropriate solution to the problem of cruelty to children. After a century of investigations into what a suffering child might mean, that is, the figure of the Inspector represents the end point of intervention—the one who decides finally what that child means and what should be done on its behalf.

Chapter 1
Creating Cruelty to Children: Genre, Authority, and the Endangered Child

In a study that purports to trace the ways in which a broadly imagined narrative becomes more narrowly defined once encapsulated within the modern welfare state, it might seem problematic to focus so intensely on one institution, and a private charity at that. It is my contention, however, that the emergence of the NSPCC represents a key transitional moment in the cultural imagining of child endangerment. While child-protection agencies pre-existed (and co-existed with) the NSPCC,[1] none played so central a role in the definition of cruelty to children, in the production of propaganda that made it a recognized concept, and in the development of laws that made it a crime. Furthermore, in its desire to professionalize and in its battle on behalf of the national, rather than the local, the NSPCC presents us with an early precursor of twentieth-century child-protection agencies. But perhaps most importantly for this study, the NSPCC's changing use of narrative in its construction of cruelty to children provides a clear illustration of the relationship between genre, authority, and the delineation of social ills and their amelioration so central to this project.

In its very early years, the Society presented its work as primarily informative: drawing upon the genre of the case study, which had been used before by reformers such as Mary Carpenter and Frances Power Cobbe, for example, the NSPCC sought to create a connection between the readers of its journals and the suffering children of London. Such a connection, I argue, relied upon a sympathy "ready-made" (in George Eliot's words), upon cultural narratives of child endangerment that had been developing throughout the nineteenth century. But within a few years of its emergence, the NSPCC's narrative shifted. No longer merely informative, the NSPCC's narratives of abuse instead underlined and supported the singular

---

[1]   George K. Behlmer notes that "A bewildering array of charitable institutions were created to make life less harsh for the young. *The Charities Register and Digest* for 1884 distinguished between those offering the child 'relief in affliction,' 'relief in sickness,' 'relief in distress (permanent),'—this category alone fills 72 pages—'relief in distress (temporary),' 'reformatory relief,' and miscellaneous services such as emigration. The most elaborate mechanisms for promoting juvenile welfare was the child-rescue agency. By the mid-1880s three organizations dominated this work, Dr. Stephenson's Children's Home, the Church of England Waifs and Strays Society (the CEWSS), and the Barnardo group" (George K. Behlmer, *Child Abuse and Moral Reform in England, 1870–1908* [Stanford: Stanford University Press, 1982], 57–8).

authority of the Society itself. That authority, however, was not entirely stable, for the very narratives of child endangerment upon which the NSPCC based its own construction of the abused child remained within and worked to contradict the logic of "child protection" as effective ameliorative action.

Social Control, Faultlines, and the Child

In 1897, William Clarke Hall, the NSPCC's barrister, wrote *The Queen's Reign for Children*, which outlined the various changes that had taken place in child life in England during Victoria's reign. This history was, ostensibly, a means of showing gratitude to a Queen who had done so much to protect "the most helpless of her subjects" in her 60 years on the throne, but it also served to place the NSPCC within a larger history of child endangerment in the nineteenth century. As Waugh states in his introduction to the text,

> Could we bring to the sympathetic imagination of the inhabitants of these Islands a picture of the condition under which children lived in the year 1837, when the Royal lady, now in the golden ripe of her reign, a tender girl, ascended the throne, the result of the contrast would be a mingled incredulity, amazement, and thankfulness such as no other contrast of the reign could inspire.[2]

While the thankfulness this narrative is meant to inspire is owed to England's Queen, it is important to note that Waugh identifies the "great awakening of the nation to a true and full recognition of the rights of children"[3] with the passage of the Children's Charter in 1889. By placing the Society at the end of a glorious reign marked by increasing care and concern for children, Waugh and Hall's history depicts the NSPCC as the sole inheritor of a grand tradition, begun with the anti–child labor activism of the 1830s and 40s, continued in the work on behalf of juvenile delinquents, and finally brought to fruition in the NSPCC's work on behalf of children.

The narrative of *The Queen's Reign* is compelling, not least because it is so familiar. As late as the 1980s, theorists such as Lloyd DeMause would refer to the "evolution" of human society as something that could be measured in its progressively more humane and caring treatment of children.[4] However, the story of the emergence of the abused child as a legal subject, and of the NSPCC as

---

[2]   Benjamin Waugh, "Introduction," in *The Queen's Reign for Children*, by William Clarke Hall (London: T. Fisher Unwin, 1897), vii.

[3]   Ibid.

[4]   DeMause famously opens his article on "The Evolution of Childhood" with the claim that "The history of childhood is a nightmare from which we have only recently begun to awaken." He continues, saying that "The further back in history one goes, the lower the level of child care, and the more likely children are to be killed, abandoned,

a centralized body responsible for the surveillance of and legal intervention on behalf of that child and its home, is also the familiar story of the rise of social control in the nineteenth and twentieth centuries. The use of case studies, statistics, and categorization as a means of combating real and imagined social ills was not unique to the NSPCC, and has indeed become the primary method of monitoring and controlling populations in contemporary society. Instead of reading the emergence of child protection as the triumph of compassion over cruelty, or as a narrative of progress in the treatment of children in Western society, therefore, it can and is read as emblematic of disciplinary tactics.[5] In *Policing Gender, Class, and Family: Britain, 1850–1940*, Linda Mahood identifies "the late nineteenth-century child-saving movement" as "part of a massive intervention into private life" by government and charitable institutions.[6] Such an intervention can be seen as part of what Michel Foucault identifies as the rise of "discipline"—that is, the construction of new forms of information, and new ways of ordering and controlling space and bodies as a means of domination—in the eighteenth and nineteenth centuries. Foucault argues that "there is no power relation without the correlative constitution of a field of knowledge, nor any knowledge that does not presuppose and constitute at the same time power relations,"[7] and in terms of this study, it would certainly be possible to identify the emergence of the NSPCC and its development of casework, by which it first "created" and then identified and prosecuted the crime of cruelty to children, as one such example of a "field of knowledge" that came to constitute a particular set of "power relations" in England: as representative of what Jacques Donzelot identifies as the transition from "a government of families to a government through the family."[8]

While the NSPCC and its discursive and policing strategies can be understood as one instance of "a complex system of production and distribution of knowledge which, once in circulation, acquires a truth value placing it in a position of

---

beaten, terrorized, and sexually abused," (Lloyd DeMause, *The History of Childhood* [New York: The Psychohistory Press, 1974], 1).

[5]   Harry Hendrick, for example, argues that "The NSPCC was of vital importance in reshaping public opinion away from the view that the family was inviolate, towards a view which recognized that if the ideal of the family were to be realized, then a certain amount of interference by outside bodies was essential for the purposes of education and, occasionally, prosecution .... The work of the NSPCC, then, was directed at the reformulation of responsibilities and codes of behaviour" (Harry Hendrick, *Child Welfare: Historical Dimensions, Contemporary Debate* [Bristol: The Policy Press, 2003], 32.

[6]   Linda Mahood, *Policing Gender, Class, and Family: Britain, 1850–1940* (London: UCL Press Limited, 1995), 2.

[7]   Michel Foucault, *Discipline and Punish: The Birth of the Prison*, trans. Alan Sheridan (New York: Vintage Books, 1979), 27.

[8]   Jacques Donzelot, *The Policing of Families*, trans. Robert Hurley (London: Hutchinson, 1979), 92.

domination," it is important to recognize that this position was far from absolute.[9] As Louise Jackson has pointed out, "Despite the high profile role of the NSPCC on a national level, it should not be assumed that the society monopolized child welfare work … The NSPCC was simply the largest society of many"[10]—and as such, the Society faced competition in its efforts to define the endangered child, while also continually asserting the authority of its singular vision. Furthermore, the NSPCC faced attacks from other quarters: from working-class parents who accused the NSPCC of targeting lower class families; from other SPCCs who resented the NSPCC's failure to respect local cultures and politics; and from organizations such as the Charity Organisation Society, which accused the Society of mismanaging its funds.[11] These many assaults upon the NSPCC speak, in part, to the controversial nature of its work: work that, as Lord Shaftesbury famously declared, was of so "private, internal and domestic a character as to be beyond the reach of legislation."[12] I would further argue, however, that what allowed so many attacks upon the fledgling organization were the contradictions at work within the Society's own narratives of abuse. In examining the emergence of the NSPCC, therefore, I am interested not so much in simply identifying the NSPCC as a means of discipline and surveillance, as I am in tracing the residual narratives, tactics, and strategies that persist within and problematize the NSPCC's own understanding of cruelty to children, and of child protection as a discourse and as a practice.

A crucial theoretical concept for understanding the displacement of some of the multiple representations of child endangerment with the somewhat unified (if still unstable) representation of the abused child is what Mary Poovey identifies as the "disaggregation" of epistemological domains. In *Making a Social Body: British Cultural Formation, 1830–1864*, Poovey describes the process by which epistemological domains—such as "the social"—emerge and eventually become separated from pre-existing domains, such as the "political" and the "economic." These emergent domains do not "immediately replace their predecessors, however, but [are] mapped onto them in a process that entail[s] the negotiation and eventual redrawing of the boundaries between kinds of knowledge, kinds of practice, and kinds of institutions."[13] Importantly, Poovey emphasizes the "incoherence that results from the uneven process of disaggregation itself": "Because emergent domains develop out of and retain a constitutive relationship to preexistent, or residual, domains, the rationalities and forms of calculation that are involved in new domains tend to carry with them traces of the rationality specific to the

[9]   Marie-Christine Leps, *Apprehending the Criminal: The Production of Deviance in Nineteenth-Century Discourse* (Durham and London: Duke University Press, 1992), 4.

[10]   Louise Jackson, *Child Sexual Abuse in Victorian England* (London and New York: Routledge, 2000), 53.

[11]   See Behlmer, *Child Abuse and Moral Reform*.

[12]   Qtd. in Behlmer, *Child Abuse and Moral Reform*, 20.

[13]   Mary Poovey, *Making a Social Body: British Cultural Formation, 1830–1864* (Chicago: University of Chicago Press, 1995), 7.

domain in which they arise."[14] These traces of a pre-existing rationality create contradictions, irrationalities, or "faultlines" in the emergent domain, a condition that, Poovey argues, "explodes the idea that power could ever be monolithic or merely repressive."[15]

The instability of the construction of cruelty to children, here represented in the discourse of the NSPCC, results, in part, from the instability of its object—childhood itself. The conceptualization of the abused child in the 1880s was in part the result of a model of childhood that came into its own in the nineteenth century: specifically, that of childhood as, ideally, a protected, carefree time and space that should be enjoyed by all children, regardless of class. In *The Children of the Poor: Representations of Childhood Since the Seventeenth Century*, Hugh Cunningham argues that the distance between the children of the rich and the children of the poor was "emphasized and celebrated" in the seventeenth and eighteenth centuries, but "came to be deplored" in the nineteenth and twentieth centuries.[16] English society increasingly began to believe that "all children were ... entitled to enjoyment of the experiences of what constituted a 'proper childhood,'" or "the kind of childhood which was being constructed in the middle-class world."[17] This "proper" childhood was constructed around issues of dependence, and "Autonomy, both economic and social, was now an adult prerogative. Children's right was to a 'natural' childhood state of innocence and irresponsibility: any whose knowledge and responsibility were 'adult' needed rescue."[18] A child enjoying an appropriate childhood was therefore, ideally, excluded from supporting the family financially, because childhood, it was increasingly believed, should be a space free from excessive labor.[19] Instead, the child became "the repository for certain valued and post-Enlightenment traits such as innocence, liberty, and naturalness."[20] The emergence of childhood as a protected time and space to be shared by all children, therefore, resulted in the transformation of the child from an economically useful member of a household to an "economically 'worthless' but emotionally 'priceless'" figure in society.[21]

---

[14]   Ibid., 14.

[15]   Ibid., 17, 18.

[16]   Hugh Cunningham, *The Children of the Poor: Representations of Childhood Since the Seventeenth Century* (Oxford: Blackwell, 1991), 1.

[17]   Ibid., 1, 3.

[18]   Anna Davin. *Growing up Poor: Home, School and Street in London, 1870–1914* (London: Rivers Oram Press, 1996), 4–5.

[19]   This is not to suggest that such conditions actually existed in reality, nor that they were universally desired. Children worked throughout the nineteenth century, at a variety of occupations.

[20]   Laura Berry, *The Child, the State, and the Victorian Novel*, 6.

[21]   Viviana A. Zelizer, *Pricing the Priceless Child: The Changing Social Value of Children* (Princeton: Princeton University Press, 1985), 3.

The emergence of "childhood" as a new domain overwrote existing epistemological frameworks for understanding youth and infancy, and as such, retained residual narratives about, most importantly for this study, the children of the poor. The reality of social and economic disparity in nineteenth-century England meant that children of the lower classes were unlikely to enjoy what was increasingly conceived of as a proper childhood, and, judging from the omnipresence of the impoverished child in Victorian fiction and social discourse, this distance between children of the poor and children of the rich was a source of much anxiety. Texts such as the *Children's Employment Commission* (1842–1843), and Frances Trollope's *The Life and Adventures of Michael Armstrong, a Factory Boy* (1840) deplored the conditions children faced working in the factories; Mary Carpenter's *Juvenile Delinquents* (1853) and Charles Dickens's *Oliver Twist* (1837–39) questioned the fitness of trying and punishing child criminals under the same laws as adults; and waif novels, such as F. W. Robinson's *Mattie: A Stray* (1864) and exposés such as Henry Mayhew's *London Labour and the London Poor* (1851–1852) revealed the harsh living conditions faced by impoverished or orphaned children on the streets. That the children of the poor were so often represented as endangered in social discourse and fiction speaks not only to the existence of social problems brought on by economic disparity, but also to a willingness, on the part of the Victorian public, to see such disparity—at least where children were concerned—as problematic and, ultimately, unacceptable.

Although the "children of the poor" were often represented as endangered in nineteenth-century texts, they were by no means the only ones. In Victorian literature, in particular, the children of the middle and upper classes were also often represented as victims in need of rescue and protection. Questions of labor and delinquency were not as much a focus in these texts as in the former, but because the new conception of childhood entailed not only increased material demands upon parents but also increased affective demands, anxiety about whether or not these demands were being met was equally a concern in terms of middle- and upper-class homes. Residual conceptions of childhood as a time of innate moral depravity, bolstered by the growth of Victorian Evangelicalism, meant that fear and discipline were the norm in many Victorian households; as Jacqueline Bannerjee argues, many parents believed that "early struggles tend[ed] to strengthen the spirit in the end."[22] Throughout the nineteenth century, then, this conception of childhood as a time of innate sinfulness had to contend with the emergent "idea of childhood as properly a time of happiness."[23]

The existence of these two contending views of childhood in the nineteenth century is evident in such works as Dickens's *Dombey and Son* (1846–1848). Flora Dombey enjoys material wealth and security; however, her father emotionally neglects her, and as a result, her childhood is spent in loneliness and isolation.

---

[22]   Jacqueline Bannerjee, *Through the Northern Gate: Childhood and Growing Up in British Fiction, 1719–1901* (New York: Peter Lang, 1996), 54.

[23]   Cunningham, *The Children of the Poor*, 152.

Bannerjee argues that Dickens's depiction of Flora's childhood "is by no means unexpected" given the often harsh climate of Victorian child-rearing, but I would argue that Dickens's presentation of Flora as a victim demonstrates the extent to which such an upbringing, if not entirely unusual, was increasingly viewed as unacceptable.[24] Furthermore, Dickens's representations of suffering childhood are hardly unique: Charlotte Brontë's *Jane Eyre* (1847), George Meredith's *The Ordeal of Richard Feverel* (1859), Wilkie Collins's *Hide and Seek* (1854), and later texts describing Victorian childhood, such as Samuel Butler's *The Way of All Flesh* (1903) and Edmund Gosse's *Father and Son* (1907), all contain depictions of endangered childhood that focus less on physical discomfort than they do on emotional isolation or lack of love.

With the growing acceptance of the idea that childhood should be "the happiest time in life," a child's unhappiness—as a result of physical hardships, or the lack of love and care—became a sign of that child's victimization.[25] As James Kincaid observes in *Child-Loving: The Erotic Child and Victorian Culture*, "An unhappy child was and is unnatural, an indictment of somebody: parent, institution, nation."[26] Although the endangered child's body in Victorian discourse speaks volumes, therefore, so too does the child's interior state. This focus on the suffering child's feelings of unhappiness served, I would argue, to bolster a concept of childhood that cut across class lines, for while it is obviously true that some children were more likely to face harsh labor and starvation than others, it could also be argued—largely as a result of the depictions of children in Victorian novels—that children of all classes experienced isolation, fear, and unhappiness. The construction of the child as a "feeling subject," as a victim in need of aid, was essential to the eventual emergence of cruelty to children at the end of the nineteenth century.

The narrative of child protection that emerged with organizations like the NSPCC owed much to representations of the feeling, suffering child, particularly because the possibility that every child could be a victim, regardless of class, was a central tenet of the NSPCC's definition of cruelty to children. That such a definition was dependent upon the new conception of childhood Cunningham describes is undeniable, because the construction of child abuse as a crime that could occur in the homes of the poor and wealthy alike was only possible if a childhood without pain, labor, or hunger was understood to be something all children should enjoy. The inclusion of things such as "begging," "exposure," and "improper employment" as categories of child abuse testifies to this change in the social value of children, and demonstrates the extent to which the distance between the children of the rich and the children of the poor had become problematic. While the necessity for children of the very poor to beg or to go hungry was largely accepted as a fact of life a

---

24   Jacqueline Bannerjee, *Through the Northern Gate*, 54.

25   Cunningham, *The Children of the Poor*, 134.

26   James R. Kincaid, *Child-Loving: The Erotic Child and Victorian Culture* (New York: Routledge, 1992), 80.

century earlier, by the mid-century, such a necessity was deemed unacceptable, and by the 1890s, criminal.

However, the fact that "begging" became a crime of cruelty, rather than a social problem unconnected to a lack of parental love, says much about the role that residual narratives played in child-protection discourse. Social casework and propaganda, proposing, as it does, to consist merely of a recording of significant "facts," has to operate according to a variety of cultural assumptions—about the problem itself, and about the best means of addressing it. Cut loose from their original contexts (the interiority of the subject as represented in the novel, the enumeration and statistical calculation of social ills as depicted in individual case studies), however, these assumptions lose much of their complexity, and remain as irresolvable contradictions in the NSPCC's construction of child abuse. Furthermore, narratives that were appropriate to a genre, and specific to a particular social issue, become unevenly applied within the new context. The child who labors becomes the child who is not loved; the parent who allows his or her child to beg becomes the very picture of the rapacious factory owner, motivated by money, rather than by starvation. In other words, actions by parents that might once have been placed within the social domain are instead placed firmly within the realm of the individual and the affective.

This is not to suggest that earlier literary texts did not perform a disciplinary role in Victorian society. As theorists such as Nancy Armstrong and D. A. Miller have pointed out, though the novel as a genre was traditionally "felt to celebrate and encourage misconduct, rather than censure and repress it," it is important to recognize the "possibility of a radical *entanglement* between the nature of the novel and the practice of the police."[27] As observed earlier, the early to mid-nineteenth-century novel in England was particularly significant in terms of developing new narratives about the plight of the lower and working classes and of the plight of the child. As Miller observes, "perhaps no openly fictional form has ever sought to 'make a difference' in the world more than the Victorian novel, whose cultural hegemony and diffusion well qualified it to become the primary spiritual exercise of an entire age."[28] And, of course, even those "fictions that purport to deal with private life, particularly the private domain of the family, nevertheless intervene in public and social debates."[29] Writers such as Charles Dickens, for example, though not always necessarily engaged in writing what are now identified as "social problem" novels, nevertheless used the novel as a space in which to make claims on behalf of England's suffering subjects.

And no subject's suffering was more "real," more significant, in Victorian fiction than that of the child. Whether the endangered child was the protagonist of the text, as in *Oliver Twist*, or an exemplar of innocent suffering as in Gaskell's

---

[27] D. A. Miller, *The Novel and the Police* (Berkeley: University of California Press, 1988), 1, 2.

[28] Ibid., x.

[29] Laura Berry, *The Child, the State, and the Victorian Novel*, 6.

Mary Barton, representations of children in the nineteenth-century novel were crucial in the reconfiguration of the child as a worthy object of social intervention. This is not to say that social-scientific studies of endangered childhood were insignificant or were not authoritative, but rather to suggest that the meaning and significance of the endangered child was still very much under construction during the mid-Victorian period, and that literary representations allowed for a more flexible, because imaginative, negotiation of that figure.

By the early twentieth century, however, the novel that engaged openly with social issues had become somewhat passé, and writers such as Virginia Woolf would complain openly about novels that take on "work that ought to have been discharged by Government officials" and that are "interested in something outside" the book itself.[30] The work of representing the disenfranchised and the endangered in society was no longer that of the novel, but of social-scientific discourse. With the emergence of groups such as the NSPCC, the endangered child of Victorian fiction became the abused child, a figure that was bound within and defined by newly authoritative modes of representation: the case study and casework. However, these newer modes of representation both engaged in the same debates as the earlier literary precursors and utilized and built upon similar rhetorical and narrative structures. Further yet, the kinds of narratives of child abuse employed by the NSPCC relied upon a logic of child endangerment that had been constructed, largely, in Victorian literature. The NSPCC's construction of cruelty to children as a classless crime, one connected to individual character flaws rather than social environment, demonstrates the influence of novelistic narratives in which child suffering is the result of crimes of "feeling"—of a failure to love, a failure to protect on the part of the guardian. Such failings on the part of guardians in novels such as *Jane Eyre*, *Nicholas Nickleby*, and *Armadale*, for example, may speak to a larger social ill—such as the hypocrisy of the middle classes, or the injustice suffered by children in an industrial world—but these failings are still, nevertheless, the sins of the guardian. The ability of the Victorian novel to recast social problems as domestic problems, to find both the solution and the blame for social ills within the private space of the home and the heart and soul of the individual, finds its way, I argue, into the late nineteenth-century social-scientific narratives of the NSPCC. That is, where child abuse is a problem in the home, the NSPCC, as we will see, often locates the root cause of this abuse in the abusive parents' failure to feel proper emotions towards their children, rather than in the family's necessity or suffering.

---

[30] Virginia Woolf, "Modern Fiction," in *The Common Reader* (New York: Harcourt, 1925), 152 and "Mr. Bennett and Mrs. Brown," in *Collected Essays: Volume 1* (New York: Harcourt, 1925), 327.

The Origins of Child Protection

This study concerns itself with the emergence of child protection in England, but the concept of "cruelty to children" as a specific crime first came into being with the Mary Ellen case in the United States. In 1873, Etta Angell Wheeler, a Methodist social worker, discovered Mary Ellen badly beaten and chained to a bedpost in her home.[31] Wheeler approached the police and child-saving institutions to intercede on Mary Ellen's behalf, but to no avail, supposedly because "the right of parents to chastise their own children was still sacred, and there was no law under which any agency could interfere, to protect a child like her."[32] Mary Ellen Wilson was not, in fact, the daughter of Mrs. Mary Connolly; she had been obtained "on a term of indenture when she was just two years old."[33] Wheeler was unable to find assistance for the child, and therefore contacted Henry Bergh, the President of the American Society for the Prevention of Cruelty to Animals (ASPCA), and "as the result of efforts initiated by Etta Wheeler and Henry Bergh, a bruised and battered Mary Ellen McCormack was brought into a New York courtroom" where she was "represented in court by the Counsel for the ASPCA."[34] The judge "granted a writ *de homine replegiando*, a special writ provided for by Section 65 of the US Habeas Corpus Act, removing Mary Ellen from the custody of the Connollys. Mrs. Connolly was arrested 13th April, and found guilty ... of felonious assault against Mary Ellen on 21st April."[35] After this case, the New York State legislature "enacted laws permitting the chartering of Societies for the Protection of Children. The New York Society for the Prevention of Cruelty to Children [SPCC], founded on 15th December 1874, was the first child protection organisation in the world."[36]

The Mary Ellen case is significant for a number of reasons, not least because the ASPCA's involvement on her behalf has been used—at the time, and in the present day—to suggest that animals received greater protections under the law than did children.[37] What the ASPCA provided in this case, however, was instead the willingness to become involved and to represent the child in court; the ASPCA did *not* represent Mary Ellen under laws that had been passed to protect animals

---

[31]   Nicholas Malton, "The Story of Mary Ellen and the Founding of the New York Society for the Prevention of Cruelty to Children," http://firststop/archive/Mary.Ellen.htm.

[32]   Samuel X. Radbill, "A History of Child Abuse and Infanticide," in *The Battered Child*, ed. Ray E. Helfer and C. Henry Kempe (Chicago: The University of Chicago Press, 1968), 13.

[33]   Susan J. Pearson, "'The Rights of the Defenseless': Animals, Children, and Sentimental Liberalism in Nineteenth-Century America" (PhD diss., University of North Carolina, 2004), 3.

[34]   Malton.

[35]   Ibid., 3.

[36]   Ibid.

[37]   See Chapter 2.

(as some child protection historians have erroneously claimed).[38] In fact, no new laws were necessary, either to remove Mary Ellen from her abusive home, or to charge her caregivers with abuse. What the Mary Ellen case demonstrated, then, was not that children needed the same legal protection as animals, or that children necessarily required separate and distinct legal protection from adults, but that abused children required advocates to represent them under the law. In other words, the major significance of the Mary Ellen case was that "public conscience was galvanized as never before, and for the first time an agency was set up specifically encourage [sic] reporting of child abuse and to investigate and pursue the interests of abused children."[39] The formation of the SPCC in America, then, represented the first step toward providing advocacy on behalf of abused children.

Furthermore, the success of the SPCC in the United States provided an "organizational blueprint"[40] for the formation of similar societies in England and in 1882, Samuel Smith, Liberal MP for Liverpool, "attended a local meeting of the Royal Society for the Prevention of Cruelty to Animals ... where he converted a proposal for the formation of a Dog's Home into an appeal for the defence of misused children."[41] The Liverpool Society for the Prevention of Cruelty to Children was formed as a result, making it the first organization of its kind in England. This organization gained immediate and influential support: from Baroness Angela Burdett-Coutts, one of England's premier philanthropists; from Hesba Stretton, best-selling author of evangelical books for children; and from Florence Davenport-Hill, author of *Children and the State*, and a key figure in child education. As well, articles on cruelty to children began to appear in *The Times*, the *Pall Mall Gazette*, and the *British Medical Journal*.[42] By 1883, child abuse and the need to provide protection for children had become a topic of public debate in England. As public interest in the issue grew, SPCCs were founded in numerous centers. London was an obvious choice for a local SPCC, and in May 1884 the London SPCC was formed.

Benjamin Waugh, a former pastor, was appointed the Honorary Secretary of the London SPCC at its inception. Waugh had written several books and been the

---

[38] Radbill claims that "They were able to have Mary Ellen removed from her parents on the grounds that she was a member of the animal kingdom and that therefore her case could be included under the laws against animal cruelty" (Samuel X. Radbill, "A History of Child Abuse and Infanticide," 13). Malton also points out that "Jacob Riis, in his influential 1882 book *The Children of the Poor*, said that animal welfare laws had to be resorted to in this case, but this does not actually seem to have proved necessary" (Nicholas Malton, "The Story of Mary Ellen").

[39] Ibid., 3.

[40] Behlmer, *Child Abuse and Moral Reform*, 52.

[41] Ibid., 53.

[42] Ibid., 56–7.

editor of *The Sunday Magazine*[43] before he took up his position with the London SPCC, which meant that, in him, the Society gained someone experienced in negotiating the world of journalism. Furthermore, Benjamin Waugh had ties to W. T. Stead, which, as George K. Behlmer suggests in *Child Abuse and Moral Reform in England, 1870–1908*, allowed "Waugh, and by extension his organization, to reap the benefits of the 'new journalism'"[44] "New Journalism" is the name given by Matthew Arnold to the "historic shift" in journalism in the nineteenth century "from a press limited by its own traditions and the modest demands of its readers" to one driven by a new market composed of readers from all classes.[45] The development of new technologies and the growth of the market affected the content and style of news-reporting, and "innovation became commonplace: bold headlines, gossip columns, sports reading, pictures, and 'news stories' whose appeal derived from a subjective interest in the evolving human drama."[46] Waugh was to bring the personal, often sensational style of New Journalism to the London SPCC, and although the Liverpool SPCC was founded earlier and had greater experience in the field of child protection, the London SPCC quickly emerged as the leading child-protection organization in England, primarily as a result of Waugh's propaganda. In January, 1887, the London SPCC published the first issue of *The Child's Guardian*, with Waugh as the editor. *The Child's Guardian* was a monthly journal aimed at increasingly public awareness and understanding of the problem of child abuse; in the opening editorial, Waugh argued that "Interest in children, and horror at what is suffered by them at the hands of brutal, ill-living parents is common enough, but it is largely without knowledge of the provision of the law for children's protection."[47] The London SPCC addressed this lack of knowledge through the publication of case studies and legal cases within the journal in the hopes of informing "such persons as are already interested in the condition of little victims of cruel treatment, wrongful neglect, and improper employment what they can and cannot do about these evils."[48]

---

[43]   Waugh published *The Gaol Cradle, who rocks it?* in 1873, and *Sunday Evenings with my Children* in 1881. He also wrote extensively for *The Sunday Magazine*, which "contained a distinctive collection of late Victorian writings on Christian, humanitarian, and philosophical themes …. It gave Waugh many opportunities to expand his exhortative and at times (to modern ears) sentimental writing for young audiences, many of his books first appearing in serial form in *The Sunday Magazine*" (Andrew Fletcher, "The Life and Times of Benjamin Waugh" [NSPCC: 1994], 13).

[44]   Behlmer, *Child Abuse and Moral Reform*, 83.

[45]   Joel H. Wiener, "Introduction," in *Papers for the Millions: The New Journalism in Britain, 1850s to 1914*, ed. Joel H. Wiener (New York: Greenwood Press, 1988), xii.

[46]   Ibid.

[47]   Waugh, untitled editorial, *The Child's Guardian* 1.1 (January 1887), 1.

[48]   Ibid.

The launch of this journal also served to provide the London SPCC with an "official voice"[49] and, importantly, with a space in which to defend its work. As Behlmer notes, "As operations expanded from a total of 95 cases in 1884-85 to 258 in 1886-87, so also did the risk of public censure" because "allegations of hostility to the poor threatened to discredit the organization in working-class neighbourhoods."[50] In response to such allegations, Waugh used *The Child's Guardian* as a platform to express his opinion that the Society's work was "no class work," and that it had "a single eye to putting down cruelty to children, which will be turned aside by neither the poverty nor the wealth of their wrong-doers."[51] Moreover, the case studies printed in *The Child's Guardian*, particularly in the first few years of its circulation, worked to support this assertion, always depicting children and families from a variety of backgrounds, from the poorest of the poor to the very wealthy. Cruelty to children, according to the London SPCC, was a classless crime, inspired by "vile pleasure" and an "ill-conditioned disposition," and the battle to bring about greater protection for children was one which, the Society believed, superseded questions of class and poverty.[52]

Although *The Child's Guardian* consisted primarily of often quite sensational case studies that served to define and delimit the problem of cruelty to children, it also included narratives about the differing success the organization met in the courts while endeavoring to prosecute parents for cruelty. Through accounts of cases in which the Society had to break the law in order to provide protection for an abused child, the journal served as a platform for the Society's efforts to bring about new legislation to further that aim. The London SPCC and the Liverpool SPCC both compiled handbooks on current legislation protecting children as a means of addressing the gaps within the law that affected child protection agencies. As Behlmer notes, however, "when Waugh invited the Liverpool, Edinburgh, and Glasgow societies to discuss possible parliamentary action, the London society had already drafted a concrete proposal. At the ensuing meeting, provincial delegates discovered that legislative confirmation, not consultation, was the order of the day."[53] Although the independent SPCCs in Liverpool, Hull, and Birmingham were also committed to bringing about new legislation, the role of the London SPCC in drafting the bill, and in developing a national presence through its expansion into the provinces and through the work of *The Child's Guardian*, meant that the proposed legislation became associated primarily with Waugh and the London SPCC.

---

[49]   Behlmer, *Child Abuse and Moral Reform*, 82.

[50]   Ibid.

[51]   Waugh, "Notes," *The Child's Guardian* 3.36 (December 1889), 224, and Untitled, *The Child's Guardian* 1.1 (January 1887), 1.

[52]   Henry Edward Manning and Benjamin Waugh, "The Child of the English Savage," *Contemporary Review* 49 (May 1886), 696.

[53]   Behlmer, *Child Abuse and Moral Reform*, 81.

In Spring, 1888, "A. J. Mundella, President of the Board of Trade in Gladstone's third government and a skilled parliamentary tactician, agreed to take charge of the bill" and introduced it to parliament on 10 August.[54] The London SPCC supported the bill by distributing a letter "along with 10,000 copies of 'Street Children,'" an article written by Waugh, "to every corporation in England. This tactic produced resolutions in favor of the bill from 87 municipalities."[55] Such a tactic also closely associated the London SPCC with the new bill, and when the Act for the Prevention of Cruelty to Children passed on 16 August 26, 1889, it was perceived by the English press to be the work of Waugh and the London SPCC, a fact that did not sit well with other SPCC organizations or with A. J. Mundella himself. As Behlmer records,

> One month later, Mundella reflected bitterly on what he saw as misplaced praise
> for the victory: "Stead has deliberately set himself to ignore all the labor and
> sacrifice of Lord Herschell and myself in reference to this important measure,
> and to call it Mr. Waugh's Bill, and assume that all Mr. Waugh had to do was
> draw some vague and unworkable clauses and insert them in the "Pall Mall" and
> they would go through Parliament in a breath.[56]

Mundella's comments are significant in that they, however "bitterly," acknowledge the role that journalism played in gaining public knowledge of and support for the new law. While Mundella undoubtedly did the hard work of pushing the bill through parliament, it was the work of Waugh and *The Child's Guardian* that created the crime of cruelty to children in the public mind.

"The Child of the English Savage"

But how did early child-protection groups define "cruelty to children"? The Liverpool SPCC, in a review of its work undertaken in 1884, "found child abuse to be a complex problem."[57] In its analysis of the "apparent cause of trouble" in child-abuse cases, the Liverpool SPCC discovered

> that mistreatment of the young rarely stemmed from personal characteristics of
> adults ('hasty temper') or children ('wilfulness'). Rather, the Society's statistics
> suggest that child abuse was, at base, an environmental problem, and as such,
> its elimination would require drastic improvement in the social and economic
> conditions of inner-city life.[58]

---

[54]   Ibid., 98.

[55]   Ibid., 101.

[56]   Ibid., 108–9.

[57]   Ibid., 71.

[58]   Ibid., 73.

The connection uncovered by the Liverpool Society between child abuse and the "social and economic conditions of inner-city life" meant that the problem of "cruelty to children" had much in common with the concerns identified in Mary Carpenter's work with juvenile delinquents and even in social investigations such as those of Henry Mayhew. It also meant, however, that the work of child protection might do little to solve the problem. It is not surprising, Behlmer therefore notes, that "the Liverpool SPCC declined to elaborate on findings that could be interpreted as showing the futility of its own work."[59]

By contrast, the London SPCC managed to convey a clear message to the public about what child abuse was and how its own Society could address the problem. Rather than grappling with the different causes of abuse, the London SPCC instead depicted cruelty as the result of character flaws in the abuser. In "The Child of the English Savage," co-written by Cardinal Manning and Benjamin Waugh and published in the *Contemporary Review* in May 1886, the origins of cruelty are located in the "peculiarity of spirit of the adult abuser of the child."[60] They argue that "Men become addicted to cruelty as they become addicted to drink and gambling. It is a vile pleasure in which they indulge, some occasionally, some persistently; making their homes into little hells."[61] Such a construction of abuse— i.e., one that severed the problem from any social or environmental explanation— allowed for an "all-encompassing narrative" of abuse that could account for the kinds of situations that the London SPCC might encounter.[62] What caused the "English savage" to be savage, that is, was less important than describing the behavior associated with such savagery:

> His clenched fist could have broken open a door at a blow, and with it, in his anger, he felled a child three years and a half old, making the little fellow giddy for days, and while he was thus giddy felled him again; and because the terrible pain he inflicted made the child cry, he pushed three of his huge fingers down the little weeper's throat—'plugging the little devil's windpipe,' as he laughingly described it.[63]

Such sadism as Manning and Waugh describe here is typical of the London SPCC's early depictions of cruelty to children. The parent is very often described as physically strong, as emotionally volatile, and as entirely unrepentant, while the child victim is physically weak, submissive, and forgiving: "a more docile child,

---

[59]   Ibid.

[60]   Manning and Waugh, "The Child of the English Savage," 696.

[61]   Ibid.

[62]   Cunningham, *The Children of the Poor: Representations of Childhood Since the Seventeenth Century* (Oxford: Blackwell, 1991), 144.

[63]   Manning and Waugh, "The Child of the English Savage," 694.

or one more ready to twine his arms round your neck, you seldom find than was the little fellow he again and again made giddy with his deadly blows."[64]

According to Manning and Waugh, therefore, the crux of child abuse lies in the contrast between two opposing natures and temperaments: they identify "the real root of persistent savagery" in "a sullen, ill-conditioned disposition" and "a cowardice which limits its gratifications to unresisting and helpless things."[65] Such an understanding of cruelty is very similar to Frances Power Cobbe's concept of "heteropathy," which "consists in anger and cruelty, excited by the signs of pain": "the more the tyrant causes the victim to suffer the more he hates him, and desires to heap on him fresh suffering."[66] However, the London SPCC argued that cruelty to children was unique in that it was, in part, a crime entirely connected to the singular nature of "the child" itself. That is, while Manning and Waugh are careful to explain that cruelty to children "is not due to peculiarity in the spirit of the abused child," their argument that cruelty is aroused by "unresisting and helpless things"—of which, they argue, children are the most exemplary—does suggest that cruelty to children is different from other forms of cruelty.[67] As Waugh proclaims in "The Prevention of Cruelty to Children," "it is almost universally true that the more innocent and simple the child is—the better looking-glass does it make for its haters to see their own black villainy in."[68] The individual child might not be the cause of the abuse through any actions of its own, but Waugh suggests that childhood itself, and in particular, its contrast with the savagery and violence of the abuser, is both what incites child abuse, and what makes it particularly heinous.

Because the London SPCC located the cause of cruelty within the individual, rather than the environment, it could argue that child abuse was a crime that defied class or gender boundaries. An "ill-conditioned disposition" could be found in individuals from every class and either gender, and while Manning and Waugh acknowledge that "Cruelty to offspring people tacitly accept as the accompaniment of great poverty, squalor, and social misfortune," they stress that "against the poor, the terribly poor, [the Society] can bring hardly a complaint."[69] Instead, abusers exist "anywhere and everywhere."[70] Furthermore, Manning and Waugh are careful to relate stories of female "savages" who also torture their children, saying of one

---

[64]   Ibid.

[65]   Ibid., 696.

[66]   Frances Power Cobbe, "Wife-Torture in England," in *Criminals, Idiots, Women, and Minors: Victorian Writing by Women on Women*, ed. Susan Hamilton (Peterborough: Broadview, 2004), 119.

[67]   Manning and Waugh, "The Child of the English Savage," 696.

[68]   Waugh, "Prevention of Cruelty to Children," *Dublin Review* 110 (January 1892), 143–4.

[69]   Manning and Waugh, "The Child of the English Savage," 691.

[70]   Ibid., 699.

such case, "The child was the mother's own, her only one, and she was in good earnings."[71]

"The Child of the English Savage" is primarily concerned, however, with the male abuser; because fathers had sole custody of their children, it was their rights the London SPCC sought to challenge, and as a result, the "English savage" is often male. Furthermore, Manning and Waugh's attack is leveled at the "Englishman's castle," for it is there, they argue, that cruelty's "doer is most secure from detection."[72] As long as the English savage is allowed sole rule over his home, the savage's "castle" will remain a "dungeon" for tortured and abused children.

Both the complaint that the "Englishman's castle" permits the abuser to be secure from detection and the description of the home as a dungeon suggest that cruelty to children occurs in secret places, hidden from the public eye; such a suggestion does not, however, entirely encompass the London SPCC's understanding of abuse. The English savage might be protected by his private rights over his own home, and cruelty might go undetected in that space, but Manning and Waugh also argue that child abuse is known, is recognized, and is, in fact, only unseen because society chooses to turn a blind eye. In recounting a case in which two children were starved to death, they exclaim, "how much of this horrible guilt is society's! ... there were no neighbours' curses on the woman; no blows drove the man from his work. Folks get to think that these things are to be allowed."[73] The failure of parliament, Manning and Waugh reason, to "place the child of the savage on the same level as his dog," results in an assumption that parents can treat children as well, or as poorly, as they choose.[74]

By depicting child abuse both as hidden and unknown, and as known and recognized, yet ignored, Manning and Waugh were able to create a definition of abuse that encompassed the wide variety of situations in which the Society was involved. Some abuse, because of the relative wealth or status of the family, could be hidden, and the fear that abuse could be entirely obscured from the public eye can be seen in Manning and Waugh's description of a case in which the abused child "did not live in a crowded slum, but in an isolated cottage, surrounded by a garden."[75] Like Frances Power Cobbe, who believed that domestic violence against women existed "in the upper and middle classes rather more ... than is generally recognized," the London SPCC may have understood that certain homes provided greater security from detection than did others.[76]

What was important, therefore, in cases of abuse was to make the abuse visible to the right people; that is, to those who would feel the proper sympathy and be

---

[71]   Ibid., 698.

[72]   Ibid., 689.

[73]   Ibid., 693.

[74]   Ibid., 698.

[75]   Ibid., 695.

[76]   Cobbe, "Wife-Torture in England," 113.

moved to provide the proper help. With the founding of *The Child's Guardian* in January 1887, the London SPCC found the means by which to reach "such persons" and instruct them as to "what they can and cannot do"[77] Through his appeal to those "already interested" in child abuse, Waugh acknowledges that there is sympathy in place; however, he further argues that although "Interest in children, and horror at what is suffered by them at the hands of brutal, ill-living parents is common enough ... it is largely without knowledge of the provisions of the law for children's protection."[78] The reality of cruelty to children might have been known and recognized in England; according to Waugh, however, the law and the protections it might offer to the child were not, and the London SPCC's role was therefore to mobilize and bring together both the public and the state on behalf of abused and suffering children. This stance would ensure that when new legislation was passed in 1889, it was largely credited to Waugh, the London SPCC, and *The Child's Guardian*.

Representing Social Ills

The success of the London SPCC and of its journal can be attributed to the abuse narratives published within it, narratives constructed so as to make both the suffering child a object of sympathy and the reader a willing participant in that child's rescue. Waugh opens his article on "The Story of the Shrewsbury Case," for example, with "the story runs thus":

> "Spell 'fox,'" said the mother. "F-o-k-s," replied the child. "You know better," said the mother. "F-o-x," the child rejoined. "Now, you knew all along; I know you did, and if you say you didn't I'll punish you," said the mother. "I know'd all the time," the little girl said, to the promise of punishment if she did not say so. The child might have "know'd all the while," yet it needs no deep insight to see how, under the look of a hard face, and the sound of a domineering voice, she could forget that fox had only three letters. "I knew you did; I shall punish you," was the mother's reply. Punishment she was to have. If she said she did *not* know—punishment; now she had said she did know—punishment—punishment either way.[79]

The influence of novelistic writing is very evident in this passage. Waugh uses dialogue both to give a sense of urgency to the passage by transforming the reader into an eyewitness and to capture the child's voice, stressing her youth through the ungrammatical structure of her speech. As well, he creates a bond of sympathy

---

[77]   Waugh, untitled editorial, *The Child's Guardian* 1.1 (1887), 1.

[78]   Ibid.

[79]   Waugh, "The Story of the Shrewsbury Case," *The Child's Guardian* 1.2 (February 1887), 9.

between the child and the reading audience by urging the reader to imagine being "under the look of a hard face, and the sound of a domineering voice."

Furthermore, by beginning with such a seemingly innocuous and everyday occurrence in family life (a parent instructing a child and losing patience with her failure to perform correctly), Waugh demonstrates how the combination of the parent's unreasonable expectations and the child's inability to meet them accelerates into an abusive situation:

> It seems as if the father was the first to whip the child; he continued for twenty
> minutes … in a minute or two the whipping began again. This time it was the
> mother, a lady of no uncommon stature and strength, who wielded the whip; and
> blows and abuses, and little hysterical screams, continued until the whipping
> had lasted half an hour. Though the child was a girl-child of only three, the
> weapon used was not fit for the hide of a horse. She was set to write a copy; her
> eye black; her head bruised and aching; and the little hand that grasped the pen,
> swollen.[80]

In describing the abuse, Waugh is careful to include certain details: that both the mother and the father participate; that the instrument used and the length of the beating are incommensurate with the age of the child, or with the child's "offence"; and that the strength of the abusers is in great contrast to the stature of the little "girl-child." As well, the story clearly indicates throughout that the family is of a higher class, because Waugh mentions that the abuse had been seen and reported by servants within the home, and he observes at the end of the tale that "To persons in the position of the prisoners it must be an exceedingly painful thing to be placed on trial on such a charge."[81] Waugh's narrativization of this particular incident, then, serves to support and dramatize the conception of abuse put forward in "The Child of the English Savage": the abuse is irrational, the child is innocent, and the crime is unrelated to issues of class or poverty.

Although the abuse in this case is not the *result* of poverty, class is, nevertheless, an important issue in the narrative. The reason why the abuse that goes on in this home does not remain a secret, in spite of the fact that it is perpetrated, literally, behind closed doors (as Waugh observes, "the door was shut" and "the door was again closed" throughout the child's beating) is because "some of the servants (five were kept) stood about the house listening, all too well knowing what was going to happen."[82] If the child's suffering in this home is known to the servants, however, it only becomes known to the public through the nurse alerting the police, and through the work of *The Child's Guardian*, both of which allow the courts (and the reading audience) to see what goes on in the secret places of this privileged home. At the end of the story, Waugh records that

---

[80] Ibid.

[81] Ibid., 10.

[82] Ibid., 9.

The Society pressed only the minor charge, believing that a conviction on that would be enough to prevent cruelty, not in this mansion alone, but in all where, through this case, it became known that even servants can bring punishment on gentlefolks' heads if they be cruel to a child. And in this aspect we wish the case to be widely known.[83]

If there is a moral to this story, it is that where cruelty to children is concerned, knowledge is important, and once obtained and used, such knowledge can empower even "servants" to mete out justice to "gentlefolks." This narrative, therefore, is empowering, because it clearly delineates both what constitutes abuse and what can be done when abuse is witnessed or suspected.

Furthermore, the focus on the punishment to the upper-class parents, visited upon them on behalf of their little "girl-child" through the actions of their servants, suggests a leveling of authority: the witness (and, to a certain extent, the victim) is granted power and redress against the abuser through the action of the law, and through the work of the London SPCC. "The Story of the Shrewsbury Case" suggests that one can be empowered by knowledge, and transformed from helpless servant to active participant in justice. As Waugh notes of the primary witness in this case, "The nurse ... Like most people who witness cruelties ... scarcely knew what to do. But, at her wit's end, she conceived the idea of writing to the police."[84] The nurse, through being forced to witness violence against her charge, is herself a kind of victim of this act of violence. But by choosing to speak out, rather than silently suffer, she brings amelioration to the child and, by association, to herself.

Through its investigative work and through the publication of its case studies, therefore, the London SPCC offered to give agency to those who witnessed acts of violence against children, and to recognize the action that, according to the opening editorial of *The Child's Guardian* in 1887, had already been taken by such witnesses: "Some specially gifted farmer compassionates a child on the high road, and stops it to talk; a suspicious school-mistress follows up the return 'Unwell' as the reason for an always poorly and timid-looking scholar; a kindly publican observes the little slave, night after night...."[85] This description of child savers is all-inclusive, suggesting that every person, in every station, is capable of detecting and ameliorating cruelty to children.

But such narratives go further, demonstrating not only that every person could be empowered to intervene on behalf of a suffering child, but that there is a moral imperative to do so. As such, these narratives draw upon what Thomas Laqueur has identified as the "humanitarian narrative"; narratives that "speak in an extraordinarily detailed fashion about the pains and deaths of ordinary people in such a way as to make apparent the causal chains that might connect the action

---

[83]   Ibid., 10.
[84]   Ibid., 9.
[85]   Waugh, untitled editorial, *The Child's Guardian* 1.1 (January 1887): 1.

of its readers with the suffering of its subjects."[86] These narratives center upon "detail as the sign of truth," on the "personal body, not only as the locus of pain but also as the common bond between those who suffer and those who would help," and finally, upon the possibility and moral imperative of "ameliorative action."[87] Laqueur argues that such narratives co-evolved within a variety of discourses, including "The realistic novel, the autopsy, the clinical report, and the social inquiry."[88]

Just how such narratives evolved was very much dependent, of course, on the genre in which they were found. The dilemma of how to represent social ills so as to provide an accurate depiction of a particular problem and of its solution plagued social reformers, writers, and the English government throughout the nineteenth century. In *States of Inquiry*, Oz Frankel notes that "The *social* enters public consciousness in times of crisis: war, riot, major accident, epidemic, or natural disaster."[89] In Victorian England, the "two Englands" debate constituted such a crisis; the perception that "distinct social blocks lived completely ignorant of each other" and that "the social sphere, spatially conceived, had grown thoroughly divided between segments that were known and familiar and those that were designated hidden"[90] inspired numerous discursive interventions, from the literary to the social-scientific. Organizations such as the National Association for the Promotion of Social Science and key documents such as James Phillips Kay's *The Moral and Physical Conditions of the Labouring Classes* (1832) and Edwin Chadwick's *Report on the Sanitary Conditions in England* (1842) drew upon statistics as a means of providing what was felt to be a comprehensive depiction of social problems in England. These studies, according to Kay, allowed an "approximation of truth," relying as they did on both "minute and accurate" information and on the first-hand knowledge of the investigator.[91] As a result of such claims and of a culture that "had already been conditioned to associate print with the rendering of facts, either in journalism, science or, as importantly, the law,"[92] statistical studies increasingly became an authoritative means of accessing and assessing populations, and of describing social ills to the English public.

Studies such as Kay's were certainly "minute and accurate," but his army of facts about the working classes also tended to flatten out the subjects he describes: in his report, all poor homes in England merge into one tiny infested flat, filled

---

[86] Thomas Laqueur, "Bodies, Details, and the Humanitarian Narrative," in *The New Cultural History*, ed. Lynn Hunt (Berkeley: University of California Press, 1989), 177.

[87] Ibid., 177, 178.

[88] Ibid., 177.

[89] Oz Frankel, *States of Inquiry: Social Investigations and Print Culture in Nineteenth-Century Britain and the United States* (Baltimore: Johns Hopkins University Press, 2006), 6.

[90] Ibid.

[91] James Phillips Kay, *The Moral and Physical Condition of the Working Classes, Employed in the Cotton Manufacture in Manchester* (London: James Ridgway, 1832), 18.

[92] Frankel, *States of Inquiry*, 11.

with savage unrecognizable beings.[93] This flattening is in some ways effective, as it allows Kay to make sweeping generalizations about the subject at hand; however, it is also an important failing in his document. The aim of statistics might have been able to help Victorian social reformers "reduce their changing and bewildering environment to manageable terms,"[94] but Kay's statistics are bewilderingly oppressive, producing a sense of the social body as massive, uncontrollable, and beyond enumeration. This criticism could be leveled at the industry of "blue-book" production in general, where the "glut of minutia in reports from the poor-law, prison, and other inspectorates"[95] led some to question the "dead weight of that which the public would not even desire to know.[96]

Those who chose to represent social ills through the medium of literature often questioned the ability of statistical studies to do the same. Charles Dickens famously mocked the Victorian fascination with statistics through the character of Gradgrind in *Hard Times*, and George Eliot argued in 1856 that "the tendency created by the splendid conquests of modern generalizations, to believe that all social questions are merged in economical science, and that relations of men may be settled by algebraic equations" was a mistake that could not "co-exist with a real knowledge of the people."[97] According to Eliot, only the "great artist" could create the conditions necessary for the development of "moral sentiment," because the kinds of generalizations found in statistical studies and even, Eliot argued, in social novels, "require a sympathy ready-made, a moral sentiment already in activity."[98] Criticism was leveled at those authors who too closely adopted blue books as blueprints for their work; as Frankel notes of Charles Reade, for example, "it was said rather dismissively that his great gift was to convert parliamentary reports into works of fiction."[99] Sheila M. Smith, however, suggests that even

---

[93]   Rather than focus on exemplary individuals, for example, Kay instead relies on generalizations of "the labourer," "the artisan," and his family. His primary interest is in the eating and sleeping habits of these families, in which he sees ample proof of the degeneration of the lower classes: "The family sits round the table, and each rapidly appropriates his portion on a plate, or they all plunge their spoons into the dish, and with an animal eagerness satisfy the cravings of their appetite" (Kay, *The Moral and Physical Conditions of the Working Classes*, 23). Kay is particularly concerned about the "lower Irish" immigrants, who he perceives as "resembling savages in their appetites and habits" (Kay, 34).

[94]   Sheila M. Smith, "Blue Books and Victorian Novelists," *Review of English Studies: A Quarterly Journal of English Literature and the English Language* 21.81 (February 1970), 23.

[95]   Frankel, *States of Inquiry*, 65.

[96]   Qtd. in Frankel, 65.

[97]   George Eliot, "The Natural History of German Life" in *Essays of George Eliot*, ed. Thomas Pinney (London: Routledge and Kegan Paul, 1963, 271.

[98]   Ibid., 270.

[99]   Frankel, *States of Inquiry*, 30.

though texts such as Disraeli's *Sybil* (1845) and Charles Kingsley's *Yeast* (1848) "used the novel as though it were a popular form of Blue book," they did so "in order to make their readers explore the social problems and give them evidence to draw some conclusions."[100]

The relationship between the literary and the "factual," between novels, poems, and blue books did not work solely in one direction; Frankel argues that "Government manufactured its papers with an eye to literary genres, as well as to the formats of review or scholarly journals. They shared with them not just sensibilities and language but also publishing strategies, such as serialization."[101] In many case studies, such as those employed by Mary Carpenter in her work on juvenile delinquents, and later, in those of the NSPCC, a balance is struck between narratives of exemplary individuals that employ the "'reality effect' of the literary technique through which the experiences of others are represented as real"[102] and statistical tables and classification systems. Such a balance succeeds in presenting social problems as widespread, yet individually experienced. Dramatizing individual tales of suffering or even allowing subjects to tell their own histories, these texts utilize a supple form of representation in which the needs of the investigator—to find and evaluate suffering individuals—and the needs of the public—to feel that a relationship had been formed between them and the sufferer—can be met.

The Emergence of the NSPCC

Though the London SPCC in its early years published case studies that worked by employing a "humanitarian narrative," it very quickly moved away from these kinds of cases. Cases such as "The Story of the Shrewsbury Case" worked by imaginatively placing the reader inside the abusive home, and thus by constructing sympathy between suffering child and active reader, but the Society soon began to represent the public as ignorant, skeptical, and incapable of addressing the problem. As early as its second year of publication, *The Child's Guardian* would proclaim that the Society's "first work is to make a happily incredulous public know the existence, extent and horribleness of the hidden evils we have come into existence to destroy."[103] Waugh continues by noting that the journal "shall try to annihilate the bliss of ignorance of any but [its readers'] own happy homes," and that "In this country, at least, if children perish, it is for the lack of brave people's knowing about it."[104] Here the claim made is not just that people in England do not know the law, but also that they do not even realize that child abuse exists. The public is now constructed as "incredulous," suggesting that even when reports of

---

[100] Susan Smith, "Blue-Books and Victorian Novelists," 29.

[101] Frankel, *States of Inquiry*, 9.

[102] Laqueur, "Bodies, Details, and the Humanitarian Narrative," 177.

[103] Waugh, "Our New Year," *The Child's Guardian* 2.13 (January 1888): 1–2, 1.

[104] Ibid., 1, 2.

child abuse are made known, they may not be believed. Child abuse is "hidden" and the work of the London SPCC becomes, as a result, revelatory as opposed to merely informative.

The London SPCC's authority, Waugh asserts, comes from the knowledge to which it alone has access:

> We do not write these things without pain and tears. We send no thrill of horror abroad which we ourselves have not first felt. We are moved not by the poor inadequate words in which we try to convey our terrible facts, but by the presence of little frightened faces, hollow voices, timid habits, bandaged heads, bruised and blistered limbs …. We have sought by word sketches to convey sensations to our readers which small living children had first conveyed to us.[105]

Here Waugh suggests that the abuse narratives in *The Child's Guardian* consist merely of "poor inadequate words," of "sketches" that cannot hope to approximate the real "presence" of the abused child itself, or even the "terrible facts" of the cases. Waugh still argues that "Knowledge is the deliverer,"[106] but the knowledge obtainable by the Society's reading audience is necessarily incomplete—the reader can feel only "sensations" that are already at a remove from the sensations directly experienced by the Society and its inspectors (both of which are themselves at a remove from the experiences of the abused child).

Waugh's profession of the inadequacy of language in this particular editorial, I argue, marks a key moment in the development of the London SPCC's rhetoric. By its second year of publication, *The Child's Guardian*'s target audience appeared to be those who were either completely ignorant of the issues the London SPCC addressed, or at the very least, were ignorant of the realities of the cases the Society and its inspectors had to face. No longer were farmers and servants capable of being empowered with child-saving knowledge; instead, the Society began to represent its own inspectors as uniquely qualified to undertake the task of saving children. Such a shift can be attributed to the Society's growing professionalization. At the beginning of 1888, the Society had only two inspectors, but by December of that same year, it had employed 15.[107] Furthermore, by April 1889, Waugh would argue that even the police were unqualified for child-saving work, claiming that "however strong their human feeling, [the police] were never the agency for dealing with poor little starved and beaten children …. It is the work of altogether different men to decoy these broken little hearts into confidences, and get a story from small, pale, dying lips on which a Bench can convict their wrongdoers."[108] This particular claim goes beyond a frustration with the "inadequacy of words" in

---

105   Ibid., 1.
106   Ibid., 2.
107   Waugh, "Notes," *The Child's Guardian* 2.24 (December 1888), 119.
108   Waugh, "Police and Ill-Used Children," *The Child's Guardian* 3.28 (April 1889), 53.

that it suggests that even the "languid little originals"[109] can only be made to speak, to give a "story," to the Society's own inspectors. What is required to address the issue of abuse is no longer simple knowledge and good will, but specialized knowledge and specialized skill.

Moreover, even before the abused child could be made to speak, it had to be identified, a task that, Waugh suggested, the Society's inspectors alone could undertake. In an article entitled "No Cruelty Here" (a phrase that would become the future NSPCC's rallying cry), Waugh claims that "but for us, the cruelties would have remained the mere secrets of homes."[110] These same cruelties went unnoticed by church and school board officials, Waugh attests, because

> As the fly has many eyes, so has man; and which he sees with, depends on the main aim of his life. We all fall into limited habits of sight. This is the result of our particular vocation. With a new vocation, facts come to light which before had been as little noticed as they are now conspicuous …. We live to observe suspicious facts in child-life, to follow their lead, and to give days, if needs be, to the doing of it.[111]

Here, Waugh not only defends what he perceives as the London SPCC's singular authority, but also appeals to a notion of specialized training that belies the possibility of broader approaches to social problems. Waugh argues that anything less than the development of expertise leads to a kind of blindness—to "limited habits of sight." According to the understanding of social amelioration Waugh presents here, those not directly concerned with child abuse and child suffering will simply be unable to see it. Only the Society's inspectors follow the "vocation" that develops the particular "habits of sight" required for that work.

The shift in the Society's narrative of abuse from something that was known, yet not addressed, to something that it alone had the skills and abilities to investigate and to ameliorate, provided ample justification for the Society's reconstitution of itself from the London SPCC to the NSPCC in 1889. Following the passage of the "Children's Charter," Waugh rejoiced that the new legislation "is an embodiment of the large spirit of the Society that promoted it. That Society knows neither London children nor Birmingham children, but only English children, and all of them."[112] By this logic, a national law requires a national organization, and although Waugh suggests that this legislation empowers "the British public," his direct association of the new law with the new NSPCC—"The principle of the Society is right. It is right for legislation. It is right for administration. We are dealing with

---

[109] Waugh, "Our New Year," 1.

[110] Waugh, "No Cruelty Here," *The Child's Guardian* 2.13 (January 1888), 4.

[111] Ibid.

[112] Waugh, "Prevention of Cruelty to Children," *The Child's Guardian* 3.32 (August 1889), 133.

a national evil. As a nation we unite to protect our injured children"[113]—instead suggests that the most important aspect of the legislation is that it empowers the NSPCC. Furthermore, Waugh's proclamation that the NSPCC "knows ... only English children, and all of them" speaks to the connection between knowledge and the centralization of power. Just as revealing cruelty to children, according to the Society's rhetoric, requires those trained with specialized "habits of sights," so too do the nation's children require a unified, centralized, national organization to fully "know" and address their sufferings.

The reconstitution of the London SPCC as the NSPCC marks another significant transition in the Society's representation of itself in relation to the public and in relation to other organizations. The NSPCC certainly argued that such a transformation from local to national satisfied purely practical demands upon child-protection work; in 1892, for example, in response to a "suggestion made the by Mayor [of Birmingham] to the effect that it would be better for Birmingham to stand alone with a separate society than to continue a part of the National Society," the reply was that "If each large town stood alone, smaller towns and country districts, unable to support societies of their own, would receive no assistance; and the children in such districts would rarely benefit by the Act."[114] In other words, the centralization of the organization allowed wealthier districts to support smaller, poorer districts, and thus provided equal representation across England. The NSPCC also argued, however, that a uniformity of *method* in the investigation and prosecution of child abuse cases was necessary in order to combat the problem. While some in England argued that "the National Society's desire to cover the land with its agencies is of mere envy and ambition," the NSPCC suggested that, in fact, it was other SPCC organizations that chose to remain separate from the NSPCC, such as the Birkenhead and Wirral SPCC and the Liverpool SPCC, that were failing in their duties towards abused children. Articles such as "The National Society's Position in Liverpool," published in 1896, argued that children in Liverpool were not receiving the full benefit of the new law, and cited as the reason "the difference between the methods employed by the Liverpool Society and the National Society."[115] When the NSPCC established its own committee in Liverpool, it "discovered" abuse that had gone unnoticed: "alas! a ghastly light is cast upon the neglected children which the Liverpool Society has unhappily practised in the years that are gone!"[116]

What abuse was found by the NSPCC that had gone "neglected" by the Liverpool SPCC is difficult to ascertain, but the differences between the number of cases undertaken by both organizations suggests that seeing abuse had as much to do with what one considered *to be* abuse as it did with uncovering unspeakable

---

[113]   Ibid.

[114]   NSPCC, "Our National Scheme," *The Child's Guardian* 6.1 (January 1892), 6.

[115]   NSPCC, "The National Society's Position in Liverpool," *The Child's Guardian* 10.3 (March 1896), 35.

[116]   Ibid.

deeds done in darkness. The "Children's Charter" allowed for a broad construction of "cruelty," a fact attested to by the wide variety of categories used by the NSPCC to classify its own cases: "General Ill-Treatment," "Assault," "Neglect and Starvation," "Abandonment and Exposure," "Begging Cases," "Dangerous Performances," "Immorality," and "Other Wrongs."[117] The Liverpool Society had always endorsed a mandate of "moderation" in which that Society "endeavoured 'to deal directly with the parents, and to reform the home rather than to punish the culprits.'"[118] However, in NSPCC discourse, the Liverpool Society comes to represent instead a failure to protect; a failure that is, importantly, linked to the lack of a proper "system." Truth and knowledge, according to the NSPCC, could only be obtained through the Society's casework, and such casework was, of course, inherently connected to the NSPCC's inspectorate and to the NSPCC's training:

> As a great public institution [the NSPCC] always has many well-qualified men applying to it for posts as Inspectors, and from these it can pick out those who, after a searching examination, appear to be the fittest. These candidates then go through a course of training in the laws that affect children, and in the Society's principles and practice as regards dealing with cases. The consequence is that an Inspector of the NSPCC is a picked expert, thoroughly trained, and competent to carry out the work of the Society, a work that demands most careful and delicate handling.[119]

Obviously, the trained and hand-picked cruelty man depicted here in 1896 provides a sharp contrast to the well-meaning and "specially gifted farmer" who helps an abused child in the opening editorial of *The Child's Guardian* in 1887. From a charity dedicated to educating the public about child abuse, the NSPCC had become a professional organization, devoted to its own "principles and practices" as the best means of carrying out child-protection work. The public's role, in terms of such an organization, was only that of working to ensure the NSPCC's prosperity so that it could continue the work of finding abuse, even that which was "hidden" in plain sight.

NSPCC Casework

Such a transformation in the field of child protection, I argue, had a significant effect on the ways in which child abuse was understood and on the ways in which it was represented. As the NSPCC's caseload increased throughout the 1890s,

---

[117]   NSPCC, "Quarterly Return of the Society's Cases," *The Child's Guardian* 5.11 (November 1891), 116.

[118]   George K. Behlmer, *Child Abuse and Moral Reform*, 55.

[119]   NSPCC, "The System of Dealing with the Suffering Child: The 'Local' versus the 'National,'" *The Child's Guardian* 10.8 (August 1896), 109.

for example, and as the work of its propaganda changed, the abuse narratives recounted in *The Child's Guardian* also began to change. Longer narratives such as "The Story of the Shrewsbury Case" appeared far less frequently, replaced instead with tables listing the "Month's Return of the Society's Cases" or with "Court Cases Proved True During the Last Recorded Month." These tables, which were devoted entirely to statistics, were sometimes followed by "Sample Cases" or "Courts and Children's Cases," in which abuse narratives appeared in greatly abbreviated forms. For example, one case from Rochester reads as follows:

> At the Rochester Country Police Court, Henry Barrand and Marion Riley were indicted for neglecting their eight children …. It appeared that the man was in receipt of regular wages of 21s. per week, and could afford to get drunk. The children were neglected, underfed, underclothed, and altogether in a very filthy condition. Inspector Cole proved having cautioned the defendants owing to their neglectful conduct to their children, whom he had found in a room almost without furniture or bedding, sleeping upon rags …. The woman asked for time to get straight, which he granted her; but a month later the place and the children were in a worse state than before, some of them were breaking out in sores. The male defendant was found guilty and sentenced to two months' hard labour. The defendant Riley was sentenced to one month with hard labour.[120]

Unlike "The Story of the Shrewsbury Case," this case does not construct a "reality effect" in order to place the reader in the role of eye-witness. The only details provided are those needed to make the case: the family has sufficient money, the children are given insufficient care, and the defendants are punished according to the law. The home life is only described in ways that materially relate to the proceedings, such as the father's implied drunkenness, the mother's failure to address the children's needs, and the filthy conditions of the home, all of which serve to support the accusations of neglect and abuse. The children themselves are important only as evidence of their parents' abuse, as the text does not indicate their fate once their parents are arrested.[121] The important aspect of this case,

---

[120]   NSPCC, "Courts and Children's Cases," *The Child's Guardian* 9.5 (May 1895), 65.

[121]   The NSPCC rarely mentions, in cases reported in *The Child's Guardian*, what happened to children who were apprehended from their homes. In its early years, the London SPCC ran a temporary shelter for children at its Harpur Street address. As well, it is evident from various "Notes" in *The Child's Guardian* that children apprehended by the Society had either been placed in "homes" (for example, 1.2, 12–13) or had emigrated (3.26, 26). For the most part, however, such information is not recorded in the journal. Behlmer, however, records that "Even when jailed for severe neglect or assault, offenders usually returned to their young" (George K. Behlmer, *Child Abuse and Moral Reform*, 175). Furthermore, he notes that "Of the 754,732 children on whose behalf the society intervened between mid-1889 and mid-1903, only 1,200—far less than 1 percent—were removed from

therefore, as suggested by its place in "Courts and Children's Cases," is the result: the parents are indicted, the case against them is "proved," and the sentences are handed down, all through the Society's efforts.

The difference between cases such as this and "The Story of the Shrewsbury Case" is, in essence, the "story." The Rochester case is not a "story" of abuse, it is a narrative of the NSPCC's casework, and as such, it does not include the novelistic elements of the Shrewsbury case. It is not meant to create outrage, but to demonstrate efficiency, and as such, it relies less upon the reader's sympathy than on the reader's trust. Because the Society can see abuse where others cannot, and because the Society is trained to deal with offenders, its work on behalf of abused children is authoritative. Cases such as this from Rochester, therefore, are about demonstrating that the public can trust in that authority to do the work of "protecting children," and to do it well. If information is missing, such as the relationship between the parents and the children, the reaction of the children to their parents' arrest, or even the whereabouts of the children after the arrest, its lack makes the information seem unessential—unrelated to the "facts" of the case and to its conclusion.

The alteration in the kinds of abuse narratives published in *The Child's Guardian* is tied, I would argue, to a shift in genre from the case study to narrativizations of casework. The case study, as I have suggested, works to create bonds between the reader and the suffering subject, to make that suffering recognizable and real to those who might be moved to ameliorate it. Casework, by comparison, represents the specific details and evidence required by a specific organization in order to achieve a specific task. The questions asked and the information gathered within casework are therefore limited: limited to what are considered the requisite questions and the requisite information. Casework records an individual's entrance into a system already in place, and it operates on assumptions about what constitutes a problem and how that problem should be addressed. It does not suggest a cure; instead, it assumes the means of amelioration are already in place. Where case studies and statistics rely on "sympathy ready-made," casework relies on authority ready-made. In its first few years, when it was still establishing itself, the London SPCC published case studies such as the "Shrewsbury Case," which still worked within the residual genres of the novel and the case study. By the 1890s, however, the abuse narratives printed in *The Child's Guardian* record the "important" details of the case, the result, and nothing else.

But what gets lost? Casework, connected as it is to a particular organization's own needs and interests, necessarily limits what can be understood or said about the object of its concern. With the emergence of this genre as the dominant mode of representing child abuse in English society, the meaning and significance of the endangered child itself became limited. While I am interested in tracing the persistence of the concerns and language of literary narratives of child

---

parental custody. Magistrates placed a few of these children with relatives, but sent most to orphanages, industrial schools, and, as a last resort, workhouses" (Ibid.).

endangerment within the new rhetoric of child protection, I am therefore also intent on elucidating that which gets repressed with the replacement of one dominant form of representing childhood peril with the other. That is, though a genre such as the Victorian novel was a vested genre that limited what was sayable about the endangered child, it also, in its imaginative depictions of that figure, demonstrated the complex reactions to and understanding of a concept that was still, largely, under construction. In an examination of a variety of narratives about endangered children in the nineteenth century, I hope to elucidate some of the possibilities for understanding the child, its relationship to its family, and the nature of its endangerment that remain as irresolvable contradictions in the (still) dominant narrative of child protection.

Chapter 2
"Animals and Children": Savages, Innocents, and Cruelty

Understanding how children came to be considered worthy objects of unique legal protections at the end of the nineteenth century requires recognition of the extent to which these protections were modeled on those provided to animals. The fact that animals received protection *first* has been used to demonstrate the low value accorded children in English society: for example, James Kincaid argues that the Victorian era was "comparatively neglectful of the young in its reforms," and as proof offers the fact that the NSPCC was not formed until 1884, "though the Society for the Prevention of Cruelty to Animals had existed since 1824."[1] In this observation, Kincaid echoes the concerns of Victorian child advocates; as one late nineteenth-century commentator put it, "It does seem anomalous that it should be easier to punish a man or woman for ill-treatment of a dog or cat than for cruelty to their own children; but such is the state of the law at present."[2] A mere recitation of the facts on both the development of anti-cruelty societies and the passage of anti-cruelty legislation would seem to support these assumptions: the Royal Society for the Prevention of Cruelty to Animals (RSPCA) was founded in 1824 (the prefix "Royal" was granted in 1840), with the first laws against cruelty to animals passed in 1835,[3] whereas the Liverpool Society for the Prevention of Cruelty to Children (the first of its kind in England) was not founded until 1883, with the passage of the "Children's Charter" occurring in 1889.

These facts misrepresent, however, the actual status of children under the law in nineteenth-century England. Though there may be evidence to suggest that cruel neglect of an animal was punishable by law *before* similar laws were imposed regarding neglect of children, in terms of violence against children, at least, such was not necessarily the case.[4] In *Forgotten Children: Parent-Child Relationships from 1500 to 1900*, Linda Pollock records a magistrate's response in 1824 to a defendant who thought that "every father had the right to do as he pleased with his

---

[1] James R. Kincaid, *Child-Loving: The Erotic Child and Victorian Culture* (New York: Routledge, 1992), 77.

[2] NSPCC, "The 'Morning Advertiser' On Our New Bill," *The Child's Guardian*, 2.19 (July 1888), 58.

[3] Martin's Act, preventing cruelty to cattle, was passed in 1822. In 1835, it was extended to all domestic animals.

[4] Martin's Act of 1822 aimed to prevent "The cruel and improper treatment of cattle," for example, the "improper" certainly leaving room for interpretation.

own child": "the law must teach the defendant that this doctrine of his was very erroneous."[5] From her examination of newspaper reports of court cases from 1785 to 1860, Pollock concludes that the

> manner in which the cases were reported by the newspaper provides an indication of the attitudes of the time to cruelty to children. The fact that the majority of cases were found guilty meant that the law and society condemned child abuse long before the specific Prevention of Cruelty to Children Act appeared in 1889. Parents who abused their offspring were generally considered "unnatural" and the cruelty as "horrific" or "barbaric."[6]

Pollock's conclusion is further supported by historians who argue that "brutal treatment of children was deplored" in working-class neighborhoods, and that "a whole range of both formal and unofficial strategies for dealing with sexual abuse, for example, existed in working-class neighbourhoods long before ... the founding of the NSPCC."[7]

The fact that violence against and abuse of children in England was condemned—both in society and before the law—before it became a distinct crime in 1889 demonstrates the inappropriateness of citing the late emergence of the NSPCC as evidence of a widespread lack of concern for abused children. And yet, it is an enduring and deeply held belief that English humanitarianism resulted in a "sentimental" attachment to animals that displaced proper concern for children. This discrepancy between the actual status of children and animals under the law and the perception of that status is captured perfectly in Benjamin Waugh's complaint, published in *The Child's Guardian*, that "if wretched children were only dogs, what sunlight would fall into their doomed and dismal lives!"[8]

The anxiety latent in this statement—that English children were somehow displaced as objects of charity by animals—ostensibly speaks to the low status of children, but it also springs from, in part, a desire to assert difference between two concepts that had long been used to define each other. The emergence of humanitarian discourse in the Enlightenment period necessitated discussion of what makes humans both human and "humane." In such discourse, animals were often represented as the victims of child cruelty, because the concept of humane behavior was linked to the desire to understand how humans initially responded to the world around them: whether "innocently," with a desire to do no harm, or "sinfully," with the desire to cause pain and suffering. Growing concern about the place of the child in industrial England, however, reconfigured this narrative,

---

[5]   Linda Pollock, *Forgotten Children: Parent-child relations from 1500 to 1900* (Cambridge: Cambridge University Press, 1983), 94.

[6]   Ibid., 93.

[7]   Anna Davin, *Growing up Poor*, 37, and Louise Jackson, *Child Sexual Abuse in Victorian England*, 31.

[8]   Benjamin Waugh, "Notes," *The Child's Guardian* 3.39 (May 1889), 84.

allowing for representations of the child and the animal as companions in their suffering, as blameless victims of an uncaring, adult society. Such a connection of the child with the animal as similar "feeling subjects"—and the accompanying severance of the child from the adult world—was a necessary precondition of the development of the crime of "cruelty to children." But if the linkage of the child and the animal allowed for a productive, if problematic, space in which to examine questions about the nature of the child, the relationship between humans and the "lower creation," and the concept of cruelty itself, this connection also, ultimately, proved to be a liability within the new rationality of child protection.

"Distaste for Cruelty"[9]

In *The Family, Sex and Marriage in England, 1500–1800*, Lawrence Stone traces the emergence of a "broad philosophical movement, which gathered strength throughout the mid- and late-eighteenth century," that he identifies as "a growing antipathy to cruelty." According to Stone, this aversion to cruelty

> seems to have been concurrent with, and related to, the spread of Enlightenment ideas throughout Europe. Even then, it was at all times a state of mind confined to a relatively small part of the population. But it was a highly articulate and ultimately very influential part which slowly learned to employ all the devices of mass persuasion available in what was increasingly an educationally literate and politically open society.[10]

This "part" of society was "responsible for such things as the abolition of the slave trade, the suppression of most cruel sports, prison reform, and reform in the treatment of the mentally sick."[11]

Although one must find fault with Stone's ready acceptance of what he identifies as a culture of feeling as the primary cause behind a growing "antipathy to cruelty" in English society—Foucault observes that the gradual disappearance of torture has been "attributed too readily and too emphatically to a process of 'humanization,' thus dispensing with the need for further analysis"[12]—it can at least be said with some certainty that physical torture and abuse became increasingly unacceptable in English middle-class society. The complexities of this change in social mores have certainly been argued at length,[13] but what I am particularly interested

---

[9]   Lawrence Stone, *The Family, Sex and Marriage in England, 1500–1800* (Middlesex, England: Penguin Books, 1979), 163.

[10]   Ibid., 62.

[11]   Ibid.

[12]   Michel Foucault, *Discipline and Punish*, 7.

[13]   James Turner's *Reckoning with the Beast: Animals, Pain, and Humanity in the Victorian Mind* (1980), James A. Hammerton's *Cruelty and Companionship: Conflict*

in here is Stone's assumption that "In its effect on family life, the connection between hostility to animals and to cruelty to children is clear enough."[14] Stone presumes that his reader will follow along with this statement quite readily—that a society that is against "cruel sports" will necessarily behave kindly towards its children. His logic here is based on his inclusion of both children and animals in the category of "the helpless," and his assumption is that compassion to one will result in compassion to the other.[15] This assumption is fundamentally flawed, however, in that it suggests that the culture of feeling Stone traces is concerned with the victim, when in fact, Enlightenment ideals were more concerned with the effects of cruelty upon the perpetrator. Such a distinction demands a reassessment of the place of children within early humanitarian discourse.

Stone's alignment of "the suppression of cruel sports" with prison reform demonstrates his argument that cruelty to animals was closely related to cruelty to humans. He supports this alignment through reference to Hogarth's *The Four Stages of Cruelty* (1751), which, as the title suggests, traces the origins and development of a man's cruelty and lack of compassion. The series begins with a young boy's mistreatment of animals, and ends with the man's "reward" for committing murder (dissection, presumably after his own execution). Hogarth's "stages of cruelty" aptly depict what many Enlightenment philosophers believed: that if, according to Immanuel Kant, a person "is not to stifle his human feelings, he must practise kindness towards animals, for he who is cruel to animals becomes hard also in his dealings with men." The antipathy towards cruelty expressed by Hogarth and Kant demonstrates not only, and certainly not primarily, a desire to protect the welfare of the animal, but more specifically, the need to cultivate and protect the development of a humane, civilized self. One of the earliest writers on animal suffering, Richard Dean, demonstrates this same concern in his *An Essay on the Future Life of Brutes* (1767): "for a man to torture a brute, whose life God has put into his hands, is a disgraceful thing, such a meanness of spirit as his honor requires him to shun. If he does it out of wantonness, he is a fool, and a coward: if for pleasure, he is a monster." While animals are "brutes," he argues, yet they "have sensibility," and to behave cruelly towards them is to betray "the attainments of

---

in *Nineteenth-Century Married Life* (1992), Moira Ferguson's *Animal Advocacy and Englishwomen, 1780–1900: Patriots, Nation, and Empire* (1998), J. Carter Wood's "A Useful Savagery: The Invention of Violence in Nineteenth-Century England" (2004), Martin Wiener's *Men of Blood: Violence, Manliness, and Criminal Justice in Victorian England* (2004), and Lisa Surridge's *Bleak Houses: Marital Violence in Victorian Fiction* (2005), for example, all provide excellent analyses of the ways in which nineteenth-century responses to violence, pain, cruelty, and suffering were inflected by issues of class, gender, and nation.

[14]   Stone, *The Family, Sex and Marriage*, 162.

[15]   Ibid., 163.

science," "the improvements of natural reason," and "the dispensation of religious light."[16]

Antipathy towards cruel treatment of animals was therefore motivated as much by a desire to construct the civilized subject as it was by compassion. What is important to realize, of course, was that children in this period were not necessarily included in the category of the humane subject. Instead, children represented the untutored, savage self, and as such, were often depicted as the natural tormentors of animals. The boy who abuses animals in *The Four Stages of Cruelty* goes on to more heinous acts of violence because his cruelty is unabated. He lacks proper instruction, and the "progress" Hogarth depicts is meant to be a warning that cruelty must be caught in its early stages. Higher than animals, yet lower than adults, children required education as a means of controlling their natural cruelty. Moreover, strict discipline (which might imply the beating of a child in a time when beating was still a very suitable choice for discipline) was suggested as a means of curbing this cruelty; as Henry Fielding remarked, "a boy should, in my opinion ... be severely punished for exercising cruelty on a dog or cat,"[17] and as David Perkins observes, "One might even recommend cruelty in order to extirpate it."[18]

The assumption that the child was naturally depraved and savage can be traced to what is often termed the "Original Sin" conception of childhood, generally considered to have originated with the Puritans. Though the Puritan habit of "injecting considerable severity and erudition into the lessons designed for the young"[19] did not derive from the same impulses as did rationalist texts for children written in the late eighteenth century in England, the perception of children as inherently depraved and in need of tutelage is shared by both the earlier religious and the later secular discourse. The clearest expression of the latter can often be encountered in stories written for children, such as Mary Wollstonecraft's *Original Stories from Real Life* (1791), which centers on the eminently rational Mrs. Mason and her two female charges. In three chapters on "The Treatment of Animals," Wollstonecraft demonstrates how Mrs. Mason observes Mary and Caroline's "cruel sports," before gently instructing them as to how they should respond to the creatures they "despise":

> The domestic animals I keep, I provide the best food for, and never suffer them
> to be tormented; and this caution arises from two motives:—I wish to make them
> happy; and, as I love my fellow-creatures still better than the brute creation, I

---

[16]   Both essays are in *Awe for the Tiger, Love for the Lamb: A Chronicle of Sensibility to Animals*, ed. Rod Preece (UBC Press: Vancouver, 2002), 174, 157, 156.

[17]   Henry Fielding, "Covent Garden," in *Awe for the Tiger*, 135.

[18]   David Perkins, *Romanticism and Animal Rights* (Cambridge: Cambridge University Press, 2003), 22.

[19]   Patricia Demers, "Puritan 'Hell-Fire': Warnings and Warmth," in *From Instruction to Delight: An Anthology of Children's Literature to 1850*, ed. Patricia Demers (Don Mills, Ontario: Oxford University Press, 2004), 46.

> would not allow those I have any influence over, to grow habitually thoughtless
> and cruel, till they were unable to relish the greatest pleasure life affords,—that
> of resembling God, by doing good.

Because Mary and Caroline's education "has been neglected," they need Mrs. Mason's lessons in order to advance from a state of taking pleasure in cruelty, to one of being like God, and making "the brute creation" as happy and comfortable as possible. Kindness to animals, according to Mrs. Mason, is what separates human beings from the lower creation, because "man is allowed to enoble his nature, by cultivating his mind and enlarging his heart." Cultivation and education are therefore key to the transformation of children from a state of cruelty to one of compassion.[20]

That the children can be taught—in other words, can be rational—is a central tenet of this kind of literature for children, a fact that problematizes any easy association of rationalist stories such as this with "original sin" constructions of childhood. Instead, what Wollstonecraft's text attempts to encounter and instruct is the "natural" child—a far more complicated and complex figure than the inherently sinful product of earlier religious discourse. Drawing upon the philosophies of Locke and Rousseau, rationalist tales often focused upon issues such as cruelty and the development of the humane subject. Within such narratives, animals and children are continually linked because children are encouraged to understand themselves—both the children within the narrative, and the children who, presumably, make up the reading audience—through a comparison of their own feelings and needs and those of animals. Narratives of this kind would persist throughout the nineteenth century, in essays such as *Some Remarks on Cruelty to Animals* (1865), Clara Balfour's *Cruelty and Cowardice: A Word to Butchers and their Boys* (1866), and, particularly, in animal rights journals such as the *Band of Mercy Advocate* and *Animal World*. Because an understanding of just what it is that causes a child to be cruel was central to an understanding of the humane subject, philosophers and writers of children's literature often embraced shared narratives of animal/child relations.

The characteristics of that narrative, however, were often complicated. The idea that children were naturally sadistic and cruel, and required the light of reason and civilization to make them otherwise, was not universally held. As early as 1713, Alexander Pope wrote that "almost as soon as we are sensible what life is ourselves, we make it a sport to take it from other creatures"; he argues, however, that children are "bred up" into cruelty. The "license of inflicting pain upon poor animals," he states, is "one of the finest pleasures we allow them." The use of "license" and "allow" here suggest the corollary of the power relationship Wollstonecraft describes in her *Original Stories*. Where there is a hierarchy in which one proves one's humanity through mastery over the "lower" creation, such

20   Mary Wollstonecraft, *Original Stories from Real Life* (Otley: Woodstock Books, 2001), 5, 5–6, 3, 11.

mastery can become the right to exercise cruelty. Pope suggests that such cruelty is not, however, inherently natural, but is instead the result of socialization—of how one is "bred."

He goes on to add, however, that "a very good use might be made of the fancy which children have for birds and insects."[21] Here, he assumes that children do have some inherent connection with animals—a natural "fancy" that can, with proper instruction, create that humane subject discussed earlier. The construction of the child and the animal as sharing some kind of inherent connection is developed further in the work of Jean-Jacques Rousseau. In *Emile* (1762), Rousseau argued that the child best learns sympathy for animals, not through rigorous moral discipline, but through natural instruction of their shared characteristics:

> To become sensitive and pitying, the child must know that there are beings like him who suffer what he has suffered, who feels pain as he has felt, and that there are others whom he ought to conceive of as being able to feel them too. In fact, how do we let ourselves be moved by pity if not by transporting ourselves outside of ourselves and identifying with the suffering animal, by leaving, as it were, our own being to take on its being.[22]

According to Rousseau, in order for the child to learn empathy—both towards animals and towards other human beings—the child must embrace its closeness to nature, must come to "know" it intimately. Rather than a hierarchy of nature, in which children learn—through evil actions or good ones—that they must have power over animals in order to affirm their humanity, what Rousseau argues for is instead a recognition of sameness.

The Romantic Child

Importantly, it is the child who is most able to embrace this sameness, as "closest to nature, [the child] had natural purity and sensibility and innate tendencies to virtue."[23] What is focused upon in Rousseau's text as a means of connection between child and animal is not virtue, however, but instead the shared experience of suffering. This conflation of a kind of natural innocence and of suffering captured the imagination of many of the Romantic poets. In *Romanticism and Animals Rights*, David Perkins notes that "By 1775 [animals] might incarnate a pristine innocence, a spontaneous joy in life that adult human beings lacked," and though his text focuses solely on the animal as the subject of Romantic discourse,

---

21   Alexander Pope, "On Cruelty to the Brute Creation," in *Awe for the Tiger*, 28.

22   Jean-Jacques Rousseau, *Emile, or, On Education* (London: Everyman's Library, 1974), 184.

23   Penny Brown, *The Captured World: The Child and Childhood in Nineteenth-Century Women's Writing* (New York: Harvester Wheatsheaf, 1993), 6.

his inclusion of "adult" points to the implicit connection that existed between animals *and* children in that discourse. That same misanthropy, that hatred for "the displacers, abusers, tormentors, and destroyers of the creatures you sympathized with"[24] that Perkins proposes as a key element of Romantic literature, also extended sympathy, I argue, to the child, who also fell outside the flaws and boundaries of human society into what Judith Plotz identifies as "the differentness of childhood and the separateness of the child world."[25]

That world might be constructed as separate from adulthood, but it was also constructed through sameness to the innocent animal, because both shared a natural goodness that, while making them playful and joyful, also made them defenseless against the violence inflicted upon them by society. In "To a Young Ass: Its Mother being tethered near it" (1794), Samuel Taylor Coleridge laments, "Poor little foal of an oppressèd race! ... Do thy prophetic fears anticipate, / Meek child of misery! thy future fate?" Though the mother ass shares the speaker's pity, it is the foal whose fate is most painful, as "(most unlike the nature of things young) / ... earthward still thy moveless head is hung." The foal is a child, in its way, and therefore its "ragged coat" and "dulled spirits" are an especial cause of misery, because the speaker can imagine "how thou wouldst toss thy heels about in gamesome play, / And frisk about as lamb or kitten gay!"[26]

The association of the animal with the child becomes even more evident in William Blake's *Songs of Innocence and Experience* (1794). In "Spring," the child narrator proclaims,

> Little Lamb
> Here I am,
> Come and lick
> My white neck.
> Let me pull
> Your soft wool.
> Let me kiss
> Your soft face.[27]

The lamb and the child share a special kinship in this poem, as both are soft, white, and presumably innocent—a kinship that is also evident in Blake's "Holy Thursday": "The hum of multitudes was there but a multitude of lambs / Thousands of little boys & girls raising their innocent hands."[28] There is obvious religious

---

[24]   David Perkins, *Romanticism and Animal Rights*, 3, 4.

[25]   Judith Plotz, *Romanticism and the Vocation of Childhood* (New York: Palgrave, 2001), 2.

[26]   Samuel Taylor Coleridge, "To a Young Ass: Its Mother being tethered near it," stanza 1, lines 1, 9, 10, 7, and 8; stanza 2, lines 31–2.

[27]   William Blake, "Spring," stanza 3, lines 19–26.

[28]   William Blake, "Holy Thursday," stanza 2, lines 7–8.

symbolism operating here, symbolism that tinges Blake's depiction with sharp irony. The lamb, though the figure of soft innocence, is also a victim—the lamb who will be led to the slaughter, whose soft wool will be pulled, not by the child, but by the shearer. By so closely associating the child and the lamb, Blake demonstrates the fragility of their shared innocence and the inevitability of its loss.

The presence of complex symbolism in Blake's and in Coleridge's poems also speaks to, however, the problematic nature of reading these texts in the same way that one might read the philosophical texts or even the children's literature cited earlier. Though they too participate in a discourse that links the child with the animal, the poetry of the Romantics is not as directly concerned with the delineation of the social as were the latter. As Penny Brown notes in *The Captured World: The Child and Childhood in Nineteenth-Century Women's Writing*,

> as a result of the social and political ferment at the end of the eighteenth century, the spiritual and intellectual conflicts and the atmosphere of national and personal doubt and questioning, the child becomes a potent literary symbol of the subjective exploration of the self, of the writer's sense of uncertainty and vulnerability, and of simplicity, innocence and feeling in the face of the increasingly dehumanized industrial age.[29]

In other words, the Romantic poets—drawing again on the misanthropy Perkins calls attention to—were, in many ways, in retreat from the social. This is not to suggest that Romanticism had no effect upon social discourse, nor that Romantic poets were unconcerned with the suffering of actual animals and children. Instead, it is to argue that the representations of the animal and the child found within poems such as those cited here must also be understood for their symbolic significance: that is, the ability of these figures to act as exemplars of innocence, nostalgia, and longing in an industrial age. The child and the animal operate, therefore, as Edenic representatives—ones to which, the Romantics feared, the changing social and political landscape of England was anathema, and for which their poems must act as memorials.

One can trace a change, then, in the status of the child in relation to the animal in the eighteenth century. Though conceived of within rationalist discourse as the animal's natural and sadistic predator, the child, within Romantic poetry, instead shares with the animal a quality of transcendent, yet fragile innocence. The influence of both narratives continues into the Victorian period, where the impetus behind legislative action on the behalf of children is, on the one hand, concern for the child's innocent, mute suffering, and on the other, fear of the child's animalistic savagery.

---

[29]   Penny Brown, *The Captured World*, 6.

Animal-Child Companionship in the Victorian Novel

Nineteenth-century novels often both engaged the imagination and participated in larger political and moral debates, and this is very much the case in novelistic representations of the suffering child in Victorian England. Laura Berry argues, for example, that "Victorian representations of childhood are more likely to ... position their discourse in relation to social reform projects and debates" than are those of the Romantics.[30] Works such as Dickens's *Nicholas Nickleby* (1838–1839) and Anna Sewell's *Black Beauty* (1877), for example, represented animals and children not just as suffering subjects with whom the reader might empathize, but also as potent symbols of the need for social change. Dickens's depiction of the abuse within the Yorkshire schools and Sewell's depiction of the suffering of cab-horses both use the imaginative space of literature to encourage readers to see the real-life counterparts of Smike and Black Beauty in their midst. This is not to suggest that children and animals were not idealized during this period, but rather to argue that images of suffering children and animals were all the more effective as calls for legislation and intervention *because* the objects of suffering were seen as exemplars of mute innocence and helplessness.

Representations of children and animals as companions in shared suffering reoccur continually in Victorian literature.[31] The two are not solely represented as symbolically linked, as they are in Romantic poetry, but are instead often represented in moving depictions of fellowship between child and animal. In Dickens's *Barnaby Rudge* (1854), for example, the mad hostler Hugh is left "a puny child" who "should have died in a ditch" after his mother is hanged at Tyburn.[32] At the moment of his own execution many years later, he asks if "there is some person who has a fancy for a dog; and not then, unless he means to use him well. There's one, belongs to me, at the house I came from; and it wouldn't be easy to find a better .... You wonder that I think about a dog just now .... If any man deserved it of me half as well, I'd think of *him*."[33] Hugh recognizes that, to most, his care for a dog will seem misplaced, but he is careful to explain his attachment as resulting from his ill usage at the hands of fellow human beings. Furthermore,

---

[30]   Laura Berry, *The Child, the State, and the Victorian Novel*, 17.

[31]   Though there are depictions of relationships between middle-class children and animals—such as Dora and Jip in Dickens's *David Copperfield* (1850) and Flora and Diogenes in *Dombey and Son* (1848)—many depictions of animal/child relationships focus on lower-class children. Waif novels such as F. W. Robinson's *Owen: A Waif* (1862) and Maria Cummins's *The Lamplighter* (1854) both focus on how physically abused and neglected children find solace in animal friendship, as does Arthur Morrison's novel, *A Child of the Jago* (1896). In journals such as *Animal World* and *The Band of Mercy Advocate*, as well, this narrative of the lonely and abandoned child and his or her faithful pet is very common.

[32]   Dickens, *Barnaby Rudge* (London: The Waverly Book Company, n.d.), 104.

[33]   Ibid., 345.

Hugh believes that the dog is more worthy of his care, that the animal is a better being than the humans to whom Hugh has been exposed. In an earlier passage, in which Hugh recalls his mother's hanging, he comments that

> Such a dog as this, and one of the same breed, was the only living thing except me that howled that day .... Out of the two thousand odd—there was a large crowd for its being a woman—the dog and I alone had any pity. If he'd have been a man, he'd have been glad to be quit of her, for she had been forced to keep him lean and half-starved; but being a dog, and not having a man's sense, he was sorry.[34]

Hugh's explanation of the dog's pity—that it lacked "a man's sense"—mirrors his own grief at the death of his mother. Though her last wish was that her son "might live and grow, in utter ignorance of his father, so that no arts might teach him to be gentle and forgiving,"[35] yet Hugh mourns her death. Both the grieving child and the pitying animal lack the "sense" to judge her harshly, but both have the sensibility to exhibit sorrow at her death. Because "sense" is equated with a lack of compassion, Hugh's comment can be seen to support an "original innocence" conception of childhood, in which society is understood as the source of cruelty, and in which children and animals (because closer to nature) display natural feeling.

Representations that linked the animal and the child in such a way demonstrate the role that literature played in constructing both animals and children as "feeling subjects." While animal welfare discourse often focused on the animal's ability to feel physical pain—"we should never forget that the animal over which we exercise our power has all the organs that render it susceptible of pleasure and pain"[36]—fictional representations that linked the animal and the child could also represent the animal's capacity to feel, for lack of a better term, emotions. In such depictions, animals and children love and suffer "beyond sense"—that is, beyond the capacity of adults to do the same. Furthermore, it is this very quality that makes them most vulnerable because, as in the case of the dog, Hugh, and his mother, neither animal nor child retaliates against the lack of caring they receive from their supposed caregiver. In *Armadale* (1866), similarly, Wilkie Collins depicts a child and his animal "brothers" who give affection to each other and to the man who mistreats them. When "Ozias Midwinter" speaks of his past, he recalls a childhood of vicious beatings and neglect. After running away from a miserable school experience, he is found by "a sturdy old man with a fiddle ... [with] two dancing dogs in scarlet jackets."[37] He is given the name of the senior Ozias Midwinter and is taught "to dance the Highland fling; to throw somersaults;

---

34 Ibid., 106.

35 Ibid., 335.

36 Thomas Erskine, qtd. in *Awe for the Tiger, Love for the Lamb*, 226.

37 Wilkie Collins, *Armadale* (New York: Peter Fenelon Collier, n.d.), 90.

to walk on stilts; and to sing songs to his fiddle."[38] Though his adopted father beats him and the dogs, both of whom the young Ozias considers his "brothers," they all still feel affection for him: "Didn't I tell you just now, sir, that I lived with the dogs? and did you ever hear of a dog who liked his master the worse for beating him?"[39] This attachment to the "master" is defended as learned behavior, but it is significant that it is behavior learned from the dogs. The tendency to love beyond sense, to care for an owner or a father who is cruel, is depicted here as an essentially "animalistic" quality.

The attachment the boy and his "brothers" have for the man who beats them is also, however, entirely pragmatic, as evidenced by the even greater suffering they experience after the master's death: "The dogs and I did badly … our luck was against us. I lost one of my little brothers—the best performer of the two; he was stolen, and I never recovered him …. These misfortunes drew Tommy and me—I beg your pardon, sir, I mean the dog—closer together than ever."[40] As with Hugh, the adult Ozias feels the need to defend, or at least explain his attachment to his "brother," and again it is suffering that creates the intense bond between the two. Ozias continues:

> I think we had some kind of dim foreboding on both sides, that we had not done our misfortunes yet; anyhow, it was not long before we were parted for ever …. Young creatures, even when they are half-starved, cannot resist taking a run sometimes, on a fine morning. Tommy and I could not resist taking a run into a gentleman's plantation; the gentleman preserved his game, and the gentleman's keeper knew his business. I heard a gun go off—you can guess the rest. God preserve me from ever feeling such misery again, as I felt when I lay down by Tommy, and took him, dead and bloody in my arms![41]

The world in which this boy and his dog brothers live is shown to be one of hardship and danger. While the man who keeps them also beats them, he at least provides them with protection and a means of gaining a living. Their affection for him, therefore, must be understood not only as a kind of instinctual devotion, but also as a learned response to the harshness of their environment.

By aligning the child with the animal as a victim in shared suffering—and shared cruelty—writers such as Dickens and Collins both critiqued English society and defined those most endangered by it. Hugh and his dog and Ozias and his brothers are all victims of an adult human regime that abuses the most innocent and helpless in its midst, making the child and the animal the most likely victims. This is not to say that animal and child companions were always represented as victims; while these pairs and others suffer, other children and

---

[38]   Ibid., 91.
[39]   Ibid.
[40]   Ibid., 92.
[41]   Ibid.

other animals in literature enjoy a petted existence.[42] However, both Dickens and Collins depict animals and children as sharing traits, such as dependency, loyalty even in the face of cruelty, and perhaps more importantly, the ability to feel and to be wounded by these feelings—to feel "such misery" as Ozias does—that make these particular creatures particularly helpless in an adult, human-oriented world. Such a construction of child and animal suffering obviously owes much to the Romantic conception of the child of nature. Ozias Midwinter's description of the need for him and his brother to play, for example, and of his own grief at the death of his companion, shares the same assumptions about the nature of youth and of its suffering as seen in Coleridge and Blake, because like the young ass and the lamb, Ozias and his brothers are defenseless against the violence inflicted upon them.

The Savage Child

The child and the animal were not always, of course, represented as meek and defenseless. Although Hugh and Ozias are both, in their childhood, depicted as figures deserving of sympathy, both also show a capacity for violence in childhood, a capacity that their lawless actions in later life bears out. The conception of the child as somehow closer to nature is, as I have argued, certainly associated with ideas of meekness and innocence, but as James Kincaid also observes, the "child of feeling, "though also associated with Rousseau and the 'cult of sensibility, unleashes dangers not usually associated with mere 'innocence.' If the child of nature is figured not as an emptiness but as one more in touch with primal sympathies, we have a creation more complex and threatening."[43] To be "primal," to be entirely feeling, that is, suggests a capacity for violence and savagery as much as for love and affection. Hugh's mother believes that "arts" might "teach

---

[42]   In "'The Rights of the Defenseless': Animals, Children and Sentimental Liberalism in Nineteenth-Century America," Susan J. Pearson argues that "Long associated with economic uselessness and the mis-investment of (adult) emotional energies, the esteem of the 'pet' rose with industrialization and the separation of home and work, a process during which children, and many domestic animals, were removed from the labour force and valued precisely for their helplessness, dependence, and innocence of worldly ways" (58). Pearson traces the representation of children and animals sharing roles as "pets" in nineteenth-century American literature, but such representations were as likely to be found in British texts. Anti-cruelty to animal journals such as *Animal World* and the *Band of Mercy Advocate* featured continual narratives, poems, and images that depicted both cherished "pets" enjoying each other's company, and similar representations can also be found in novels such as Dickens's *David Copperfield*, where Dora, David's "child wife" share close kinship with her petted dog, Jip. The child as cherished pet could also be a source of endangerment to the child, however, as seen in Clara Balfour's *Drift* (1861), in which the eccentric Miss Keziah Pendrainly replaces her (repeatedly poisoned) dogs with a child foundling named, aptly, "Birdie."

[43]   Kincaid, *Child-Loving*, 74.

him to be gentle and forgiving,"[44] and without the presence of, presumably, proper moral guidance and instruction, Hugh does indeed grow in violence. Similarly, Ozias relates that after Tommy's death, "the keeper attempted to part us—I bit him, like the wild animal I was."[45] In claiming that he was "a wild animal," Ozias erases any distinction between himself and his animal brother. However, unlike his earlier dog-like behavior of demonstrating affection even in the face of cruelty, in this instance, the characteristic he shares with animals is that of violence. The child and the animal, both of whom act and feel without a "man's sense," can act and feel with violence, as well as with devotion. To be uncivilized is to be unspoiled. But such closeness to nature, representations such as those of Dickens and Collins suggest, also makes one dangerously "savage"—someone or something existing outside the bounds of adult, civilized society.

The savage child was a common figure in Victorian fiction and social discourse, though the association of children with savages was not always pejorative. According to Hugh Cunningham, the child of nature often went hand in hand with the concept of the "noble savage," the "ideal state in which man lived in harmony with nature, and [was] imbued with its virtues."[46] At the end of the eighteenth century, "the qualities associated with noble savagery were projected wholesale onto childhood" and "These children were often portrayed as flowers in intimate contact with nature, both physical and animal, and deriving from it 'great physical beauty....'"[47]

As Cunningham goes on to describe, however, fears about the unemployment of children, which proliferated when child labor was restricted in the 1830s and 40s, led to more unpleasant associations of children with animals. Commenting on Lord Ashley's response to street children in London, Cunningham argues that Ashley searches

> for a language to describe what he had seen, though unhappily aware that "language is powerless to describe the truth." The children of the streets were, he wrote, a "tribe—bold, and pert, and dirty as London sparrows, but pale, feeble, and sadly inferior to them in plumpness of outline" ... These "independent urchins" or "young maniacs" had their own way of life, and were increasing in number. They were quite separate from "the category of poor but peaceful children." They were "a wild and lawless race" with "roving habits," the "wild colts of the Pampas," the "Arabs of the metropolis."[48]

While Cunningham focuses, quite rightly, on the racial significance of Ashley's descriptions, I would like to focus on the extent to which these children were

---

44   Dickens, *Barnaby Rudge*, 335.
45   Collins, *Armadale*, 92.
46   Cunningham, *The Children of the Poor*, 99.
47   Ibid.
48   Ibid., 106.

figured as wild animals. The term "street Arab," though undoubtedly racial in
its implications,[49] originally referred to the breed of horse, rather than to Arab
peoples. Other phrases from the nineteenth century, such as "ownerless dogs,"
and "predatory hordes"[50] also clearly signify the connection between children and
wild animals, and Cunningham concludes that "Animal analogies were indeed
common: John Hollingshead wrote of 'human child-rats,' Blanchard Jerrold of the
'claws' of the 'wretched children' in the street."[51]

It is tempting to resolve the contradictory aspects of the "child of nature"
through a class analysis, arguing that middle-class children represent the "lambs"
and the "pets," with their sweetness, innocence, and gentleness, while the street
"Arabs" represent the wild, untamed, and potentially violent half of the dichotomy.
Such a resolution would not be far off the mark; texts that linked children with
animals and "savages" often did so as a means of registering their distance from
the ideal, middle-class child. Thus, in his description of "Deputy," "the hideous
small boy" who stones Mr. Durdles in *The Mystery of Edwin Drood* (1870),
Dickens relays Jasper's horror at the contrast between what a child should be,
and what this boy appears to be, "a little savage": "'Do you know this thing, this
child?' asks Jasper, at a loss for a word that will define this thing."[52] The "creature"
(as Jasper continually refers to him) is only questionably a child, more definitely a
"thing." Moreover, he is only one of a crowd of "young brutes" identified as either
"twopenny lodgers or followers or hangers-on of such" who themselves fall upon
the boy, "as if attracted by some carrion-scent of the Deputy in the air, start into
the moonlight, as vultures might gather in the desert, and instantly fall to stoning
him and one another."[53] As this depiction attests, although the representational
linkage of children with animals could be employed to highlight the helplessness
and defenselessness of both, it also served to register anxiety about the perceived
depravity of the children of the poor. Precisely because the "child of nature" could
be both helpless and dangerous, both guileless and "savage," and both dependent
and independent, it could be used to register complex and often contradictory
reactions to childhood and endangered childhood.

As the construction of childhood as properly a sanctified, protected space
became increasingly dominant in England, however, the "savage" child primarily
elicited concern. When writers were confronted with the animalistic child of the

---

[49]   For an excellent analysis of these implications, see also Lindsay Smith, "The Shoe-
Black to the Crossing Sweeper: Victorian Street Arabs and Photography," *Textual Practice*
10.1 (1996): 29–55, and Lydia Murdoch, *Imagined Orphans: Poor Families, Child Welfare,
and Contested Citizenship in London*, 24–32.

[50]   Cunningham, *The Children of the Poor*, 108.

[51]   Ibid., 122.

[52]   Charles Dickens, *The Mystery of Edwin Drood* (New York: Pantheon Books,
1980), 33, 34.

[53]   Ibid., 34.

street, their response was therefore often one of horror: "Can these be *children*?"[54] The goal of social reformers, particularly those working with street children, juvenile delinquents, and child prostitutes, then, was to restore these animalistic children to the proper childhood that had been denied them. A child that was allowed to be untamed, unrestrained, and unlawful, was a child that questioned the sanctified space of childhood itself. As Mary Carpenter observes in *Juvenile Delinquents: Their Condition and Treatment* (1853),

> Juvenile Delinquents! The very term is an anomaly, and should startle us as something monstrous and fearful; something which should lead us to think, 'How can this be so? And if it be so, what can each one of us do to remove so dreadful an evil?' For we are speaking of children,—of young beings but recently come from the hands of their Maker, of whom the Saviour has said ... 'Whosoever shall receive one of such in my name receiveth me,' and the care of whom as his 'lambs he committed with twice repeated injunctions to that apostle whom he appointed to be the rock on which his church should be built. Yet these are called, perhaps are, delinquents; not only *perishing* from lack of knowledge, from lack of parental care, of all that should surround childhood, but they are positively *dangerous* ....[55]

Carpenter suggests that these children are literally dangerous, that their violence and unlawfulness present a physical threat to civilized people. These "savage" children, who "seem monstrous and fearful," are shocking, however, because they are or should be "lambs." Carpenter's use of this term is not precisely the same as Blake's, for while both uses are religiously inflected, Carpenter's does not rejoice in the "naturalness" of these children. Rather, her rhetoric refers solely to the "child of God," as opposed to the "child of nature"—the child whose soul, as well as its life, is in desperate need of salvation.

The Child of God

The "holy child" had a long history before the Victorian period, emerging in Puritan texts as exemplars of God's grace embodied in infant form. At the beginning of the nineteenth century, "the Evangelical movement, a surviving strain of Puritanism, which had already had fifty years of mounting influence behind it associated with the Methodist revival, began to come into its own."[56] Penny Brown argues that

---

[54]   Micaiah Hill, qtd. in Cunningham, *The Children of the Poor*, 111.

[55]   Mary Carpenter, *Juvenile Delinquents: Their Condition and Treatment* (Patterson Smith: Montclair, 1970), 15.

[56]   Brown, *The Captured World*, 41.

the portrayal of the child in Evangelical writing revealed the duality which corresponded to the legacy of, on the one hand, the Puritan and Wesleyan traditions, and on the other, the Rousseau-istic and Romantic. The child was thus either seen as the product of Original Sin and hence burdened by the innate depravity of mankind which had to be recognized, battled with and overcome through individual conversion before salvation could be achieved, or, particularly later in the century, as a version of the 'innocent' child, a symbol of purity and grace.[57]

The influence of Evangelicalism and the belief in the child as a product of "original sin" can be seen in the depiction of the often harsh and isolating childhood experience now often associated with Victorian child-rearing. However, as the belief in childhood as a safe, protected space gained ground, "The latter view became, in fact, a firm favourite with many Victorian writers, gaining ascendancy over the 'Original Sin' approach as the century advanced."[58]

The innocent holy child of Victorian fiction is characterized by its innate sense of right versus wrong actions and, as Kincaid observes, by its obedience: "A kind of reverence for the child and a concern for its purity contributed to the manic insistence on obedience .... The pure child is thus the absolutely obedient child, the child of God (and a joy to its parents)."[59] The precociously virtuous child can be seen throughout Victorian literature, most famously in Dickens's Little Nell in *The Old Curiosity Shop* (1841), but it is particularly present in Evangelical tracts and literature, in which young boys and girls escape the cruelty and depravity of their environments through religious encounters. The "street-arab evangelist" can thus be found in the mid- to late nineteenth century works of writers such as Hesba Stretton and Mrs. O. F. Walton, whose characters display a "naïve or unconscious religiosity" or, at times, "a conscious and relentless evangelizing."[60]

Brown suggests that such characterizations of children were "symptomatic of the flood of sentimentality in fiction which peaked in the 1880s and 1890s," but Cunningham locates the emergence of the sentimentalized holy child into public discourse with the transition in the treatment of endangered children. He proposes that "The year 1866 may be said to mark the beginning of the sentimentalizing of children of the poor, for the emphasis began to shift from evangelical work towards rescue."[61] In February of that year, "Shaftesbury entertained to supper one hundred and fifty street boys, 'wild, wandering lads, the wandering vultures of the metropolis.'"[62] During the course of the supper, the boys "spoke about their lives" to great effect upon the spectators: "The hearts of the spectators were much moved

---

[57]   Ibid., 43.

[58]   Ibid.

[59]   Kincaid, *Child-Loving*, 80–81.

[60]   Brown, *The Captured World*, 88.

[61]   Cunningham, *The Children of the Poor*, 134.

[62]   Ibid.

at the forlorn spectacle before them, and many friends were so touched at the sad condition of these immortal beings that it was impossible with some to restrain their tears."[63] Through relating their own sad stories, these boys are transformed for their audience from "wandering vultures" to "immortal beings." No longer mere animals, these boys are, instead, souls in need of salvation, and after working to place them in refuge homes and on training ships, Shaftesbury proclaims that

> It had already been proved that if they would take out of the streets of London all the homeless, most friendless, and most destitute of lads, polish them gently, and apply the hand of skill and affection, they would turn out to be diamonds— and diamonds, too, as clear and bright as had ever adorned the most splendid crown.[64]

Shaftesbury's discovery of the gem-like nature of these former street "vultures" separates them utterly from the animals to which they had been compared. For while an animal will always be an animal, a child has an immortal soul—and in the case of street children, a soul that requires saving. Therefore, unlike Ozias, Hugh, and their animal counterparts, who command the sympathy of their readers by virtue of their shared capacity to feel pain and suffering, Shaftesbury's street children demand protection by virtue of what should be their *distance* from animals, because it is the existence of these children's immortal souls that makes it possible for society to reclaim them, polish them, and save them.

The virtuous, godly, endangered child of Victorian sentimental and Evangelical discourse must not, therefore, be confused with the "child of nature." The child of God—recently arrived from the hands of the maker—requires only the proper environment and instruction in order for his or her innate goodness to emerge. Unlike Rousseau's version of the "originally good" child, this child is not corrupted by society itself, only by the wrong kind of society. The child cannot be blamed for his or her behavior, nor can that behavior be understood as a learned response to the child's environment. A child who displays "savagery," violence, independence, or ignorance of religion is a child who requires rescue, and after that rescue, proper training to ensure that child-like innocence, dependence, and purity can be maintained. Of course, these children were not necessarily saved to an ideal life of middle-class childhood (the "homes" they were sent to being quite different from the middle-class home), but they were, at least, "saved" from—it was hoped—a life of crime and indigence to a life of useful service to society.

---

63   Lord Shaftesbury, qtd. in Cunningham, *The Children of the Poor*, 134.
64   Ibid., 134–5.

"The Child of the English Savage"

It is the wholly innocent, helpless child of God who Cunningham argues is most common in early child-saving rhetoric, because "A sentimentalizing of the child was ... built into the dynamics of the situation of those who worked for the rescue of children."[65] In early London SPCC and NSPCC writings, allusions to animalistic savagery refer solely to the abusive parent, never to the abused child. The abusive parent is a "reckless brute," "whom no pretty words, no tender caresses could mollify."[66] In the "Notes" section of the *Child's Guardian* in 1887, Waugh explains that the Society has been forced to abduct a child who had to "plead for money to keep the large animal who owned her in drink,"[67] while in another article, he describes the "cat-like killing of a child."[68] In his article on "Prevention of Cruelty to Children," Waugh describes a parent "fixing big jaws of teeth in the fat of the thigh while child under bed [sic] for refuge, dragging it out, standing up with it, and shaking it 'as a dog shakes a rat.'"[69] And in "Child-Life Insurance," Waugh provides an extensive description of parents who murder their children for money. He argues that "There is in England a herd of cruel reckless married and unmarried creatures with maternal organism, whom, for morbid villainy towards their young, hot-blooded and cold-blooded beasts and reptiles fail to supply figures of speech to describe; and there are males to match them." Having dismissed the fitness of the animal kingdom to supply metaphor, however, he goes on to state that these parents are "lazy as sloths, lustful as monkeys, crafty as serpents, savage as tigers."[70] From these and other descriptions, it is evident that the animal world, in fact, provided very useful imagery for describing the abusive parent, imagery that separates parental cruelty from social conditions, locating cruelty in the "savage" nature of the parent. Furthermore, by linking violent parents with animals, Waugh highlights the extent to which such cruelty is inhuman, outside of the bounds of civilized society.

Such depictions of animality and savagery were, of course, quite commonly applied to lower-class subjects. In 1832, James Phillips Kay argued that "To condemn man" to unremitting labor is "in some measure, to cultivate in him the habits of an animal. He becomes reckless. He disregards the distinguishing appetites and habits of the species," and he and his family, "with an animal eagerness satisfy the cravings of their appetite."[71] The animalistic lower classes,

---

65   Cunningham, *The Children of the Poor*, 146.

66   Manning and Waugh, "The Child of the English Savage," 694.

67   Waugh, "Notes," *The Child's Guardian* 1.3 (March 1887): 22.

68   Waugh, "A Righteous Call to a Universally Neglected Duty," *The Child's Guardian*, 1.5 (May 1887): 34.

69   Waugh, "Prevention of Cruelty to Children," *Dublin Review*, 110 (January 1892): 140–51, 151.

70   Waugh, "Child-Life Insurance," *Contemporary Review*, 58 (July 1890), 53.

71   Kay, *The Moral and the Physical Condition of the Working Classes*, 22–3.

while undoubtedly objects of concern in texts such as Kay's, were also, and perhaps more so, objects of fear. As J. Carter Wood points out, "Identifying the 'dangerous class' increasingly preoccupied" middle-class commentators on "refinement" and "civilization."[72] Wood suggests that

> Middle-class culture emphasized self-restraint, aspiring at least to the appearance of control over "passion," which was often linked directly to violence. Consequently, "violence … acquired a symbolic currency in political discourse, for middle-class men pointed to their own self-control as a justification for their claims to political power, while attacking the working class as too violent to deserve the vote."[73]

"Savagery," therefore, was not just a trait that distinguished the lower-class child from the middle-class "pet," but also that which separated the lower-class adult from the refined middle-class adult.[74]

Interestingly enough, the "savagery" and perceived animalistic behavior of the lower classes was registered not just in their violence towards and against each other, but also in their treatment of animals. The fact that bear-baiting was attacked as a cruel sport long before hunting says much, again, about the perception that lower-class cruelty was of a more "savage" order than that of the upper classes. But if working-class violence justified middle-class political power, it also had disturbing implications for the social order. As Moira Ferguson points out,

> In their jousting with animals … generally powerless common people wielded a semblance of control over their material conditions, claiming an agency that worried employers and other interested groups who sought working-class complacency. By fighting animals, workers gained a reverse power, a control that transcended class-based subservience.[75]

Furthermore, groups of "savage" working-class people engaged in cruel sports or physical fights called to mind more organized working-class violence that could possibly threaten social order. Manning and Waugh's description of the abusive parent as "savage," then, demonstrates the extent to which their construction of child abuse relied upon residual classed discourses and fears while also disavowing class as a contributing factor to abuse.

---

[72]   J. Carter Wood, 'The Invention of Violence in Nineteenth-Century England," *Journal of Victorian Culture*, 9.1 (Spring 2004): 22–42, 33.

[73]   Ibid., 32.

[74]   See also Lisa Surridge's *Bleak Houses: Marital Violence in Victorian Fiction* (Ohio University Press, 2005) and Martin Wiener's *Men of Blood: Violence, Manliness and Criminal Justice in Victorian England* (Cambridge, 2004).

[75]   Moira Ferguson, *Animal Advocacy and Englishwomen, 1780–1900: Patriots, Nation, and Empire* (University of Michigan Press: Ann Arbor, 1998), 28.

Though the parent might be "savage," the child of such a parent was never described as such. Instead, as seen throughout Manning and Waugh's article, the child of these parents is always represented as inherently "other" to them. Like Hugh, Ozias, and their animal counterparts, the abused child of "The Child of the English Savage" possesses a greater capacity to feel—both affection and pain—than do adults, and a greater helplessness and defenselessness that makes the child particularly deserving of protection. Unlike Dickens's and Collins's children of feeling, however, the abused child here bears no hint of savagery, no capacity to respond with violence to violence inflicted upon it. Instead, the child is wholly innocent, wholly helpless, and wholly separate from the savagery that surrounds it.

The opening sentence—"The Christianity and the civilization of a people may both be measured by their treatment of childhood"[76]—immediately places this argument within a religious framework, and Waugh and Manning continue this framework in their description of ideal domesticity:

> The love of Fatherhood was revealed in the Eternal Father; and the love of Motherhood in the Mother of the Eternal Son. A new and divine consanguinity bound man to God and man to man. It has thereby entered the sanctity of the home and the charities of domestic life. We were already children of God our Maker; we are now children of God by a new birth, and by sonship in Jesus Christ.[77]

The exemplary familial relationship here is the Holy Family, and through it, the family itself is constructed as holy. The home is "sanctified" and the family is the earthly sign of God's consanguinity to humanity. To fail to live up to this example or to respect and maintain that "sanctity" is, therefore, to defile the relationship between God and man. Such a construction of the family works to place an added injunction against child abuse, as cruelty to the child becomes almost blasphemous in its defilement of the family's godly purpose.

Moreover, it is the child who is most like God, and who best represents this divine-human relationship: "A child is not only made in the image of God, but of all His creatures it is the most like to Himself in its early purity, beauty, brightness, and innocence. It has an immeasurable capacity of joy and bliss, and of eternal union with God in the beatific vision."[78] The similarities between Manning and Waugh's child of God and the Romantic child of nature are quite explicit here, for in both versions of the child, it is the child's supposed "purity, beauty, brightness, and innocence" that is admired. As well, the child of Waugh and Manning's article shares the deep feeling of the Romantic child, both in its "immeasurable capacity of joy and bliss" and in its capacity for suffering:

---

[76] Manning and Waugh, "The Child of the English Savage," 687.

[77] Ibid., 687.

[78] Ibid., 688.

> What a mystery is pain in a child. Death reigns over them even in their early innocence. The feeble texture of their frame is quick in every nerve with the sense of suffering. To wound a child, then, is brutal. And if pain in childhood is a mystery, how much more wonderful is the sorrow of a child. The whole soul of childhood is open to the sting of sorrow.[79]

Like Ozias, Hugh, and their "brothers," Waugh and Manning's child deserves and demands sympathy by virtue of its peculiar capacity to feel pain—both physically and emotionally. Such a construction of the child goes beyond the "humanitarian narrative," which works through making the reader identify with the pain and suffering of another. A child's pain, according to Manning and Waugh, is greater than that of an adult, and is therefore more objectionable than that of an adult.

The child's weakness and helplessness is, Manning and Waugh argue, unique precisely because it is a sign of the child's tenuous connection to this world. This child of God is not connected to nature; rather, through its connection to the divine, the holy, innocent child is, instead, almost *too* good for this world. Paradoxically, while this otherworldliness is a sign of the child's connection to the divine, it is manifested in the child's fragility:

> Nevertheless, a child is the most helpless and defenseless of the creatures that God has made. The offspring of the lower creation is no sooner born into the world than it can, for the most part, care for itself. A child does not even know its own dangers. It is thrown for protection, guidance, and nurture upon its parents and upon us.[80]

This child of God, then, is not the robust, independent, deeply feeling child of nature Rousseau describes. This child is marked by weakness, by a mysterious "feebleness" that makes it more prey to pain and death and sorrow than are the infants of the "lower creatures." Although their depiction of the child shows the influence of Romantic conceptions of childhood, therefore, Manning and Waugh create a distinctive break in the association of children with animals. The child and the animal are no longer equally helpless, nor equally sensitive. An infant animal can "care for itself," whereas a child requires "protection, guidance, and nurture." As well, the animal cannot be said to have the same religious significance as does the child, because it does not represent any relationship between God and man, and as a "lower creature," it has no part in the sanctified domestic space. Rather than a mute, feeling victim, the animal is depicted as hardy—as if formed by God to be able to cope without humanity's aid or assistance. By implication, then, animals are not as deserving of aid as are children, lacking as they do the child's dependence "on us with an absolute need."[81]

---

[79]   Ibid., 688.
[80]   Ibid., 688.
[81]   Ibid.

The RSPCA and the NSPCC

Though Manning and Waugh's comparison of the infant animal and the infant human would seem to suggest that any linkage between the two as objects of concern would be problematic at best, such linkages were in fact still quite common at the end of the nineteenth century. As Susan J. Pearson notes,

> Efforts to protect animals and children from abuse and neglect spread rapidly. The first animal protection society in the United States had begun in 1866 and by 1908, there were 354 active anticruelty organizations in the United States. Of these, the plurality, 185 of them, were humane, or dual societies; 104 were exclusively animal societies; and 45 were dedicated solely to child protection."[82]

The connection of cruelty to animals with cruelty to children was as prevalent in England as it was in the United States. As noted earlier, the first anti-cruelty to children society in England, the Liverpool SPCC, came into being at an RSPCA meeting originally held to propose the founding of a dog's home. With the RSPCA, the fledgling child protection movement found both a ready-made membership and a model with which to combat cruelty to and abuse of children. The ties between the two movements became even stronger with the founding of the London SPCC— initially, the London SPCC and the RSPCA shared facilities (the RSPCA's board room at Jermyn Street, London); as well, "a significant overlap existed between RSPCA and London SPCC officials."[83] The London SPCC also received significant financial support in its early years from RSPCA members: as Behlmer notes, "32 RSPCA subscribers contributed £178 to the London SPCC's coffers (20 percent of its total income) between July and December 1884."[84]

Furthermore, the London SPCC gained significantly from the RSPCA's experience. John Colam, the secretary of the RSPCA, served on the London SPCC / NSPCC Executive Committee until 1894, and "provided useful guidance on planning the structure of the NSPCC," and his son, Roger Colam, served as the "SPCC's chief legal counsel."[85] With this guidance, the London SPCC adopted the same organizational structure as the RSPCA (a national committee with various branches throughout the country), similar membership and organizational structures (like the RSPCA, the London SPCC would employ secretaries, branch officers, and inspectors), and, significantly, similar methods of propaganda. *The Child's Guardian*

---

[82] Pearson, "'The Rights of the Defenseless,'" 3.

[83] Ibid., 67. According to the NSPCC, "Of the 119 London officers listed in its first annual report, 20 belonged also either to the RSPCA or the Victoria Street Society for the Protection of Animals from Vivisection" (NSPCC, "Links Between the NSPCC and the RSPCA," http://firststop/archive/RSPCA/RSPCA.htm [accessed June 26, 2002],1).

[84] Behlmer, *Child Abuse and Moral Reform*, 67.

[85] NSPCC, "Links," 1 and Behlmer, *Child Abuse and Moral Reform*, 67.

was modeled on the RSPCA's *Animal World*, and in 1891, the NSPCC's youth auxiliary, the Children's League of Pity was modeled after the RSPCA's own Band of Mercy.

Such close cooperation between two moral reform groups was not necessarily unusual; as Brian Harrison points out, moral reformers in general "shared many personalities, attitudes, and techniques." Many organizations were

> connected indirectly, many directly; and there [were] links between rival organizations operating in the same policy area. The institutional history of these bodies was riddled with disputes between reformers whose objectives were similar; yet ... these schisms did not preclude strong personal linkages between warring institutions.[86]

Such combined cooperation and competition certainly characterized the relationship between the NSPCC and the RSPCA. Initially, cooperation between the two served the needs of both organizations. The London SPCC, in its early years, gained much from the RSPCA's support, guidance, and assistance, while "the advocacy of a separate organization for child protection would have been politically expedient for the RSPCA. As early as 1870 letters appeared in *Animal World* calling for the inclusion of children in an enlarged 'Society for the Prevention of Cruelty to Children and Dumb Animals'"; however, the RSPCA, "to safeguard its status as a moderate extra-parliamentary reform group, had to resist the demands for uncompromising reform made by extremists." One way to circumvent these demands, Behlmer notes, was "to encourage enthusiasts to form distinct agendas for narrower ends."[87] By supporting the formation of a society exclusively devoted to the prevention of cruelty to children, then, the RSPCA was able to maintain its original mandate and purpose and continue to resist expansion into other areas.

While at the outset, a proposal for a "Society for the Prevention of Cruelty to Children and Dumb Animals" was perceived as a logical, if not politically expedient way to address issues of cruelty in England, within only a matter of years such a proposal was greeted with ridicule. In a December 1893 commentary in *The Child's Guardian*, Waugh records that

> We have heard with surprise that the "Harrogate and District Society for the Prevention of Cruelty to Animals" has determined to enlarge the scope of its operations so as to include children. No doubt, in a free country any combination of words may be employed to describe a particular combination of people. It is, therefore, quite open to these particular persons in Harrogate to include the

---

[86]   Brian Harrison, "State Intervention and Moral Reform," in *Pressure from Without in Victorian England*, ed. Patricia Hollis (London: Edward Arnold, 1974), 290.

[87]   Behlmer, *Child Abuse and Moral Reform*, 68.

names of "Animal" and "Children" in the same title, but it is not the less a ridiculous and practically impossible combination.[88]

What had once been a necessary and practical separation between two similar organizations had become a "ridiculous and practically impossible combination." Waugh's assertion betrays not only the growing resentment of the NSPCC towards the financial success of the RSPCA, but also the fact that aligning children with animals had become—at least in NSPCC rhetoric—a narrative impossibility. The representation of children and animals as sharing a unique form of victimization certainly allowed, at least initially, for the formation of similar societies for their protection, and for the sharing of resources and membership between those two societies, but by the end of the nineteenth century, such a connection, at least as far as the NSPCC was concerned, was no longer desirable. For while the NSPCC did not attack or slight the RSPCA itself, its rhetoric increasingly suggested that the care and protection of animals was a morally suspect endeavor—one that was not only ethically inferior to the rescue of children but also, essentially, antagonistic to child-protection work itself.

In "The Child of the English Savage," for example, Waugh and Manning describe a family in which the child is starved to death, even though the family "bought meat for their cat."[89] Similarly, an article on "The Children's Bread to the Dogs," published in *The Child's Guardian* in 1887, demonstrates a failure on the part of a father to provide the same nourishment for his children as for his pets. The choice of these parents to care for animals before their children is a sign of their savagery, of their failure to respect and protect the sanctified space of the home. As the NSPCC never failed to point out, however, such a preference for animals over children was not restricted to the lowly English savage. Just as the "children's bread" went to animals in abusive homes, so too did moneys the NSPCC felt would be better spent on children go toward the support of societies for animal welfare:

> Referring to Legacies, we are not a little amazed at the fact that we receive so little from the wills of benevolent persons. It is not the dogs but the children to whom fall the crumbs from these tables. It is highly creditable to the lovers of animals that their last charities include handsome shares for the objects of their love. We give once more a form of bequest, which benefactors are earnestly desired to use.[90]

While Waugh acknowledges that it is "creditable" that those who love animals should give so generously to the cause of their care and protection, the obvious parallel between the stories of abusive homes in which animals are fed and children

---

[88] Waugh, "Notes," *The Child's Guardian*, 7.12 (December 1893), 166.
[89] Manning and Waugh, "The Child of the English Savage," 696.
[90] Waugh, "Notes," *The Child's Guardian*, 11.11 (October 1897), 130.

are not and Waugh's assertion that it is the children who receive "the crumbs from these tables" (while the dogs, one presumes, are well fed) encourages the reader to view the priorities of these "benevolent persons" as morally suspect.

Even in its earliest years, when the London SPCC was benefiting from the support and expertise of the RSPCA, it also, at the same time, used the success of that organization to bolster its own arguments about the devalued place of children in English society. The article "Dogs of London," originally published in the *Contemporary Review*, was reprinted as "Sir Charles Warren on Our Society" in the third issue of *The Child's Guardian*. In this article, Warren[91] argues that the "advance from solicitude for the welfare of animals only to that of human beings, is one of which the nation may well congratulate itself; for the latter will always be found to comprehend the former."[92] Although many organizations existed to protect children, Warren's statements make it appear as though "solicitude" for children only came into being with the formation of the London SPCC. Moreover, he suggests that with the emergence of this society, the nation has become enriched, because "Those who are kind to their fellow-creatures will always be found to be also kind and considerate to animals; while, on the contrary, those who are merely fond of animals are known to be often averse to children, and to care little for the welfare of the human race."[93] The "advance" to which Warren referred earlier is here attributed to the belief that those who care for children are themselves more "advanced" in their compassion; their consideration extends to all, whereas the love of animals (as represented, presumably, by animal welfare advocates) is described as less encompassing, more narrow in its object. According to Warren, this narrowness of compassion can be attributed to the fact that

> the love of animals in itself is very frequently merely a liking for them so far as they pander to our own selfish amusements; and in many cases the love extends to them as it does to inanimate objects, our goods and chattels, and no further. So much is this the case that the kindly feeling goes as far as our own children—that is to say, it is not uncommon to meet with persons who are fond of their own children and their own dogs, but who care little for the children of others. The feeling alluded to, however, as now spreading the country, is beyond all this; it is the love of humanity which is springing up and influencing so many—love for those who are not known; and with this comes also a feeling for animals, of a higher nature than that possessed by those who may love animals only, but who dislike what they call "gutter children."[94]

---

[91]   Sir Charles Warren was the Chief Commissioner of the Metropolitan Police in England from 1886–1888.

[92]   NSPCC, "Sir Charles Warren on Our Society," *The Child's Guardian*, 1.3 (March 1887), 20.

[93]   Ibid.

[94]   Ibid.

Warren is not directly attacking the RSPCA or any other animal welfare organization, and in fact, his critique of those who view animals as their own "goods and chattel" was very much in keeping with animal-welfare discourse of the time. His critique of "the love of animals in itself," of "those who may love animals only" is, however, based upon the assumption that animal welfare somehow displaces or perverts the proper feeling of love and compassion for humanity. Moreover, he specifically states that those who betray this perverted sensibility dislike children, because "those who are merely fond of animals are known to be often averse to children."[95]

The belief that a concern for animal welfare displaced the proper concern for human beings did not originate with the London SPCC, and, in fact, played a role in pro-vivisection writings of the nineteenth century.[96] The specific accusation that Warren levels against "animal lovers"—that this love almost inevitably excludes a proper love for children—does, however, seem to gain strength with the emergence of child-protection discourse. Because the animal and the child had been depicted throughout the nineteenth-century as sharing a kind of mute innocence that made them particularly defenseless against cruelty, and because literary and philosophical discourse had long used the two to define and describe each other, it was perhaps inevitable that the child and the animal should come to be represented as being in competition with each other for the (apparently limited) compassion of English society. Focusing on such competition, Warren presents the love of children as being of a "higher nature" than the love of animals, because it is a "love of humanity." By contrast, the love of animals, as described by Warren, has much in common with the kinds of instincts betrayed by the English "savage," because it is primarily concerned with "its own selfish amusements" above everything else. The shared membership of the RSPCA and the London SPCC obviously provides strong evidence that those who wished to protect animals were moved by an *equal* desire to protect children, but the power of Warren's rhetoric even in the face of such evidence can be attested to by the persistence of his narrative even to this day.

As the Society continued to expand and to require financial backing to support that expansion, it became more open in its critique of those who supported animal welfare organizations. In the "Notes" section of *The Child's Guardian* in 1889, Waugh writes of the financial prosperity of the RSPCA and claims that

> Without one bit of jealousy of that institution, or any other feeling than one of
> pain at the thought of its suffering to the extent of a single shilling in the interests
> of our own society for the benefit of children, it is with restless anxiety that we

---

[95] Ibid.

[96] See, for example, "The Morality of Vivisection" by Victor Horsley and "The Morality of Vivisection" by M. Armand Ruffer in *Animal Welfare and Anti-Vivisection 1870–1918: Nineteenth-Century Women's Mission, Volume Three: Pro-Vivisection*, ed. Susan Hamilton (London: Routledge, 2004), 237–50.

look to occupying the same position in the esteem of the good and the same dread of the bad; and with adequate resources it must come.[97]

Waugh's words acknowledge both the importance of the RSPCA, and the role played by that organization in terms of providing a blueprint for the London SPCC to follow—a role model, as it were, of a strong organization that the London SPCC might someday become. His next words, however, suggest that such graciousness is not entirely without the "jealousy" Waugh denies:

> What can gratify the compassionate more than the fact that during the last month, 1, 440 destitute dogs have … been captured, and there and then removed straight from the kennelless streets of the metropolis to the Home for Homeless Dogs at Battersea. Yet little hatless, homeless children, dying on charity, are left to turn into ashpits and common lodging-houses …. The difference between the nation's treatment of the two homeless things is that one is somebody's *child*, whilst the other is only his *dog*. If wretched children were only dogs, what sunlight would fall into their doomed and dismal lives![98]

Waugh's italics and tone here diminish his claim that he can regard the success of the RSPCA "without one bit of jealousy." His scathing critique of a society that will house dogs and yet leave children homeless suggests, perhaps, more outrage than jealousy, but coming, as it does, on the heels of his own plea for more funding, this critique has to extend to those who fund the RSPCA instead of the London SPCC. The answer to his question of "what can gratify the compassionate more" than the rescue and care of homeless dogs is provided in his plea for the care of homeless children, and his repetition of the phrase "only dogs" demonstrates his belief that the child is infinitely more worthy than the animal.

What interests me here is not whether the child *is* more worthy or in need of more care and protection than an animal, but instead, why the NSPCC felt such a distinction had to be made. By 1889, it is clear that the Society understood—or at the very least, represented—its financial difficulties as resulting in part from the diversion of funds from children to animals. Announcing a decision to cut back on the formation of new "Aid Committees" (branches of the NSPCC in other districts), *The Child's Guardian* explained in 1890 that "Getting at cruelty to children is like getting at coal, a costly thing at the outset."[99] Waugh goes on to clarify that

> This decision indicates no check in the prosperity of the Society. Its prosperity has been and is still unique. That fact, however, is that the increase in the Society's influence and the demands of its work, especially since the new law, have been greater than its increase in its funds. Were as many of our rich Christians as

---

97   Waugh, "Notes," *The Child's Guardian*, 3.29 (May 1889), 83–4.

98   Ibid., 84.

99   Waugh, "Notes," *The Child's Guardian*, 4.4 (April 1890), 43.

interested in the prevention of cruelty to children as they are in the prevention of cruelty to animals, the committee would have no need to check the pace of its crusade against the vilest, blackest shame of our land, the famine and pain of tiny staggerers to the grave.[100]

Again, the reader is confronted with the belief that, in terms of social evils, cruelty to children trumps all others as "the vilest, blackest shame." Unfortunately, it is suggested, the support of a lesser cause is in some ways responsible for "checking the pace" of the NSPCC's "crusade." Not only does this "Note" suggest that there is a finite amount of compassion (represented by donations, of course) to go around, but it takes as a given that more people in England concern themselves with suffering animals than with suffering children.

But this is a given without any evidence. While the NSPCC is careful, throughout the 1890s, to provide information about the funds it requires for its work, it at no point provides any figures that back up its assertion that animals received greater financial support in English society than did children. The NSPCC also fails to reveal, in these complaints, that the Society in fact continued to receive more money each year, and that the shortfall it experienced was not the result of a falling-off in funding, but of the inability of those funds to keep up with the aggressive pace of the Society's expansion. But perhaps most importantly, the NSPCC also fails to acknowledge the existence of other child-saving agencies. Certainly, organizations such as Dr. Barnardo's Homes and the Church of England Waifs and Strays Society, or any other of the multitude of children's organizations operating at the time, might be responsible for "diverting" funds of "rich Christians" away from the NSPCC. And yet, none of these organizations is ever represented as the competition in NSPCC discourse, nor are charities for temperance, for poor relief, for "fallen women," for overseas missions, or for any of the other innumerable charitable causes of the time. In reading *The Child's Guardian*, one gets the distinct impression that animals and children were the sole objects of charity in late nineteenth-century England, with the NSPCC and the RSPCA battling it out on their behalf.

This focus on competition between the two organizations, on the part of the NSPCC,[101] can be at least partially explained by the initial close cooperation between the two. Because the NSPCC shared membership with the RSPCA (and perhaps even subscription lists), the fledgling organization may have felt that its work was cut out for it in terms of winning over the support of those already committed to the RSPCA. Furthermore, the NSPCC had much more in common with the RSPCA than it did with organization such as Dr. Barnardo's Homes, and the need to distance itself from the RSPCA could be seen as an effort by the NSPCC to prove its own uniqueness. Certainly, the fact that dual organizations for the relief of animals and children were proposed before the NSPCC came into

---

[100]   Ibid.

[101]   So far as I know, the RSPCA did not engage in a corresponding discourse.

existence did seem to be something from which the NSPCC wanted to distance itself. In its criticism of the Harrogate and District Society for the Prevention of Cruelty to Animals, which had decided to expand its scope to include the prevention of cruelty to children, Waugh declared that "training for a horse doctor is not so unlike the training of a child doctor as the training of an animals inspectors is unlike that of an inspector of children ... they have no more relation to one another than have the duties of a head schoolmaster to the duties of a horse trainer."[102] Given that the NSPCC gained its organizational, membership, and employment structures from the RSPCA, and shared many of the same board members with that organization, and that dual organizations were quite common, Waugh's righteous critique of those who would align animal anti-cruelty work with child-protection rings somewhat hollow.

Nevertheless, it was a critique that could not be made often enough; throughout *The Child's Guardian* in the 1890s, there are articles, "Notes," and editorials that testify to the fact that children and animals must be represented by separate organizations, and that where there is overlap, it is the children who suffer. For example, in the November 1898 issue, it is reported that "We have received a newspaper report of 'The Prevention of Cruelty Society' in Queensland. This Society is for animals and children. As is usual in such a combination of work, the work done for animals is greater than the work done for the children."[103] The comment that the supposed slighting of endangered childhood is "usual" in such cases again relates to the idea that those who love animals are somehow ambivalent about or, worse, antagonistic towards the suffering of children. By suggesting that anti-cruelty work on behalf of children and animals is not only impractical but, in fact, antithetical, the NSPCC succeeds in distinguishing itself from the organization with which it shared so many members, and in defending its own expertise in the field of child protection.

Separating the Child from the Animal

There may be more to the NSPCC's desire to assert the separation of the child from the animal, however, than mere competition between itself and the RSPCA. Residual conceptions of the child as naturally depraved and sinful meant that many in England still believed that violence was a necessary aspect of parental discipline. In the November 1892 issue of *The Child's Guardian*, Waugh provides what he calls "a fair sample of many communications implying the triviality of our Society's work in comparison with that of the 'Society for the Prevention of Cruelty to Animals'": "Miss H. is not one of those silly sentimentalists who see an 'infant Jesus' in every peevish, squalling child, although, of course, she disapproves of cruelty both to the children and to the still more to be pitied animal,

---

102   Waugh, "Notes," *The Child's Guardian*, 7.12 (December 1893), 166.
103   Waugh, "Notes," *The Child's Guardian*, 12.11 (November 1898), 130.

as it is dumb."[104] Miss H.'s contrast between the "squalling" child and the "dumb" animal suggests the opposite of what Manning and Waugh had argued in "The Child of the English Savage," for here it is suggested that the child is more than able to speak up for itself, whereas the animal requires others to intervene on its behalf. Furthermore, the child's "peevishness" suggests that a good wallop or two will do it no serious harm, while the dumb animal, one presumes, has caused no such offense. In order for the NSPCC to venture into the terrain of parental discipline and corporal punishment, the Society had to carefully distinguish between the ill-behaved child (who, it believed, deserved corporal punishment) and the abused child, whose ill-treatment was either unrelated to any action of the child, or a response far in excess of any wrong committed by the child. Therefore, when constructing the abused child, the NSPCC carefully stressed the child's innate meekness, in order to make that child as mute and helpless as the suffering animal.[105]

But if an ill-mannered child was an unattractive object of charity, then the dangerous, "savage" child of the poor and of the streets was even more so. A letter printed in the July 1893 issue of *The Child's Guardian* from (according to Waugh) a "powerful-minded lady" suggests some of the hopelessness and fear these children aroused in the population:

> Surely it is better that these horrible people should painlessly kill their children before they can feel the horror of a loveless life …. Let us at least turn away in mournful silence while the vile of our own population put any merciful limit to their own increase …. Till there are no parents but such as love their offspring, it is far better that they should sleep on their children when they will.[106]

Though the writer refers to "loveless" homes, the reference to overlaying— a common concern virtually limited to poor families, and associated with drunkenness—suggests that the "vile of our own population" refers here to the lower classes. The woman's suggestion that death is the "far better" option to either rescue by the NSPCC or survival and the chance to contribute to the "increase" of this population, gives some sense of the work the NSPCC had to undertake in order to portray the child of abusive homes as worthy of protection. Furthermore, the woman's reference to parents putting a "merciful limit to their own increase," has echoes, of course, of discussions current in *Animal World* on the best way to "mercifully" put down animals—whether to end their suffering, or to deal with large litters of offspring. Her comments therefore underscore the more brutal aspect of associating children with animals—if both were nuisances to society

---

[104]   Waugh, "Notes," *The Child's Guardian*, 6.11 (November 1892), 136.

[105]   The NSPCC was not, however, opposed to the use of violence in parental discipline, as outlined in Chapter 5—instead, it was careful to distinguish between appropriate and inappropriate forms of discipline.

[106]   Waugh, "Notes," *The Child's Guardian*, 7.12 (December 1893), 165.

that must only suffer if allowed to live, then seeking to end their lives in the most "humane" way possible was not outside the realm of the imagination.

Obviously, letters such as the two quoted above do not necessarily provide an accurate depiction of late-Victorian attitudes towards endangered children; in fact, it is the use of such letters by the NSPCC that is particularly telling. In both cases, these letters dramatically enact the mindset the NSPCC claims as the enemy of children and of the Society's continued prosperity—that of an obvious preference for animals over children, and of a disregard for the "value" of children that the Society must (or argued it must) continually combat. The perception (and possible reality) of such opponents of child protection demonstrates why the image of the "child of God" as opposed to the "child of nature" was so important to the NSPCC. If children and animals had so much in common, it was reasonable to assume that one could choose to help the one that was soft and mute, as opposed to the one that stole one's handkerchief in the street, and that could grow up to produce more such "savages" in the future. The child *as* animal had to be replaced with the child of God, whose care was a divine and ethical injunction.

Furthermore, comparisons between children and animals were also perceived as threatening because they fell, as the second letter writer demonstrates, dangerously close to the ungodly territory of social-Darwinian or Malthusian thinking, both of which Manning and Waugh perceived to be a grave threat to the sanctity of the family: "The duty society owes to the lives of unwanted children is greatly increased by the waking-up of evil men to the modern ideas that population is a nuisance, and that God and future judgment are 'superstitions.'"[107] According to Manning and Waugh, the "new ideas" of the value of human life, separated as they were from concepts of man's consanguinity with God, inspired abusive parents to reject the sanctity of the home, and fall away from their sacred duty of caring for their offspring. Therefore, in the face of what they perceived as the waning of faith in England, Manning and Waugh argue that "As the tendencies of religious consideration are being superseded, the tendencies of legal ones must take their place, or tampering with infant life will greatly increase."[108] The NSPCC had a responsibility to inspire parliament to take over where religion had lost hold, and to combat the "secularized conscience" disseminated by "the dictation of certain apostles amongst us" who spread their ungodly creed among "even disposed men."[109] In order to make children a worthy object of protection, then, the NSPCC had to do battle with the "increasing tendency to regard human beings as protoplasm; to shake off the idea of Jesus as the living God, the Father of us all, and to account for human life by molecules," for "Child life and happiness are bound up with the Kingship of God."[110]

---

[107] Manning and Waugh, "The Child of the English Savage," 693.

[108] Ibid.

[109] Ibid.

[110] Waugh, "Street Children," *Contemporary Review* 53 (June 1888), 833.

The abused child had to be a salvageable child—not the animalistic, hopeless, and eminently "lost" children of late nineteenth-century novels such as Arthur Morrison's *A Child of the Jago,* in which there is no way out for poor Dicky Parrott but his own violent death. The concept of the "child of nature," who shared kinship with animals, and who thrived outside the bounds of society, had to be replaced with a concept of the child that fell firmly within the bounds of religiosity, so as to reject any view of the child as vicious or irredeemable, and so as to demonstrate the necessity—and possibility—of shaping that child through guidance and protection. But perhaps most importantly, the abused child had to be presented as inherently separate and distinct from the abusive parents who raised them. If the abused parent was animalistic and "savage," the abused child must be everything but—so as to, again, highlight that child's salvageability, but also to combat the idea that saving these children would inevitably allow them to increase their own "vile population."

The actual child with whom the Society came into contact, of course, did not always show the same desire to be kept separate from the abusive parent. When, during the course of a particularly brutal case in the early years of the Society, it was observed that "the child kissed her mother," Waugh relied upon an association of the child with nature in order to explain this phenomenon:

> When the science of childhood is as well understood as is the science of molluscs, it will no more occur to the legal profession to plead that the mother loves the child, than it now occurs to it that a limpet's clinging to a rock is proof that the rock loves the limpet. By sheer instinct, a little child is bound to love her parents, even those she fears and dreads; and, in spite of dangers, she must show her love.[111]

Waugh refers here to something that very much resembles the kind of love Ozias and his brothers showed towards the man who beat them. But whereas that love was a sign of both the child's and the animal's true, innocent, and feeling nature, here that same love is reduced to "instinct." The child cannot help it, and as a result, the action is virtually meaningless—or, at least, should not be heeded. While the literary representation of this moment allowed for some agency on the part of the animal and the child—or, at the very least, highlighted some admirable, if perhaps endangering aspect of their nature—Waugh's depiction of it deprives the child of any agency whatsoever. The child's actions cannot even be understood by the child itself, but only by those who understand the "science of childhood."

This brief moment of reliance upon a connection between child and animal in order to explain a child's behavior is unusual in NSPCC rhetoric, but very significant. The attitude revealed within this passage by Waugh demonstrates the most negative consequence of associating the child with the animal: that of rendering the child a mute object of concern, the reality of whose own thoughts and

---

[111]   Waugh, "Notes," *The Child's Guardian,* 1.2 (February 1887), 14.

feelings are questionable at best. But Waugh's statement also starkly demonstrates what gets lost in child-protection discourse when narratives of child endangerment are severed from the representations of shared animal-child suffering seen earlier in the period. Ozias and his brothers, Hugh and his dogs—these relationships highlight the extent to which child suffering is the result of power relations in society, of hierarchies in which the child and the animal are inevitably placed at the bottom. Waugh's easy dismissal of the child's grief at being separated from her mother reaffirms rather than reverses this hierarchy. Thus, by severing the child from the animal, the NSPCC failed to recognize the ways in which narratives of child-animal suffering might help to illuminate problems of power, cruelty, and domination.

While the initial cooperation between the RSPCA and the NSPCC had been fruitful largely because children and animals were linked in the public imagination as helpless, feeling subjects, such cooperation—between the two societies and, it would seem, between children and animals—was no longer desirable once the NSPCC established itself. Although animals and children began the century as companions, they ended it as adversaries—much, I would argue, to the detriment of both.

Chapter 3
"What Eyes Should See":
Child Performance and Peeping
Behind the Scenes

One of the more controversial aspects of the London SPCC's early efforts to bring about legislation on behalf of abused children concerned the restriction of child performance. In taking on this issue, the Society had influential support: "While on his deathbed, the Earl of Shaftesbury had purportedly sent for Benjamin Waugh, placed in his hands a book denouncing theatrical work for the young, and implored him to 'right those wrongs.'"[1] However, the figure of the child performer did not necessarily lend itself to the Society's constructions of the abused child. As with comparisons between children and animals, narratives of the child performer throughout the nineteenth century served to define both the child itself and the nature of childhood suffering, but stories about children who performed in the street, the stage, or in the circus also centered on the issue of what a child could do with its body, and what could be done to it. Specifically, these narratives focused on the child's body on display—its grace and suppleness, its exertion, its fragility. The meaning of that child's body and its gestures, therefore, varied greatly, because performance, particularly acrobatics, combined the attributes of play with evident physical exertion and, in some cases, danger. As a result, the child performer was a vexed figure, straddling, on the one side, the world of fancy, imagination, and pleasure, and on the other, the world of commerce, training and labor. Child performance could be and was variously understood as a joyful and pleasurable expression of childhood fancy, as an endangerment to the souls of the performers themselves and to their audiences, as a form of employment, and as an instance of "cruelty to children."

The duality of the child performer—both playful child and rigorously trained entertainer—has much to do with the binary opposition of the stage itself, whereby the performance one sees is both in direct contrast to, and mutually constituted by, what goes on "behind the scenes." The charming "pantomime fairy," for example, while pretty and cared for on stage, was feared to suffer from exhaustion, abuse, and exploitation when off the stage—what Ellen Barlee refers to as the "curtain's

---

[1]   George K. Behlmer, *Child Abuse and Moral Reform in England, 1870–1908* (Stanford: Stanford University Press, 1982), 104.

reverse shadow" in her 1884 exposé, *Pantomime Waifs*.[2] As a result, narratives of child performance often focused upon that which could *not* be seen—on the "reality" of the backstage, always placed in sharp contrast to the lie or deception of the performance itself. This concern was elicited by the long hours and hard labor necessary for the training of a child performer, but it was also brought forth by questions about the performing child itself. Taught to "practise the various expressions of the passions—pride, contempt, love, hatred, surprise, pleasure, etc.—until each can be assumed at command," such children, it was believed, faced endangerment from learning "the power [performance] imparts of deceiving others, and simulating right to cover wrong."[3] The child performer, throughout the nineteenth century, was therefore a source of anxiety because it encapsulated contradictory narratives about what it meant to be a child: playful versus manipulative, open and artless versus deceitful and artful, natural versus artificial.

The vexed nature of the child performer in Victorian England meant that the question of whether or not one should take pleasure in its performance was equally problematic, and both fictional and actual responses to the child upon the stage demonstrate the constantly shifting role of adult observation of, pleasure in, and intervention on behalf of that child. From enjoying the performance, to "peeping behind the scenes," to just plain peeping, the adult audience was necessarily implicated in concerns surrounding the child performer. It was also, however, invested in that performer, and where child-protection discourse sought to instruct the audience as to how it should react to the child upon the stage, resistance to that instruction (both from within and without the child-protection movement) speaks to the difficulty of constructing the child performer as the abused child— a difficulty that is itself revelatory of the conditions necessary for the latter to become an object of social concern.

"The Truth of Infancy": Child Performance and Child Labor

In *The Circus and Victorian Society*, Brenda Assael suggests that the origin of nineteenth-century circuses and fairs "had its roots in a variety of cultural sites: the ancient amphitheater, the medieval fair on the ancestral village green, the Lord Mayor's Day procession, the aristocratic court, and the eighteenth-century virtuoso's cabinet of curiosities." But "it was in the late eighteenth and early nineteenth centuries that the organization of these acts into one program performed in a tent or amphitheater was turned into a commercial enterprise."[4] The nature of theatrical employment in circus entertainment varied: some shows were more

---

[2]   Ellen Barlee, *Pantomime Waifs, or, a Plea for our City Children* (London: S. W. Partridge & Co., 1884), xiv.

[3]   Ibid., 28.

[4]   Brenda Assael, *The Circus and Victorian Society* (Charlottesville and London: University of Virginia Press, 2005), 2.

fixed in nature, being connected to permanent amphitheaters, such as Astley's Amphitheater in Lambeth, while others traveled the countryside; some were run by large companies and headed by managers, while others were smaller, and run by individual families.[5] As well, employment in the circus or fair sometimes led to employment in more urban settings, where "this talent was also displayed in the theater and later the music hall depending upon public demand."[6]

Children were often employed in circus and theatrical performance, and Assael argues that the "cottagelike" nature of some theatrical groups, "in which all the family members were involved in some aspect of the performance," was not uncommon. Children who labored in the theatrical professions, however, "In contrast to their peers in the textile and mining industries, who were affected by the Factory Acts of the 1830s and 1840s … remained untouched by legal controls."[7] This failure to acknowledge the performing child within legislation restricting child employment suggests that child performance was not understood to be labor in the same ways as was child labor in the factories and mines. In *A Voice from the Factories* (1836), however, Caroline Norton opens her exposé of child labor through an extended depiction of a young acrobat, a "stage-wonder." In this depiction, Norton makes explicit the connections between the suffering of the eminently visible child performer and the suffering of the unseen child working in the factories. This connection between these two separate groups of endangered children suggests that even though child performers did not receive legal protections until late in the nineteenth century, they still aroused concern in some members of their audience. The lack of early nineteenth-century intervention on their behalf, then, may speak more to the problem of constructing child performers *as* endangered children than to an actual lack of concern for them: a problem very much present in Norton's poem.

Norton opens her sequence poem with a dedication to Lord Ashley, in which she recognizes that "it requires but an inferior understanding to *perceive* an existing evil, while the combined efforts of many superior minds are necessary to its remedy," but argues further that "I cannot but think it incumbent on all who feel, as I do, that there *is* an evil which it behoves Christian lawgivers to remove,— to endeavour to obtain such a portion of public attention as may be granted to the expression of their conviction."[8] Norton attempts to garner this "portion of public attention" on behalf of child laborers through her poetry, and the small "stage-wonder" with which she opens her poem itself commands an audience. In describing the child's performance, Norton focuses particularly on the audience's reaction to the spectacle before them:

---

[5]   Ibid., 3.

[6]   Ibid.

[7]   Ibid., 111, 136.

[8]   Caroline Norton, *A Voice from the Factories* (Oxford and New York: Woodstock Books, 1994), vii.

Where is the heart so cold that it does not thrill
With a vexatious sympathy, to see
That child prepare to play its part, and still
With simulated airs of gaiety
Rise to the dangerous rope, and bend the supple knee?[9]

Norton's rhetorical question, "Where is the heart so cold," appeals to the power of
the child performer to elicit feeling from its audience because, Norton suggests,
there is something both natural and right about the child's ability to elicit
"sympathy." This particular child elicits a "vexatious sympathy," however, for the
part it is about to play is a dangerous one, one for which the child must "prepare."
The sympathy the audience feels is therefore distressing, because to feel with the
child is also to feel its fear and anxiety. Such fear and anxiety, however, is also
an integral part of the "thrill" the audience feels, suggesting that its members are
themselves complicit in both the child's labor and its suffering.

Complicit, because the sympathy for the child is complicated by the pleasure
that the performance itself elicits. The "supple knee" of the child acrobat suggests
that, despite the danger and the need for this child to "prepare to play its part,"
there is something natural in this child's play, as if its body is somehow made for
this particular work. Furthermore, the performance itself is beautiful, as the child
"runs along with scarce perceptible pace— / Like a bright bird upon a waving
spray, / Fluttering and sinking still, whene'er the branches play."[10] The comparison
of the child to a "bright bird" speaks to the idea of the "natural child" discussed
earlier, who revels in play and in the connection with nature such play confirms.
This child possesses an "infant skill"[11] to move fluidly, gracefully, and lightly, and
the pleasure of watching the performance is therefore that of watching the child's
body in action, a body that has an energy and a grace lost to adults.

Norton is careful to point out, however, that while this child's skill might be
natural, it is also "exertion," exertion that is necessary for the child to "earn its
bread," and that deprives the child of "wholesome slumbers."[12] This performance,
Norton clearly argues, is not play at all, but labor. The child must, however, "mime"
and put on "simulated airs of gaiety" in the commission of its performance in order
to please its audience.[13] It "lifts its small round arms and feeble hands / With the
taught movements of an artist's grace," and on its face "a joyless and distorted
smile / Its innocent lips assume; (the dancer's leer!)."[14] The "smile," the "grace,"
and the "gaiety" of the child are all here, but they are "simulated," "taught," and
"assumed." Clearly, while the actions of this child might appear spontaneous

---

9   Ibid., stanza 3, lines 5–9.
10   Ibid., stanza 4, lines 7–9.
11   Ibid., stanza 3, line 2.
12   Ibid., stanza 3, lines 2, 1, 3.
13   Ibid., stanza 3, lines 4, 8.
14   Ibid, stanza 4, lines 3–4, stanza 5, lines 1–2.

and playful, they are in fact the actions of a child "playing" its part: performing childlike "gaiety" while attempting to conceal exhaustion, fear, and necessity. This performance is not entirely successful, for while the "dancer's leer" bespeaks the moment when the child succeeds in "conquering its terror for a little while,"

> Then lets the TRUTH OF INFANCY appear,
> And with a stare of numbed and childish fear
> Looks sadly towards the audience come to gaze
> On the unwonted skill which costs so dear,
> While still the applauding crowd, with pleased amaze,
> Ring through its dizzy ears unwelcome shouts of praise.[15]

The child might momentarily "conquer" its emotions, but its experience is one of "terror," of a "numbed and childish fear" that is betrayed to the audience by its eyes, its "stare." This momentary failure to deceive in the performance represents in Norton's text a moment of truth. The "truth of infancy" she describes is that of the child's transparency—of its failure to obscure completely its own terror behind a "joyless and distorted smile."[16] Because the child is a child, Norton suggests, it cannot truly deceive, but must instead betray its true feelings, its innocence. Norton locates the true nature of childhood in this transparency, and as a result, the entire performance is represented as suspect, for grace and agility of the child notwithstanding, the "truth of infancy" would suggest that demanding that a child deceive, act, and / or perform is asking the child to go against its very nature.

Although the child fails both to perform a natural and convincing smile and even to maintain the façade of a smile, the audience is, nevertheless, captivated by the performance. That is, while the speaker sees through the performance to the "truth of infancy" that is betrayed by the child's sad and frightened gaze, the "applauding crowd," who in turn "gaze" upon the child, respond merely with "pleased amaze" and "unwelcome shouts of praise." The audience members here represent an authority figure, because, in response to the child who has entertained "obedient to the public will,"[17] they show that they are pleased, and "reward" the child for its efforts. Norton, however, suggests that too much has been asked of this "obedient" child; its skills "unwonted," its praise "unwelcome," the stage-wonder is more a victim of its natural talents, and of the audience members' demands for those talents to be put to use for their pleasure, than a child who has won praise for proper exertion and compliance.

Through her depiction of the audience's inappropriate pleasure in the child's labor, Norton instructs her reading audience in the proper response to such a spectacle by asking, "What is it makes us relieved to see / That hapless little dancer reach the ground; / With its whole spirit's elasticity / Thrown into one glad, safe,

---

[15]   Ibid., stanza 5, lines 3–9.

[16]   Ibid., stanza 5, line 1.

[17]   Ibid., stanza 3, line 4.

triumphant rebound?"[18] The use of "us" here includes both the speaker who has observed the child's terror, and the reading audience whom Norton rhetorically includes in the feeling of relief at the closure of the child's performance, thereby constructing an "appropriate" subjective response. She demands that her reading audience recognize that the "truth of infancy" is here made evident in the contrast between the child's strained performance of "simulated airs" and "taught movements," and its own "glad, safe, triumphant bound" at the completion of the performance. The appearance of the "true" child, in sharp contrast to the performed child, awakens within the speaker (and by association, the reading audience) a feeling quite different from the "pleased amaze" with which the child was greeted during the performance:

> Why are we sad, when, as it gazes round
> At that wide sea of paint, and gauze, and plumes,
> (Once more awake to sense, and sight, and sound,)
> The nature of its age it re-assumes,
> And one spontaneous smile at length its face illumes?[19]

Although the audience had responded with pleasure to the child's "joyless and distorted smile," its "dancer's leer," the speaker feels only sadness at the appearance of the child's own "spontaneous smile." In "re-assuming" the "nature of its age," the child performer reveals the extent to which the audience's pleasure in the performance was obtained by "simulated airs" rather than by the child itself. In other words, the performance of childish "grace" brings pleasure to those who fail to recognize the reality of the child's labor, that which prevents it from being able to enjoy its true nature.

But if the reality of the performance as labor complicates the ability of that performance to represent the true child, because "we feel, for Childhood's years and strength, Unnatural and hard the task hath been,"[20] Norton suggests that it is also the artifice of the stage that endangers the child, "Because our sickened souls revolt at length, / And ask what infant-innocence may mean, / Thus toiling through the artificial scene."[21] The "truth" of childhood is therefore two-fold: it is "unnatural" and "hard" for a child to labor, to "toil," but it is also unnatural for a child to be "artificial," or, to be more specific, to be exposed to and forced to occupy a space that is artificial. Norton's depiction of "that wide sea of paint, and gauze, and plumes" upon which the child gazes deliberately confuses both the adult audience—itself, perhaps, dressed up for the performance—and the costumes of the circus. Deceit, performance, and artifice are here constructed as part of adult society, and as such, unfitting for a child. The influence of Romantic

---

[18]   Ibid., stanza 6, lines 1–4.
[19]   Ibid., stanza 6, lines 5–9.
[20]   Ibid., stanza 7, lines 1–2.
[21]   Ibid., stanza 7, lines 3–5.

conceptions of the child is very evident here, because the "truth" that is revealed is that the child should be natural (i.e., transparent), that the child should enjoy the "natural world," and finally, that the child should not undertake tasks outside its "years and strength."

Norton's use of the child performer to argue that "Ever a toiling child doth make us sad"[22] provides a complex segue into her examination of child factory labor. The fact that the performance of the "hapless little dancer" excites applause as well as sadness, and that the audience members' "sickened souls" only "revolt at length"— that is, after they have received pleasure from the spectacle which eventually sickens them—strongly suggests the investment of the public in the labor of children. For of course, the "toiling" child performer elicits more applause than sadness. By encouraging her reader to see the connection between the stage-wonder and the "pent-up little wretches"[23] within the factory, Norton suggests that, like the audience watching the child performer, the people of England are complicit in the abuse of children within factories, because "in the British senate men rise up … And while these drink the dregs of Sorrow's cup, / Deny the sufferings of the pining band." [24] By revealing the "truth of infancy" behind the "paint and gauze" of the performance, therefore, Norton instructs her audience to see beyond England's gain to the suffering that has brought it about. Moreover, because the child performer is visible before all, and, even in spite of its training, is unable to obscure the truth of its "infant-innocence," it can make the suffering of those children supposedly hidden away visible to all.

The question of just how hidden away those factory children were, however, suggests further work that this stage-wonder—as a symbolic representation of the child laborer—might perform. Having the child performer represent these workers suggests that just as the performance obscures a reality behind the scenes, so too is the reality of child labor in the factories concealed from the public eye. The use of a stage metaphor therefore paradoxically relieves some of the responsibility for that labor from the English public. For while that public is exhorted to bring about change in the current system of child labor, it is also simultaneously excused from responsibility through Norton's construction of child labor as a *secret* evil. That is, while her text encourages her audiences to work towards the abolition of child labor, it also provides a transition between a not-too-distant past in which child labor was entirely accepted in England. By constructing child labor as a hidden fact of English life, as a performance which has obscured pain and suffering behind paint and spangles, Norton allows her audience to believe that they have somehow been misled or deliberately kept in ignorance about the hardships which have contributed to English wealth. The figure of the child performer, then, works as a means of transition from a residual conception of childhood, one that allowed

---

22 Ibid., stanza 9, line 1.
23 Ibid., stanza 10, line 2.
24 Ibid., stanza 16, lines 1, 3–4.

labor for children as a financial necessity, to a newly emergent conception of childhood that found such labor reprehensible.

Furthermore, Norton's use of a child performer as a means of eliciting public concern on behalf of child laborers can also be seen as, in part, a defense of her own genre. The child performer, by engaging the imagination through the practice of its art, has the ability to move its audience, to elicit feelings, and to provoke insights. So too, in a sense, does Norton defend her own work; she observes in the dedication to her poem, "doubtless there are those to whose tastes and understandings, dry and forcible arguments are more welcome than reasonings dressed in the garb of poetry."[25] Like the child performer, who serves to draw in a sympathetic audience on behalf of its less spectacular endangered laborers, Norton's poem dresses up "dry" prose in order to reach a broader audience. Norton is careful to point out, of course, that unlike the child performer whose "truth of infancy" is obscured by "simulated airs of gaiety," her own poetry has obscured no truth, because she has "in *no* instance overcharged or exaggerated by poetical fictions, the picture drawn by the Commissioners appointed to inquire into this subject"[26]—though, of course, this very defense speaks to Norton's perception that the language of the governmental reports is "truth," while poetry can be dangerously deceptive. It can also, however, reveal truths that "forcible reasonings" cannot, because, as Norton argues, "as poetry is the language of feeling, it should be the language of the multitude."[27] Fancy and imagination can obscure or exaggerate the truth, but they can also, she suggests, bring about a revolution in feeling in their audience.

If the parallel holds between the child performer, who elicits pity on behalf of children hidden in the factories, and Norton's poetry, which serves to obtain that same sympathy through the use of imaginative representation, then the stage-wonder in Norton's text is a complicated figure. Norton encourages the reader to empathize with and feel for this child, but she also, through her own use of this figure to move her audience, testifies to the stage-wonder's power. The child performer's skills might be "unwonted," but it has, nevertheless, the ability to command an audience and to make that audience feel, whether it be pleasure, guilt, or sadness. This power of the child performer to move the adult audience, and perhaps to embody imagination and fancy, would continue to be at the heart of conflicting responses to child performance throughout the nineteenth century.

Fantasy and Reality: The Child Performer in Sentimental Fiction

Although Norton is careful to point out that her stage-wonder is engaged in labor, not play, for writers of sentimental fiction such as Dickens and Collins, the image of the theater as a place of fantasy and imagination was tremendously attractive.

---

[25]   Ibid., vi.

[26]   Ibid., viii.

[27]   Ibid., vi.

For Dickens in particular, the "world of the stage and circus was the 'type' of fairyland; its inhabitants, ridiculous, feckless or pretentious as he might represent them, were by these very qualities detached from the harsh world of materialism."[28] In Dickens's novels, the world of the theater is not a place of danger, but a place of refuge from the dangers of the outside world. Furthermore, as Brenda Assael suggests, "in Wilkie Collins's *Hide and Seek* and Charles Dickens's *Hard Times* the circus girls Madonna and Sissy Jupe, respectively, embody 'fancy,' 'imagination,' 'romance,' and creativity."[29] The theater in these texts therefore comes to symbolize—as a place of play, freedom, and fancy—the ideal of childhood that was currently being constructed in the middle-class world. There is also much in these texts, however, to suggest that while both authors valorized and celebrated the world of the circus as a place of escapism for adults, neither entirely supported it as a proper place for a proper child.

In Dickens's *Nicholas Nickleby* (1838–1839) and *Hard Times* (1854) and in Collins's *Hide and Seek* (1854), the theater provides protection for those rejected or endangered by the outside world, and in particular, by the failings of their own families. Nicholas Nickleby and Smike find employment in Mr. Crummle's theater company, Thomas Gradgrind hides from the law in Sleary's circus, and in Collins's novel, the Peckovers, a circus clown and his wife, shelter the infant Madonna and her dying mother from the horrors of the workhouse. For all of these characters, the circus and the theater represent places of safety, but perhaps more importantly, these characters also find acceptance in a kind of surrogate family within the theatrical world. Smike, abused and orphaned, and Nicholas, temporarily exiled from his mother and sister, are warmly welcomed into Crummle's troupe and are there given the acceptance and support that they have failed to gain from their own families. Tom, though exceedingly surly and ungrateful for the sanctuary that he has been given in Sleary's circus, is nevertheless taken in and protected on behalf of Sissy Jupe, who considers the circus folk as a kind of extended family. And at the moment of her death, Madonna's mother gives her child to Mrs. Peckover, by whom she is raised as part of the circus family, who (for the most part) respond to her with generosity and kindness. As Mrs. Peckover relates, "She grew up so pretty that gentlefolks was always noticing her, and asking about her; and nearly in every place the circus went to they made her presents, which helped nicely in her keep and clothing. And our own people, too, petted her and were fond of her." By contrast, Madonna's own family dismisses her as a "child of sin," and suggests only that "the parish must support it if nobody else would."[30] The theater, then, rather than existing purely as a place of employment, is represented in these works as a kind of home—a place of safety, acceptance, and love.

[28]   Margaret Nancy Cutt, *Ministering Angels: A Study of Nineteenth-Century Evangelical Writing for Children* (Wormley, England: Five Owls Press, 1979), 163.

[29]   Brenda Assael, *The Circus and Victorian Society*, 141.

[30]   Wilkie Collins, *Hide and Seek* (Oxford: Oxford University Press, 1993), 90, 88.

In *Hard Times*, however, the theater symbolizes not just the home, but also a place in which lost childhood can be regained; as Paul Schlicke notes, "The values which Dickens associated with popular entertainment—including spontaneity, freedom, fancy, and release, as opposed to the life-denying forces of hard-headedness and hard-heartedness—converged in the most important image in his art, that of the child."[31] Louisa and Thomas Gradgrind have the misfortune to be raised by their own parents in their own home, and as a result, suffer greatly under their father's system of education, one that eschews imagination and fancy in favor of a hyper-Benthamite obsession with facts. Having carefully raised his children according to his "system," Gradgrind is horrified to witness his children's exposure to the harmful effects of "Sleary's Horse-riding" circus:

> the turning of the road took him by the back of the booth, and at the back of the booth a number of children were congregated in a number of stealthy attitudes, striving to peep in at the hidden glories of the place …. Phenomenon almost incredible though distinctly seen, what did he then behold but his own metallurgical Louisa, peeping with all her might through a hole in a deal board, and his own mathematical Thomas abasing himself on the ground to catch but a hoof of the graceful equestrian Tyrolean flower-act![32]

As a result of their father's educational system, the Gradgrind children are deprived of a proper childhood, and the circus for them represents a glimpse into a world that is utterly foreign to their own, a world that can reveal the limitations of their own existence. It provides access to fancy and imagination, to which—Dickens's text implies—they as children have a right, but of which they have been deprived. "Peeping with all their might," Louisa and Thomas wish to gaze upon that which represents their own lost childhood, and which will promise them a momentary escape from the constraints of their father's household.

Rather than focusing on the dangers of the circus, then, Dickens instead focuses on the kind of endangerment middle-class children are often portrayed as experiencing in sentimental novels—that of a strict, loveless home. This failure to provide "childhood," though not perhaps physically damaging, is represented as damaging to the all-important "character" of the middle-class child, and Louisa and Thomas are no exception. Louisa, in particular, is aware that she has been marred in some way by her rigid upbringing, an awareness brought home by her father's adoption of Sissy Jupe. Sissy, a circus girl, is brought into the Gradgrind home to serve as an "example" to Louisa: an example "of what this pursuit [i.e., the circus] which has been the subject of a vulgar curiosity, leads to and ends in."[33] Ironically, Sissy instead demonstrates to the Gradgrind family the benefits of imagination and play to the

---

[31]   Paul Schlicke, *Dickens and Popular Entertainment* (London: Allen & Unwin, 1985), 14.

[32]   Charles Dickens, *Hard Times* (Peterborough: Broadview Press, 1996), 50–51.

[33]   Ibid., 72.

formation of feeling, nurturing womanhood. While Louisa comes to understand that she has been irreparably harmed—"I don't know what other girls know. I can't play to you, or sing to you. I can't talk to you so as to lighten your mind, for I never see any amusing sights or read any amusing books that it would be a pleasure or a relief to you to talk about"—Sissy goes on to fulfill the normative female role of wife and mother: "happy Sissy's happy children loving her; all children loving her; she, grown in childish lore; thinking no innocent and pretty fancy ever to be despised; trying hard to know her humbler fellow-creatures, and to beautify their lives of machinery and reality with those imaginative graces and delights."[34] Sissy, the former circus girl, becomes a model of middle-class femininity, a role she shares with Madonna, the former circus girl of Wilkie Collins's *Hide and Seek*: "Deliciously soft, bright, fresh, pure, and delicate," dressed in "very pretty, simple, Quaker-like attire," and with a face "the nearest living approach they had ever seen to that immortal 'Madonna' face, which has for ever associated the idea of beauty with the name of RAPHAEL,"[35] Madonna represents the quintessential angel in the house. Compared to Louisa Gradgrind, who marries a man she does not love, who teeters on the edge of an infidelity, and who remains essentially tainted and childless at the end of the novel, Sissy and Madonna, the former circus girls, fare very well indeed.

They are, however, *former* circus girls, and there is much to indicate in these texts that, despite even Dickens's attachment to the theater as a place of fancy, he sees it as no place to raise a child, particularly a girl. That is, while both Dickens and Collins use the circus as a means of representing the joys of an ideal middle-class childhood, as well as the dangers children face in the materialistic, hypocritical, middle-class world, both writers also register concern about the actual role of children within the theater. In *Nicholas Nickleby*, Dickens's description of Mr. Crummle's daughter—the "infant phenomenon"—gestures towards some of the dangers a child may face in the theatrical profession. The phenomenon is presented to Nicholas as a ten-year-old wonder; however, Nicholas's surprise at this information is elicited not by the precocity of her talent, but by her haggard appearance:

> the infant phenomenon, though of short stature, had a comparatively aged countenance, and had moreover been precisely the same age—not perhaps to the full extent of the memory of the oldest inhabitant, but certainly for a good five years. But she had been kept up late every night, and put upon an unlimited allowance of gin-and-water from infancy, to prevent her growing tall, and perhaps this system of training had produced in the infant phenomenon these additional phenomena.[36]

---

[34]   Ibid., 88, 315.

[35]   Collins, *Hide and Seek*, 48, 50.

[36]   Dickens, *The Life and Adventures of Nicholas Nickleby* (Hertfordshire: Wordsworth Editions Limited, 2000), 262.

Dickens plays this moment for its dark humor, but there is, nonetheless, serious concern expressed here as well. Though the infant phenomenon is neither infant nor phenomenon, she has also not enjoyed an ideal childhood, and if Louisa and Thomas Gradgrind are ruined by their father's "system," there is much to suggest that Mr. Crummle's child has suffered, at least physically, from his own "system of training." Because her status is not middle-class, however, Dickens represents her lack of a childhood as somewhat comedic—perhaps because the importance of fancy in the development of proper womanhood is less a concern with a woman such as she will someday be.

Therefore, although it is true, as Assael argues, that both Sissy and Madonna embody imagination and romance, it is nevertheless important that both girls are removed from the circus in which they are found and placed within the middle-class home. Sissy's father abandons his child so that she will live a better life outside the circus, and though there is irony in the fact that it is Sissy herself who "saves" the Gradgrind family, she is, nevertheless, also herself rescued from her lower-class life into one of middle-class domesticity. Moreover, Valentine Blyth's adoption of young Madonna in *Hide and Seek*, which prevents her from performing in Mr. Jubber's circus, is depicted as nothing less than her rescue and salvation, because in that circus the young deaf-mute had faced both physical abuse and moral degradation. In fact, Madonna's deafness and muteness are both the result of her participation in the circus. Yielding to pressures from the circus' proprietor, and from Madonna's desire to "play," Mrs. Peckover consents to allow Madonna to take part in a performance: "I don't know what we should have done then, if my husband had lost his engagement. And, besides, there was the poor dear child herself, who was mad to be carried up in air on horseback, always begging and praying to be made a little rider of."[37] Again, as in Norton's text, Mrs. Peckover's words suggest that there is something natural about child performance, that the child herself can both enjoy and excel in the work to be done. There is, however, also something unnatural, something almost wild in the child's desire to perform; her adoptive mother observes that Madonna "had a sort of mad fondness for it that I never liked to see, for it wasn't natural to her."[38] The "dear" child, who is pretty and fond and petted, becomes, through the influence of the circus, infected with a desire to perform dangerous stunts. The catastrophe that ensues (Madonna is dropped by the rider who carries her and is seriously injured) results in the child's complete deafness and muteness. She can no longer "beg and pray" to perform, but is still forced to play a part, parading her deafness in a "weary pilgrimage"[39] that brings her no joy. Her madness for performance past, Madonna must continue to perform long after she herself can find pleasure in it. Performance is represented in this text, at least dangerous performance, as something that, though it might

---

[37]   Collins, *Hide and Seek*, 91.

[38]   Ibid.

[39]   Ibid., 61.

appeal to the child, appeals to some wild, savage part of the child's nature. And without that madness, the child faces nothing but labor and exploitation.

Importantly, the success of Madonna's act lies in her very failure to perform. Made to walk round the ring with her slate and chalk, performing conjuring tricks, she garners applause and sympathy by virtue of her condition and demeanor, rather than her skill:

> The face and manner of the child, as she walked into the center of the circus, and made her innocent curtsey and kissed her hand, went to the hearts of the whole audience in an instant … she began to perform her conjuring tricks with Mr. Jubber and one of the ring-keepers on either side of her, officiating as assistants. These tricks, in themselves, were of the simplest and commonest kind; and derived all their attraction from the child's innocently earnest manner of exhibiting them, and from the novelty to the audience of communicating with her only by writing on a slate.[40]

The attraction of Madonna's performance is that it is not a performance—her innocence, her earnestness, and her unique impairments are what move her audience, rather than any particular skill. It is the artlessness of her act, the appeal of her true child's nature—as opposed to her "mad," unnatural performance on horseback—that brings pleasure to those who watch her.

If Collins is clear about what appeals to the audience in his performance, he is equally clear as to the nature of the audience itself. His assurance that the protagonist Valentine's attendance at this performance "did not proceed from that dastard insensibility to all decent respect for human suffering which could feast itself on the spectacle of calamity for hire, in the person of a deaf and dumb child of ten years old,"[41] instructs the reader that Valentine's own reaction will be the proper response to such a spectacle:

> He saw the small fingers trembling as they held the cards; he saw the delicate little shoulders and the poor frail neck and chest bedizened with tawdry mock jewelry and spangles; he saw the innocent face, whose pure beauty no soil of stage paint could disfigure, with the smile still on the parted lips, but with a patient forlornness in the sad blue eyes ….[42]

Although Valentine sees and is enraptured by the child's beauty and innocence, he also, like the speaker in Norton's poem, sees beyond the pleasure elicited by the child to the suffering she herself endures. "Trembling," "frail," "sad," and "forlorn," Madonna cannot disguise the weariness she feels, even behind the "tawdry mock jewelry" and "stage paint." She is transparent, and the true nature

---

[40]   Ibid., 59–60.

[41]   Ibid., 57–8.

[42]   Ibid., 62.

of her performance is visible to all who have the wisdom, and the proper insight, to see it. The novel therefore constructs appropriate adult subjectivity in terms of response to such a child: acknowledging the seductive attractiveness of Madonna, but also suggesting that an empathetic recognition of and sympathy for her suffering should and must trump the pleasure found in gazing upon her.

Valentine further models the proper action to be taken in these circumstances, for once being witness to Madonna's suffering, he takes it upon himself to be her salvation. After seeing "terror in her eyes—terror palpable enough to be remarked by some of the careless people near Mr. Blyth"—the "careless," of course, demonstrating that no peculiar gifts are necessary to decipher a child's need—Valentine follows her backstage in order to "find out what was really going on behind the red curtain."[43] There, he discovers her being beaten for making a mistake in her performance. Unlike the actions of the "careless people" who remark on the child's fear but do nothing, Valentine demonstrates that the proper response to a child in danger is to look behind the scenes, to intervene. And intervene he does, as he arranges to meet with Mrs. Peckover to propose his own adoption of the child.

Although the adoptive mother is understandably upset at the thought of giving up her child, Valentine and his friend, Mr. Joyce, offer arguments against which she cannot defend herself. The circus world in which she lives, they argue, is one of great danger to Madonna, both because of the cruelty and abuse she faces at the hands of the proprietor and because of the even greater dangers to her innocence and purity. Mr. Joyce urges Mrs. Peckover to

> Only reflect on Mary's position, if she remains in the circus as she grows up! Would all your watchful kindness be sufficient to shield her against dangers to which I hardly dare allude?—against wickedness which would take advantage of her defencelessness, her innocence, and even her misfortune? Consider all that Mr. Blyth's proposal promises for her future life; for the sacred preservation of her purity of heart and mind.[44]

Although Madonna does grow up to be a pure and virtuous woman, she does so because she has been rescued from the polluting influence of the theater. The "tawdry jewelry" and "soil of stage paint" that she wears during her performances not only provide a sharp contrast to her own "pure beauty,"[45] but also suggest a kind of prostitution, in which her innocence is at risk—and, based upon Valentine's own reaction to her as a "Devotional beauty" and "Enough to bring the divine Raphael down from heaven to paint her,"[46] by which the audience itself can be seduced. Her body on display before the audience arouses Valentine's indignation

---

[43]   Ibid., 67.
[44]   Ibid., 104.
[45]   Ibid., 62.
[46]   Ibid., 60.

(after, of course, arousing his desire and admiration), as much from the parallel this display draws between her and other women who display their bodies, as from the exploitation of her affliction. Though Madonna is loved and cared for by the surrogate family that takes her in, they cannot provide her with the proper childhood she deserves, nor give her the proper "position" when she will become a young woman. Madonna is saved to a life of middle-class childhood, and by saving her, Valentine saves himself by transforming the desire he feels—in his transformation of Madonna from tawdry performer to beloved child—into the appropriate feelings of parental love and protection.

The fact that both Sissy and Madonna are saved from the world of the circus and introduced into middle-class domesticity points to the extent to which discourse on children in the theater centered on issues of class. Though the theatrical world could represent fancy, play, and freedom within the imaginative space of the novel, all things increasingly associated with ideal childhood, and all things represented as particularly attractive to the adult middle-class protagonists of the novel, in reality those children who grew up in the theater belonged to the working classes. The problematic nature of child performance in Dickens's and Collins's texts, therefore, speaks to the somewhat contradictory nature of the work these novels perform. These novels seek to critique middle-class hypocrisy through an appeal to the theater as the representative of lost childhood—childhood that can be somewhat regained within that magical space—but they also perform the work of constructing social consciousness in terms of the poor, the downtrodden, and the suffering. Increasing public fears on behalf of children in the theater therefore jeopardized the ability of that space to represent free play, and to act as an escape from the confines of middle-class existence. This would prove to be particularly true in those cases where children performed in the street; nevertheless, even in narratives of performing street children, the conflict so present in these texts between desire and indignation, between concern and envy, and between protection and voyeurism, persists.

Tumblers, Traders, and Prostitutes: Child Street Performance

Children who performed in the streets did so under a variety of arrangements: attached to adult street performers and entertainers (as seen in Henry Mayhew's highland dancer, and in the Italian *padroni* system),[47] working as part of a troupe, or working on their own account at tumbling or singing as a glorified form of

---

47   In the second on "Street Entertainment" in volume three of *London Labour and the London Poor*, Mayhew interviews a "Scotch piper" who is accompanied by his daughter, who performs the Highland fling and a sword dance. This Scotch piper is also a good example of how street performers in the city also, during the appropriate seasons, ventured out across the country to perform in towns and villages. The Italian *padroni* system refers to the exportation of Italian children into England as apprentices to adult street performers.

begging. Because the kind of work children found in the streets was dependent on a variety of factors (such as the weather, the time of day, and the season, as well as the living situation of the children themselves—whether they were runaways, orphans, or living with their families), street children who performed often did so on a much more casual basis than did children who were attached to a theatrical company or circus. The casual nature of this work made street children difficult to account for, and even more difficult to categorize. Nineteenth-century narratives of children who perform in the streets therefore tend to enunciate fears about street children in general: about their lack of childishness, their independence, and their perceived immorality. Such children fell far outside the idea of childhood gaining ground in Victorian society, and Cunningham notes that "A romantic idea of what childhood ought to be" is contrasted, in narratives of street children, "with the horror of the actuality of the street child."[48] This horror was especially strong, I would argue, where girl-children were concerned—for while there was room in nineteenth-century discourse for the savage boy-child to be reclaimed, the dangers of the street for the girl-child made her unsalvageable.

In *London Labour and the London Poor* (1851–1852), Henry Mayhew sets out to explore, interview, and categorize the types of labor and laborers in London's streets. His work represents an early ethnographic, sociological study, and as such, makes ample use of case studies, statistics, and tables. It also, however, draws heavily upon the novelistic tradition in those case studies and in Mayhew's imaginative use of data; as Christopher Herbert observes in *Culture and Anomie: Ethnographic Imagination in the Nineteenth Century*,

> So novelistic does Mayhew's 'survey' often seem that he has inevitably been suspected (on almost no evidence) of doctoring his informants' statements, presumably to give them an enhanced Dickensian flavor, of falsifying his image of street life by dwelling at disproportionate length on weird and picturesque individuals and occupations, and of gullibly reporting made-up stories as fact.[49]

Accusations such as the ones Herbert describes demonstrate the extent to which sociology and literature are bound up in binary oppositions of fact/fiction, data/imagination, and reality/fantasy. That Mayhew's text disrupts such boundaries Herbert makes amply clear, arguing that "These problematic aspects" must be seen "as the symptoms of Mayhew's powerful movement toward a fully ethnographic—which is to say, a fully interpretive—concept of culture; they exhibit in all their

---

Chapters 6 and 7 of Carolyn Steedman's *Strange Dislocations* provides an analysis of the responses to this particular "category" (to use Mayhew's terms) of street performer.

[48]   Hugh Cunningham, *The Children of the Poor*, 108.

[49]   Christopher Herbert, *Culture and Anomie: Ethnographic Imagination in the Nineteenth Century* (Chicago: University of Chicago Press, 1991), 207.

disruptive glory the contradictions which that equivocal concept necessarily entails."[50]

Such "disruptive glory" is evident in Mayhew's depictions of lower-class children. Within this voluminous work, Mayhew often comments upon the lives and manners of children, who, whether on their own or attached to a family, are essentially raised by the streets:

> The education of these children is such only as the streets can afford; and the streets teach them, for the most part—and in greater or lesser degrees,—acuteness—a precocious acuteness—in all that concerns their immediate wants, business, or gratification; a patient endurance of cold and hunger; a desire to obtain money without working for it; a craving for the excitement of gambling; an inordinate love of amusement; and an irrepressible repugnance to any settled in-door industry.[51]

Mayhew's focus on their "desire to gain money without working for it" and their "repugnance" to settled "industry" suggests the recognition on his part that these children must work, which in turn indicates an acceptance of the distance between these poor children of the streets and their wealthier counterparts. In this sense, Mayhew's attitude towards the children of the costermongers is influenced by residual narratives, particularly social-scientific narratives regarding the children of the poor, that focused upon the necessity of preventing idleness among children of the lower and working classes. These narratives had "a long and continuous history. Instead of the habits of industry, such children, it was thought, would acquire a propensity to crime."[52]

However, Mayhew's text also reveals anxiety about the distance between these children and what he evidently thinks a child *should* be, demonstrating the influence of changing constructions of the child. The education these children receive on the streets is one, his text suggests, that makes them unfit for a proper childhood. Street children endure privation, rather than enjoy security and comfort; they have a "precocious" independence when it comes to fulfilling their own "gratifications," rather than depend upon those who could, presumably, choose more wisely on their behalf; and though, like all children, they enjoy amusement, in their case their enjoyment is "inordinate." These are children without boundaries and restrictions, children who cannot settle "in-doors" in the proper sphere of the home, and their unrestricted freedom demonstrates the extent to which representations of childhood as a time of freedom and play strictly limited what such freedom and play might mean.

Mayhew's text therefore struggles between fears of idle children and fears for children who never play; between desire for the child-like child, and admiration

---

[50] Ibid.

[51] Henry Mayhew, *London Labour and the London Poor* (London: Penguin, 1985), 24.

[52] Cunningham, *The Children of the Poor*, 103.

for the laboring child. In all his depictions of children, Mayhew registers anxiety about what a poor child should *mean*, largely because, I would argue, his own genre straddles competing discourses about that poor child. In his interview with the Watercress girl, for example, Mayhew expresses anger and disbelief at the child who "although only eight years of age, had entirely lost all childish ways": "There was something cruelly pathetic in hearing this infant, so young that her features had scarcely formed themselves, talking of the bitterest struggles of life, with the calm earnestness of one who had endured them all." The fact that this "infant," is, "in thoughts and manner, a woman"[53] is brought home to Mayhew by his querying her on what he considers appropriately "childish subjects." Asking her about toys, parks, and playing, Mayhew is met with "a look of amazement," and he comes to the conclusion that "All her knowledge seemed to begin and end with watercresses, and what they fetched."[54] Throughout his interview with this girl, Mayhew seeks to register, through his questions and her responses, the extent to which this child is *not* a child, to which she has aged before her time, as evidenced in her body and her face, which "was wrinkled where dimples ought to have been."[55] Steedman remarks that "The child confounded him: he could not explain her: the theories of childhood and working-class life he possessed failed him," and Cunningham notes, "Rarely do two concepts of childhood at such odds with one another confront each other so directly."[56]

Though Mayhew's response to the watercress girl demonstrates his desire for this child, and other street children, to be given "Parental instruction; the comforts of a home, however humble … the influence of proper example; the power of education; [and] the effect of useful amusement,"[57] his expectations of her and other street children are also gendered. He is able, with the male street children, to recognize aspects of their lives in the streets that unite them with boys of all classes, for he asks the reader to consider the street boys in the light of "the spirit of emulation, of imitation, of bravado, of opposition, [and] of just and idle resentment among boys," the "among" suggesting that these are shared characteristics of all male children. Mayhew argues, however, that because female children belong "to the sex who, in all relations in life, and in all grades of society, are really the guardians of a people's virtue," his inquiry into the lives of "the female children of the street" is "much more important" than that of the boys.[58] In his analysis of the children of the street, therefore, Mayhew applies general rules about the proper nature of childhood that seek to register sameness between the street children he sees and the ideal, middle-class counterparts with which he implicitly compares them. Or, to be more

---

[53]　Mayhew, *London Labour and the London Poor*, 64.

[54]　Ibid., 65.

[55]　Ibid.

[56]　Steedman, "The Watercress Seller" in *Reading the* Past (Basingstoke, England: Palgrave, 2000), 20, and Cunningham, *The Children of the Poor*, 109.

[57]　Mayhew, *London Labour and the London Poor*, 185.

[58]　Ibid.

accurate, he compares these children to *respectable* working-class childhood that is itself modeled on middle-class ideals. Because the boys of the street register that sameness, their lives and habits cause him less anxiety than those of the girls, who do not measure up to the rule he applies: that girls and women in all classes of society represent virtue. This particular anxiety about the occupations, habits, and demeanor of girl street children in comparison to those of boys can be seen particularly in those of Mayhew's subjects who have nothing to sell, and who must, as a result, use their bodies as a means of earning a living.

In his discussion of the "crossing sweepers" of London, Mayhew describes this occupation as "one of those … which are resorted to as an excuse for begging."[59] The boys engaged in this work combine their sweeping with "tumbling": "When I see anybody coming, I says, 'Please, sir, give me a halfpenny, and touches my hair, and then I throws a caten-wheel, and has a look at 'em, and if I sees they are laughing, then I goes on and throws more of 'em."[60] This boy, the "King" of the crossing-sweepers, has his routine completely worked out, and the measure of his performance's success is the pleasure he brings to his audience. The boy's language would seem to suggest that he is one of those children Mayhew complains of who "desire to obtain money without working for it," because his description of "throwing" a "caten-wheel" suggests ease, rather than labor. Furthermore, in his interview with "Gander," the "Captain" of the crossing-sweepers, Mayhew himself observes what appears to be the ease and naturalness of the boy's tumbling:

> During his statement, he illustrated his account of the tumbling backwards—the "caten-wheeling"—with different specimens of the art, throwing himself about the floor with an ease and almost a grace, and taking up so small a space of ground for the performance, that his limbs seemed to bend as though his bones were flexible like canes.[61]

Mayhew here, like the audience of Norton's stage-wonder, is mesmerized by the child's body in action, by its flexibility and grace. And though his comparison of the child's bones to cane suggests disquiet on Mayhew's part, it is one that springs from recognition of the strangeness of the child's body, rather than from any sense that this movement is unnatural. Because the boy can "throw" himself about with "ease," his tumbling appears effortless, and there is as much envy in Mayhew's description as there is admiration.

Tumbling is, however, an "art," and Mayhew and the boys themselves are very careful to point out the work that has gone into obtaining this skill—if for very different reasons—and the effort it takes to perform it correctly. The "King" of the crossing-sweepers points out that "The Gander taught me tumbling," and he complains that, while he can do a caten-wheel "twelve or fourteen times running

[59] Ibid., 257.
[60] Ibid., 279.
[61] Ibid., 273.

.... It just *does* tire you, that's all."[62] The "King," as Mayhew describes, has "wondrous tumbling powers": "He could bend his little legs round till they curved like the long German sausages we see in the ham-and-beef shops; and when he turned head over heels, he curled up his tiny body as closely as a wood-louse, and then rolled along, wabbling like an egg."[63] The boy's body can do these "wondrous" things, but it is because of training, not only by Gander, but by a gentleman "as belonged to a 'suckus'": "He taught me to put my leg round my neck, and I was just getting along nicely with the splits (going down on the ground with both legs extended), when I left him. They (the splits) used to hurt worst of all; very bad for the thighs."[64] The pain of the postures the "King" assumes, and the work involved in the performance itself, backs up the boy's statement to Mayhew that "we works hard for what we gets,"[65] a statement further supported by "Mike," who says of his own tumbling, "I can't do it more than four times running, because it makes the blood to the head, and then all the things seems to turn round. Sometimes a chap will give me a lick with a stick just as I'm going over—sometimes a reg'lar good hard whack."[66] Although the tumbling of the street boys may appear natural, playful, and exuberant, it is actually a skill that must be learned, and one that both requires effort and excites little respect.

These boys and their performances are therefore quite problematic for Mayhew. While he is fascinated by the community of boy crossing-sweepers and tumblers, and shows respect for their labors in the details he provides of the "art" of tumbling itself, he also, in his discussion of the "ease" with which the boys move, suggests that while this tumbling might be hard work it is not "industrious"—there is too much of play about it, despite the exertions it requires. Paradoxically, however, the reality of the labor behind the play is also a source of anxiety, for it reveals the crossing-sweepers' performance of boyish exuberance *as* performance. This act of playing childhood is intimately connected, in Mayhew's text, to the close relationship between performance and begging. While interviewing Gander, for example, Mayhew expresses frustration at the boy's tendency to deceit:

> It was perfectly impossible to obtain from this lad any account of his average earnings. The other boys in the gang told me that he made more than any of them. But Gander, who is a thorough street-beggar, and speaks with a peculiar whine, and who, directly you look at him, puts on an expression of the deepest distress, seemed to have made up his mind, that if he made himself out to be in great want I should most likely relieve him.[67]

---

[62]   Ibid., 279, italics in original.

[63]   Ibid., 278.

[64]   Ibid., 282.

[65]   Ibid., 281.

[66]   Ibid., 272.

[67]   Ibid., 274.

Though these boys may work, and work hard, at what they do, this work is still just a glorified form of begging to Mayhew, and while they may be practicing an art, they also learn artfulness. Gander "speaks" with a whine, and "puts on" facial expressions, even in his interview with Mayhew, suggesting that the boy's performance is perpetual—a learned response to life on the streets that the boy cannot easily put off, even when hectored by his companions. Their bodies trained to be flexible, and their minds accustomed to deceit, street-boys like Gander show none of the transparency—none of the "truth of infancy"—evident in Norton's and Collins's depictions of child performers. The dangerous education they receive on the streets is therefore made manifest in the contrast between the appearance of youthful exuberance constructed by their tumbling, and the reality of their hard labor and their cunning as revealed through Mayhew's interviews of them.

Although Mayhew asserts that the "female child can do little but *sell* (when a livelihood is to be gained without a recourse to immorality)" whereas "the boy can not only sell, but *work*,"[68] he does include interviews with a few girls who work as crossing-sweepers. These girls, in turn, mention both boys and girls who work in this manner, suggesting that the occupation is not worked solely by boys. However, Mayhew is careful to elicit from both girl crossing-sweeps that they do not "stop out at night"[69] when the boy crossing-sweepers take up their tumbling. Whether or not any female children take part in this tumbling is therefore difficult to ascertain, but what is clear in Mayhew's account is that it is a particular kind of girl whom the boy tumblers encounter during their nightly performances:

> After the Opera we go into the Haymarket, where all the women are who walk the streets all night. They don't give us no money, but they tell the gentleman to .... Sometimes a gentleman will tell us to go and get them a young lady, and then we goes, and they general gives us sixpence for that. If the gents is dressed finely we gets them a handsome girl; if they're dressed middling, then we gets them a middling-dressed one; but we usual prefers giving a turn to girls that have been kind to us, and they are sure to give us somethink the next night.[70]

Boys and girls may work as crossing-sweepers together during the day, but according to Mayhew, at night their occupations are quite different. Both use their bodies as a means of earning money, but for the girls, apparently, prostitution is the only means of doing so. There is still performance involved, as the boy tumblers and girl prostitutes have a kind of routine worked out by which they both profit from gentlemen who walk the streets of the Haymarket. But if there is some admiration from Mayhew for the boys' tumbling performance, there is none here; not only are the women fallen and degraded by their occupation, but the boys too are complicit in it, participating in that fallenness.

---

[68] Ibid., 169.
[69] Ibid., 289, 291.
[70] Ibid., 268–9.

Although girls and women undoubtedly engaged in performance on the streets in the evening, Mayhew seems able only to see women who work at prostitution. In fact, Mayhew even suggests that those girls who work at selling in the streets are in fact performing as a means of procuring customers for prostitution. Remarking that "I did not hear of any girls who had run away from their homes becoming street-sellers merely," Mayhew goes on to say that "They more generally fall into a course of prostitution, or sometimes may be ostensibly street-sellers as a means of accosting men, and, perhaps, for an attractive pretence to the depraved, that they are poor, innocent girls, struggling for an honest penny." The performance these female street sellers engage in is motivated by a deceitfulness born of the streets; they perform "honesty" and "innocence," but are anything but in Mayhew's eyes, and once removed from the relative safety of the parental home (relative because even the homes of the costermongers do not provide the kind of supervision and guidance Mayhew believes girls require), "their ruin seems inevitable."[71]

Boys may tumble at night to supplement their earnings during the day, but girls, Mayhew suggests, can only sell themselves. The labor is connected, however, because both must perform, be cunning, and manipulate their audience in order to obtain a living. And, as in the case of the boy tumblers and the prostitutes in the Haymarket, their audience is the same. The gentlemen who watch the boys tumble also watch the women, as both the boys and the prostitutes put their bodies on display in the streets. What Mayhew does with his work is not so much make the boys and girls of the street visible, as they are already exceptionally so, but make them visible *as* children: that is, he calls attention to the distance between what they should be and what they are. While he succeeds in making these children appear dangerous—in their deceitfulness, their immorality, and their manipulation of the public—he also wants to show that they are endangered. He therefore appeals to a wider audience, his reading audience, to see these children, and to recognize that "They have been either untaught, mistaught, maltreated, neglected, regularly trained to vice, or fairly turned into the streets to shift for themselves. The censure, then, is attributable to parents, or those who should fill the place of parents—the State, or society."[72] These children, Mayhew asserts, require saving, not just on their own behalf, but also on behalf of the children with whom they come into contact, because "Mixed with the children who really *sell* in the streets, are the class who assume to sell that they may have the better chance to steal, or the greater facility to beg." [73] The "mixing" of the children of the street, so that those who sell come to associate (and be associated) with those who perform, and those who perform come to associate (and be associated) with those who prostitute, lends urgency to Mayhew's call for his readers to see street children differently: not to take pleasure in watching their bodies, but to think how such children can be saved.

---

[71]   Ibid., 164.

[72]   Ibid., 161.

[73]   Ibid., italics in original.

Mayhew's text therefore resolves some of the tension of his generic mélange by falling back on a narrative about the children of the poor that was present within a broad range of genres—that of rescuing or saving the poor child. His text, however, also works to erase particular kinds of child endangerment through his gendered reading of child employment on the streets. For Mayhew, girls who work are inevitably girls who sell themselves, but there is no such corresponding narrative about boy children. According to Larry Wolff, Mayhew instead relies upon gendered representations of juvenile crime that persisted throughout the nineteenth century, in which boys were perceived to fall into theft, while girls fell into prostitution. In "'The Boys are Pickpockets, and the Girl is a Prostitute,'" Wolff argues that "To recognize the male prostitute meant also recognizing the homosexual patron,"[74] a recognition that threatened, in texts such as Dickens's *Oliver Twist*, "Dickens's insistent construction of the innocent benevolence of older gentleman, [which] was essential to the Victorian vision of society."[75] By failing to recognize the ways in which his boy performers might perform in exactly the same way as their female street-walking counterparts, Mayhew safeguards his own gaze upon the performing boy's body, and displaces desire entirely onto the body of the girl.

By the end of the nineteenth century, narratives linking the female child performer and prostitution would become dominant narratives of child performance and endangerment. The problem of child street performance, and, in fact, of child presence in the streets in any capacity, was partially solved by the Education Acts of the 1870s and 1880s, which effectively removed many children from the streets and placed them within the school. Furthermore, by 1872, Lord Shaftesbury had "introduced a private bill designed to protect the lives and limbs of acrobat children."[76] The bill provoked resistance upon various points,[77] but by 1879, the Children's Dangerous Performances Act was passed into law. This Act "prohibited the employment of any child under 14 in a performance that was dangerous to life or limb," thus protecting children engaged in novelty acts, such as "acrobats, stilt-walkers, rope-dancers, children shot from cannons, [and] contortionists." However, "children employed in dangerous performances represented a tiny proportion of the industry."[78] Many feared (and warned) that the Act "would not

---

[74]   Larry Wolff, "'The Boys are Pickpockets, and the Girl is a Prostitute': Gender and Juvenile Criminality in Early Victorian England from *Oliver Twist* to *London Labour*," *New Literary History* 27.2 (1996), 238.

[75]   Ibid., 241.

[76]   Brenda Assael, *The Circus and Victorian Society*, 146.

[77]   Assael lists as some of the obstacles faced in the effort to protect child acrobats debates about the limits of state intervention, about the "age group the bill was meant to protect," and about the effect such legislation would have upon working-class families who were employed in the theatrical industry (Brenda Assael, *The Circus and Victorian Society*, 216, 217).

[78]   Steedman, *Strange Dislocations*, 132.

stop the practice" of child performance, because "the itinerant lifestyle of many of these performers made them unlikely candidates for legal control, regardless of state intervention."[79] Finally, the Act did not contain provisions restricting training, because "there remained the practical difficulty of how to police private households in which the alleged cruel training took place. The surveillance of homes, if put into law, would intrude on the rights of freeborn Englishmen to the privacy of their homes."[80]

Therefore, while the Education Acts and the Dangerous Performances Act of 1879 did much to restrict child performances, neither addressed the problem of itinerant families who worked in the theater or circus. Because "children who performed with troupes usually did not remain in any community long enough to warrant registration in a local school district,"[81] they often escaped the disciplinary apparatus of school boards. Furthermore, as long as the dangers they faced occurred within the home, and were not of a kind to be restricted as "Dangerous Performance"—i.e., one that would cause physical harm—child performers still failed to receive the protection of the law. In the later years of the nineteenth century, therefore, it was the role of the parent in child performance, and the moral, rather than the merely physical dangers faced by the child performer that were to arouse the greatest concern.

Pantomime Waifs: "A Peep Behind the Scenes" and Performance as Seduction

Because those who performed on the streets of the cities also often worked in the surrounding countryside, discourse about "theatre waifs" tended to collapse concerns about child performers with concerns about street children. As Mayhew observes of women who worked on the streets, "The muscular irritability begotten by continued wandering makes her unable to rest for any time in one place .... The least restraint makes her sigh after the perfect liberty of the coster's 'roving life.'"[82] Assael notes of child acrobats in the nineteenth century that "Despite their public role in the ring, the itinerant status of these children, who traveled with tenting companies or moved from one resident company to the next, obviously made them difficult to trace—a fact that only heightened public anxiety about their work."[83] In both cases of the "roving" costermonger and the traveling child performer, there is no home in which children can lead a "settled" existence. The itinerant nature of the work of the traveling performer, combined with concerns about both the

---

[79]   Assael, *The Circus and Victorian Society*, 149.
[80]   Ibid., 150.
[81]   Ibid.
[82]   Mayhew, *London Labour and the London Poor*, 46.
[83]   Assael, *The Circus and Victorian Society*, 136.

immorality of the stage and the physical hardship suffered by children within it, therefore made the traveling theater or circus somewhat akin to the street.

It is not surprising, then, that one of the best-selling books for children, Amy Walton's *A Peep Behind the Scenes* (1877),[84] combines an Evangelical depiction of the "street waif" with a narrative about a traveling circus.[85] For strict Evangelicals, the stage was a place of danger for children, not simply because of the physical threats it contained, but more importantly, because of the moral dangers it represented: "actors, acrobats, dancers, and magicians were all represented in Evangelical literature as hawking the trash of Vanity Fair to lure the weak and the young into the broad way of destruction."[86] Destruction by theater came about, according to Evangelicals, through the "deception" of the performance itself, through the wasted time spent participating in or witnessing such events, and through the (assumed) immorality of actors, acrobats, and performers themselves. The theater endangered, therefore, both those children employed within it, and those who were its witnesses. Acrobatics was seen as particularly pernicious, because of the "unnatural" and "immoral" postures the child assumed, but cherished English traditions such as the pantomime were also targeted in this fiction.

"Waif novels," a genre within Sunday-school fiction[87] that was "influenced by discourses on ragged children, nineteen-century didactic writing for children,

---

[84]   Amy Catherine Walton published under the name Mrs. O. F. Walton.

[85]   According to Cutt, "*A Peep Behind the Scenes* was, in its time, almost every little girl's favourite book" and "was one of the best-known children's tales of the century" (Margaret Nancy Cutt, *Ministering Angels*, 160). This assessment is supported by Penny Brown, who states that "in a survey carried out in 1884 [O. F. Walton] was one of the nine top authors among girls of 11 upwards, together with Dickens, Charlotte Yonge, Charles Kingsley, and Hesba Stretton" (Penny Brown, *The Captured World: The Child and Childhood in Nineteenth-Century Women's Writing in England* [New York: Harvester Wheatsheaf, 1993], 88).

[86]   Margaret Nancy Cutt, *Ministering Angels*, 160.

[87]   As Cutt argues, "by 1810 new writers for children were mostly Evangelicals or Evangelical sympathizers, their work being a calculated part of the Evangelical determination to reform and convert the nation and eventually the world" (Margaret Nancy Cutt, *Ministering Angels*, 20). Publishing companies such as the Society for the Propagation of Christian Knowledge (SPCK) and the Religious Tract Society (RTS) produced both the majority of fiction for children and "a constant supply of cheap printed matter," without which "children's libraries in the poorer homes of the last century would have been scanty indeed" (Ibid., 31). Early Evangelical tracts owed much to the rationalism of Hannah More's Cheap Repository Tracts, though they worked to "replace the Rule of Reason in children's books [with] the Rule of Religion" (Ibid., 18). However, by the mid-nineteenth century, Evangelical fiction showed the influence of popular literature and moved away from strict moralism towards sentiment and pathos as the primary means of instruction. The street "waif," exemplified by a poor, isolated child, surrounded by physical and moral degradation, and yet capable of piety, innocence and purity, became a popular figure within the works of F. W. Robinson, Mrs. O. F. Walton, and Hesba Stretton, to name a few.

sentimental fiction and reports by social reformers,"[88] tended to focus upon idealized depictions of slum children, in which the "poor child was the means of redemption for an adult."[89] In this genre, the savage child of the street is replaced by the innocent, inherently holy child who represents both the ideal subject of evangelizing, and the means by which the conversions of the chosen around her take place. In texts such as *A Peep Behind the Scenes*, for example, the child's endangerment is not registered through the shocked awareness of distance between the savage, impoverished child and the ideal, middle-class child—that moment when the observer must ask "is this a child?"—but instead through the recognition of the distance between the ideal child and the fallen or degraded environment in which it is portrayed. The "truth of infancy" in the Evangelical waif novel, as in Collins's text, is what allows the child to escape the ravages of its environment, and to exist not only as the means of redemption for others, but also as an appropriate candidate for rescue.

One of the most influential children's books of its time, Hesba Stretton's *Jessica's First Prayer* (1867),[90] focuses on the redemptive qualities of Jessica, a former pantomime actress and a current street waif, who brings about a change in spirit in Daniel, the miserly owner of a coffee-stall, and is in turn saved by him from her drunken mother and her life of poverty. The success of this novel "led to a stream of similar tales,"[91] a significant number of which dealt with child performers. As Assael argues,

> That a discrete body of waif novels featured the child acrobat as a subject for rescue is significant not only because many believed that the performer's real-life counterpart was in need of saving but also because the street, the stage, or the circus ring provided a provocative fictional venue where a nightmarish world beset by cruelty could be spectacularly witnessed by the reading public, which included middle-class and working-class children .... The contrast between the rational recreation of reading and the irrationality of performing as it appeared in the waif novel, could not have been made more stark.[92]

The importance of reaching a child audience with tales about the true horrors of theater and circus life was spurred by the growth of the theatrical industry in the second half of the nineteenth century. After the Theatre Regulation Act of 1843, "there followed a rapid expansion of theatrical outlets at all levels of the market,

[88]   Assael, *The Circus and Victorian Society*, 137.

[89]   Cunningham, *The Children of the Poor*, 139.

[90]   According to Cutt, "Two million copies [of *Jessica's First Prayer*] are said to have been printed by the time of [Stretton's] death in 1911, and within five years of publication, the tale was in translation all over the world" (Margaret Nancy Cutt, *Ministering Angels*, 135).

[91]   Cunningham, *The Children of the Poor*, 139.

[92]   Assael, *The Circus and Victorian Society*, 141–2.

particularly as working-class entertainment," which "increased employment opportunities on the stage for women and children of the working and lower-middles classes."[93] Furthermore, "By 1877, circus, pantomime and amateur theatricals had become accepted juvenile entertainment."[94] Evangelical novels that focused on the dangers of theatrical life, therefore, sought to save both those children who worked in the theater itself, and those children who were witnesses to the child on stage and were themselves seduced by the pleasure of its performance.

Rather than rejecting the pull of imagination and fancy, however, Evangelical writers such as Walton instead used fairy-tale structures and sentiment as a means of locating "fairyland" in the world of home, religion, and morality. In *A Peep Behind the Scenes*, Walton tells the story of Rosalie, a circus waif, who "is exploited by her drunken father, acquires a cruel stepmother and a kind of fairy godmother in the shape of a circus dwarf, Mother Manikin, and eventually finds a home with her mother's long-lost sister's family in a country vicarage."[95] Throughout the novel, Walton includes detailed descriptions of circus life, always placing them in sharp contrast to the ways in which outsiders perceive the circus. In particular, Walton demonstrates the pull of the theater for children:

> about twelve o'clock, they came up to a little village where they halted for a
> short time so the horses might rest before going farther. The country children
> were just leaving the village school, and they gathered round the caravans with
> open eyes and mouths, staring curiously at the smoke coming from the small
> chimneys, and at Rosalie, who was peeping out from the muslin curtains.[96]

Like Louisa and Tom Gradgrind, these children are fascinated by the circus, and their open-mouthed curiosity speaks to the seductive power of the theater. Rosalie herself is equally an object of curiosity, but also of envy, as witnessed by the reaction she arouses in some of the children who see her: "'Don't you wish you was her?' said one of the little boys to the other. 'Ay!' said the little fellow; 'I wish *our* house would move about, and had little windows with white curtains and pink bows!'"[97] Walton acknowledges the attraction of both the novelty of Rosalie's

---

[93]   Steedman, *Strange Dislocations*, 130. Steedman further notes that "Until the Theatre Regulation Act of 1843, only licensed theaters were allowed to present entirely 'spoken theatrical activity.' In order to stay within the letter of the law, all other places of entertainment had used the strategy of interspersing music, dance, acrobat, gymnastic, and other novelty turns with drama and melodrama …. The Theatre Act freed the theatre from monopoly, but also helped bring about the stratification of the entertainment industry, distinguishing clearly between the theatre and other premises where the sale and consumption of drink was allowed in the auditorium" (130).

[94]   Ibid., 160.

[95]   Brown, *The Captured World*, 89.

[96]   Walton, *A Peep Behind the Scenes* (Fairfield, Indiana: 1st World Library, 2005), 24.

[97]   Ibid., 8.

life, and of the circus itself, but she also allows her reader to "peep behind the scenes" to the interior of this house: "It was a very small place; there was hardly room for him to stand …. There was not room for much furniture in the small caravan; a tiny stove, the chimney of which went through the wooden roof, a few pans, a shelf containing cups and saucers, and two boxes which served as seats, completely filled it."[98] Though Rosalie's home may seem attractive and whimsical to the children watching, Walton reveals its shabbiness, as well as the pain within it, for Rosalie's mother is desperately ill and her father is violent and demanding. The house may inspire envy in those children who gaze upon it, but it is not, Walton makes clear, a home.

Although the theater allows Louisa and Tom Gradgrind a glimpse of the childhood world of fancy and imagination that they have been denied, the townschildren in Walton's text have a proper home to which they return, and "after satisfying their curiosity, they moved away in little groups to their various homes, so that they might be in time for dinner."[99] In *A Peep Behind the Scenes*, it is instead the girl in the circus, Rosalie, who is "peeping out" from the caravan in an attempt to catch a glimpse of the world of proper home and family that she herself is lacking. By comparing Rosalie, in the caravan peeping out at the town and countryside, to the children peeping in and hoping to get a glance at the magic and wonders of the circus, Walton suggests that for the waif, it is the world outside the theater that holds magic. Rosalie's gaze upon a road-side cottage and the domesticity enacted upon its front-steps, and upon a church in the town at which she catches only a "peep"—"ever so pretty, mammie dear; such soft grass and such lovely roses, and a broad gravel walk all up to the door"[100]—transforms the mundane world of everyday life into one of wonder. For Rosalie, the pull of the countryside, with its pastoral landscape, is its sharp contrast to the shabbiness of the world in which she lives.

But if the countryside seems magical and seductive to her, it is nonetheless real and true. Although the children who gaze, open-mouthed, at the caravan are deceived by the glamour of the circus, a glamour that obscures the cruelty, ugliness, and poverty of those within, Rosalie finds only truth as a result of her desire to see and to know more about the life the cottage represents. At the end of the novel, it is in a similar cottage that Rosalie begins to live happily ever after: "She was not easily deceived by the world's glitter and glare and vain show; for Rosalie had been behind the scenes, and knew how empty and hollow and miserable everything worldly was." The cottage and "green pasture" where Rosalie makes her home fulfill the promise of the pastoral landscape which had first captured Rosalie's imagination. Her education in the world "behind the scenes," therefore, makes her appreciate the benefits of respectability, and allows her to be satisfied

---

[98]   Ibid., 9.
[99]   Ibid., 24.
[100]   Ibid., 31.

with her salvation through a life of domesticity, an education in which the child readers of Walton's text are too meant to share.[101]

If through Rosalie's realization of the falseness of "the world's glitter and glare and vain show" Walton seeks to educate her child readers in the importance of accepting reality as it is, she is also careful to point out that Rosalie's nightly performances do just the opposite:

> There were many young girls there, some of them servants in respectable families, where they enjoyed every comfort; yet they looked up at little Rosalie with eyes of admiration and envy. They thought her life was much happier than theirs, and that her lot was greatly to be desired. They looked at the white dress and the pink roses, and contrasted them with their own warm but homely garments; they watched the pretty girl going through her part gracefully and easily, and they contrasted her work with theirs. How interesting, how delightful, they thought, to be doing this, instead of scrubbing floors, or washing clothes, or nursing children![102]

The danger inherent in Rosalie's performance is not just the immorality to which she has been exposed through the long hours that she works and the brutality that she faces from her father, but also the deception to which her audience is exposed. Rosalie's performance inspires dissatisfaction in those who watch her: dissatisfaction with their work, dissatisfaction with their station in life, and dissatisfaction with the benefits of respectability and homeliness.

Rosalie is therefore a somewhat problematic figure. Though her beauty and her innocence are a source of continual comment throughout the text, the proof that she is untouched by the polluting influence of the world around her, they are also the means by which she seduces and deceives her audience. When Rosalie dresses for her performance, Walton draws attention to the "contrast Rosalie looked to the rest of the caravan": "The shabby furniture, the thin, wasted mother, the dirty, torn little frock she had just laid aside, were quite out of keeping with the pretty little white-robed figure which stood by the bed."[103] Walton again uses the contrast between Rosalie in her costume and the interior of the caravan as a means of revealing the deception of the theater world, as Rosalie's rich costume only serves to highlight the miserable conditions in which she has to live. However, Rosalie's costume also serves to demonstrate the distance between the child and her surroundings. Her environment is "out of keeping" with her, and it is the costume that reveals the truth of her unfitness for the world in which she lives and works.

But if the donning of a pretty white dress—as opposed to the "dirty, torn little frock she had laid aside"—reveals Rosalie's potential for salvation, in that it demonstrates her separation from the shabbiness of her home and thus makes

---

[101] Ibid., 270.
[102] Ibid., 18.
[103] Ibid., 17.

possible her final salvation from it, it is also the means by which she seduces those who watch her. In Walton's text, the seductive power of Rosalie's performance is one that will speak to Walton's reading audience of working- and middle-class children: the promise of excitement and glamour, of pretty things, and easy labour. Barlee's comment that children who worked in the theater "when trained can earn a shilling a night," an income "too good to be lost by their natural protectors," and leading to "a career which is rarely ever quitted for any more permanent industrial calling,"[104] suggests that it is the relative attractiveness of theatrical labor, compared to the more "respectable" labor most working-class children faced, that is the actual draw of the stage. Barlee's and Walton's anxiety about this labor is therefore as much about the independence it might grant working-class children— an independence that challenges normative views of innocent childhood—as it is about the danger of the work itself. But it is also a very gendered fear, for if such girls become accustomed to their careers, they will, Barlee attests, be "unfitted for any domestic calling, and even those who become wives and mothers, make dawdling, untidy and improvident ones."[105] Like Sissy and Madonna, such girls require "rescue" from the attractions of the stage in order to be saved to lives of proper domesticity.

Because, of course, the focus on Rosalie's pretty figure upon the stage speaks to another power of seduction: that of the stage child engaging in a kind of prostitution. The danger of independence and the danger of prostitution are not necessarily separate in these texts, as concerns about the effects of the stage life upon children, particularly after the Dangerous Performances Act of 1879, centered on the extent to which that life produced in them "a precocious undercurrent, not of too refined a nature."[106] This precociousness, according to Ellen Barlee's *Pantomime Waifs* (1884), spoke both to the environment in which the children lived, to a training that tended to "the formation of artificial characters,"[107] and to the children's comprehension of their own powers, because "what marked all stage children, of whatever class, was their 'insatiable thirst for admiration.' They were children who were very used to being watched, and to seeing themselves as objects of someone else's contemplation."[108]

As Steedman notes, "some commentators of the 1880s were utterly certain of the correlation between sexual desire for the child and its public display,"[109] a correlation Barlee makes explicit in her observation that

> Although Pantomimes are supposed to be arranged for children's amusement, the number of grey-headed men and women who invariably form the larger

---

[104]   Ellen Barlee, *Pantomime Waifs*, 48.

[105]   Ibid., 51.

[106]   Ibid., 14–15.

[107]   Ibid., 28.

[108]   Steedman, *Strange Dislocations*, 136.

[109]   Ibid., 140.

proportion of the audience, prove that these entertainments, far from being suited only to children's minds, draw the world's *dilletanti*, who seemingly have no better purpose in life than the hour's amusement, and the gratification of the senses.[110]

Though Barlee's comment purports to ridicule those adults who find pleasure in performances aimed at children, there is obvious anxiety about the "gratification of the senses" such gazing might entail, an anxiety that only increased in England in the wake of W. T. Stead's "Maiden Tribute of Modern Babylon."[111] While such anxiety had been expressed about female child acrobats,[112] it was also applied to girl-children who worked in the pantomime and ballet, whose scanty costumes and, it was feared, provocative poses drew parallels between child-performance and child-prostitution. Tights, in particular, were seen as pernicious, as they "effaced the division of the leg that training for the classical dance had established (foot, ankle, knee and thigh), and ... by a single sweep of flesh-pink worsted they drew the eye smoothly upwards, towards the place where they ended."[113] While the audience, the child itself, and opponents of child employment in the theater were aware "of the sexual meaning of this clothing, and the kind of attention it attracted,"[114] however, "Pressure groups like the National Vigilance Association[115] and other parties interested in stage censorship often experienced extreme difficulty in bringing charges of obscenity against certain stage performances, because they were unable either to read or to articulate the pornographic code that made some acts so disturbing."[116] The connection between the child performer and the prostitute was commonly recognized and understood; however, it was not

---

[110]   Barlee, *Pantomime Waifs*, 29–30.

[111]   W. T. Stead's "Maiden Tribute," published in the *Pall Mall Gazette* in 1885, created a moral panic in England with its sensationalized representations of "white slavery" in England. See Chapter 5.

[112]   As Assael notes, "In *The Mountebank's Children*, Milly wears a tight bodice, and bends into a hoop ... showing her audience her frontal anatomy which, according to the author, could only serve to demoralize her," and, presumably, her audience (Brenda Assael, *The Circus and Victorian Society*, 214).

[113]   Steedman, *Strange Dislocations*, 141.

[114]   Ibid., 142.

[115]   The National Vigilance Association (NVA) "emerged in the campaign for the 1885 Criminal Law Amendment Act ostensibly to protect children, but it was increasingly concerned with all aspects of public morality. The list of prominent NVA activists reflected the close relationship between child rescue and sexual purity: Stead conceived the NVA; the Reverend Benjamin Waugh, Secretary of the NSPCC, was a council member; Samuel Smith, MP, founding father of the Liverpool SPCC, acted as chief spokesman on obscenity; and Donald Maclean, MP, acted as solicitor for both the NSPCC and the NVA" (Harry Hendrick, *Child Welfare: Historical Dimensions, Contemporary Debate* [Bristol: The Policy Press, 2003], 39).

[116]   Steedman, *Strange Dislocations*, 141.

necessarily explicit, and as such, often failed to register under the laws regulating the theater.

While the Dangerous Performances Act of 1879 did much to protect children who were physically endangered in the theatrical profession, and while the Education Acts of the 1870s and 80s did much to remove children from improper employment on the street and the stage, and provide them with "proper" (unpaid) employment within the school system, children such as Rosalie—itinerant; at the mercy of her father; and morally, rather than physically, endangered—remained essentially invisible in terms of legislation and regulation. Writers such as Walton were able to use the space of the novel to allow their readers a glimpse "behind the scenes" of Rosalie's home life, but to gain access to the actual homes, it seemed, required the advent of child protection.

Child Performance and the "Children's Charter"

Those who were concerned about the effects of performance, both moral and physical, upon the child performer, and upon the role that parents, such as Rosalie's father, played in exploiting their own children, placed great hopes in the nascent child protection movement as a means of addressing these concerns, as evident in the anecdote relating Lord Shaftesbury's request to Benjamin Waugh mentioned earlier. Child protection allowed for a new understanding of child performance: that of the child performer as the abused child. In reporting on a criminal case in 1889, for example, involving a father who had murdered the leader of a troupe in which his daughter died, Waugh was careful to explain that the Society had no desire to "prejudice the case, which must come before the approaching Assizes."[117] Yet his decision to relate the particulars of the case in order to "enable fathers to understand what it was that preyed upon the mind of the man who now stands charged with the willful murder of the master of his dead girl," demonstrates his sympathy with, if not justification of, that man's actions. Told in "the child's own words,"[118] the story describes how the girl, increasingly ill and wasting away, was forced to perform: "The doctor said I must have rest. I had no rest. I had to perform four times each day …. Master shouted at me once, I remembered, and offered to hit me."[119] Her account is very similar to Collins's and Walton's depictions of child performance, but in the context of *The Child's Guardian*, it takes on new significance. Rather than participating in a merely distasteful or even abhorrent display of cruelty, as does Collins's Mr. Jubber and Rosalie's father, this troupe proprietor commits a crime, one that the London SPCC—even before the passage

---

[117]   Benjamin Waugh, "An Invalid Child Acrobat," *The Child's Guardian* 3.31 (July 1889), 113.

[118]   Ibid.

[119]   Ibid., 114.

of the "Children's Charter"—could have stopped had the father not taken the law into his own hands.

The implication that the Society should have been alerted to the abuses occurring within this troupe points to another change brought about in the theatrical world by the emergence of child protection. Not only were child performers transformed into possible subjects of legal protection, but the audience members were themselves transformed, in the London SPCC's rhetoric, from willing participants to useful informants. In the February 1887 issue of *The Child's Guardian*, for example, readers are "urged to keep a close watch, especially on the lower kind of circus and traveling show, and to report suspicious circumstances to 7, Harpur Street" (the Society's address at the time).[120] And in an issue from 1889, Waugh asks, "Will our friends look for a traveling show with 'the celebrated female pugilist' as part of its attraction; and on finding it, at once send us word of its whereabouts. We are anxious to see it."[121] Both of these "Notes" to the readers of *The Child's Guardian* demonstrate the role that the London SPCC gave to audience members throughout England. Norton, Collins, Mayhew, and Walton all displayed anxiety within their works about the ways in which audiences watch children perform: with pleasure, with thoughtlessness, and with desire. By encouraging audiences to "keep a close watch" on child performance in order to identify possible cases of cruelty, the Society instructed its readers in the proper response to the child's body. Such instruction not only sought to regulate that response, but also simultaneously empowered the viewer, combating that "impotent watching of children's distress" so evident within the earlier texts.[122]

However, the appeal to the readers of *The Child's Guardian* to "keep a close watch" also, interestingly enough, justified that very activity. By granting power to the audience to discern cruelty and abuse when and where they saw it—or, more accurately, to know when to alert those who did have that power—the London SPCC tacitly acknowledged that not all child performance constituted cruelty; that while one must constantly observe the child performer for signs of abuse and suffering, that child performance itself was not abuse. Such a stance reflects the continued ambiguity of the child performer, even at the end of the nineteenth century, for while many saw the activity as inherently harmful to the child, there was still the belief, even among reformers like Barlee, "That the love of both dancing and acting is born with children ... as babes, their greatest pleasure is to dance to the sound of music; when older grown, what pleasure so great as that of dressing up in their elders' clothes and personating their characters?"[123] Furthermore, the pleasure adults had in watching children perform extended even into the charitable arena, where child performance was an essential aspect of fund-raising. In 1888, the Bill for the Better Prevention of Cruelty to Children met opposition from the

[120] Waugh, "Notes," *The Child's Guardian*, 1.2 (February 1887), 14.
[121] Waugh, "Notes," *The Child's Guardian*, 3.26 (February 1889), 25.
[122] Steedman, *Strange Dislocations*, 31.
[123] Barlee, *Pantomime Waifs*, 37–8.

Band of Hope movement, the youth auxiliary of the Temperance Movement, because "this group feared that restrictions on the employment of children in public entertainment might jeopardize its penny readings, parades, and choir competitions." The London SPCC, however, "sought only to discourage sending children to sing and dance in unwholesome environments (such as public houses); it had no wish to prevent performances associated with legitimate philanthropy."[124] In terms of non-philanthropic entertainment, however, the bill stood firm, calling for the "prohibition of theatrical work for those under the age of ten."[125]

This proposed restriction of child employment in the theater met with strong opposition from those who argued that such a law would cause hardship to working-class families employed in the industry and from those who "protested that the new outburst of reformist fervor threatened to destroy 'many of the performances and plays which have been popular with the British people for generations.'"[126] In the end, opposition to this portion of the bill forced an amendment "allowing children between the ages of seven and ten to perform in theaters, provided that they were licensed to do so by a magistrate."[127] "Reformist fervor" aside, child performance at the end of the century remained one of the exceptions to the rule of child labor restriction in England. The "Children's Charter" empowered magistrates to provide licenses to theatrical proprietors, allowing them to employ children "if satisfied of the fitness of the child for the purpose, and if it is shown to their satisfaction that proper provision has been made to secure the health and kind treatment of the children taking part in the entertainment."[128] Furthermore, restrictions on child performance did not apply "in the case of any occasional sale or entertainment the net proceeds of which are wholly applied for the benefit of any school or to any charitable object."[129]

The newly reconstituted NSPCC had learned, both from the experience of SPCCs in the United States, and from the opposition that it faced in its own battle to restrict child performance through anti-cruelty legislation, that child performance elicited as much pleasure as it did concern. The New York SPCC's successful restriction of child performance was met with scorn by some commentators, who asked "what cruelty is there in permitting a precocious, agile, and healthy child to dance before an audience or to take a part in any drama or musical entertainment adapted to children, when the child is not exposed to danger or physical injury?"[130] The New York Society, far from being seen as the protector of children, is here

---

[124]   George K. Behlmer, *Child Abuse and Moral Reform*, 100.

[125]   Ibid., 105.

[126]   Ibid., 106.

[127]   Ibid., 108.

[128]   William Clarke Hall, *The Law Relating to Children* (London: Stevens and Sons, Limited, 1905), 73.

[129]   Ibid., 72.

[130]   Abram Dailey, "The Conflict Between Parental Authority and the Society for the Prevention of Cruelty to Children," *Medico-Legal Journal* 10 (1892), 379.

depicted as somehow ruining their fun, imposing restrictions upon a child who longs to demonstrate its own health, grace, and agility. Furthermore, the question the London SPCC had faced during its own battle for new legislation of "What … would *Midsummer Night's Dream* be without its 'little fairies,'"[131] proves that the fight to preserve child performance in England was as much about the pleasure derived from watching them, as about the pleasure the children themselves might experience in performing.

By combating the abuses that went on within the theater rather than the theater itself, the NSPCC therefore successfully avoided the pitfalls associated with restricting performance. But perhaps more importantly, such a stance enabled the NSPCC itself to benefit from child performance. The NSPCC struggled throughout the 1890s to raise enough funds to support its rapid expansion throughout England, and in December 1891, the Society founded a youth auxiliary group, the Children's League of Pity, in response to that need. While the goal of the "Leaguers" was to raise funds for the society through canvassing amongst their friends and family, and through staging sales and performances, this work on behalf of abused children was also defended as beneficial to the Leaguers themselves, because the League provided "great chances of training up children to ennobling sentiments."[132]

The performances staged by Leaguers served the noble purpose of supporting the Society and of encouraging compassion in the Leaguers themselves, but they also succeeded in providing pleasure for their adult audiences. An article in *The Children's League of Pity Paper* entitled "Living Pictures," for example, lauds one such performance by the Leaguers of Eastbourne. In describing the tableaux, the author mentions that "The pictures were sustained entirely by children, and were admirable in every way, the set and pose of the various characters being full of charm and interest to the audience, who were loud in their praises of the little executants."[133] Here, performance by children is very much to be praised, because the children show industry in "sustaining" the performance entirely on their own, and therefore, far from being understood as pernicious, this performance is instead "admirable" and "full of charm." A performance at a "Japanese Garden Party" by the Norwich Leaguers, who are held up to the readers of the journal as "A Branch to be copied," provokes a similar reaction:

> the hands of most willing helpers quickly transformed our school dining-room and large class-room into two prettily decorated tea-rooms, when numerous Leaguers, all clothed in wonderful Japanese costumes of every colour of the rainbow, busied themselves in waiting on the guests. All subsequently adjourned to the playground, as the sun was beginning to peep through the clouds, and

---

[131]   Qtd. in Behlmer, *Child Abuse and Moral Reform*, 106.

[132]   Waugh, "Notes," *The Child's Guardian* 7.10 (October 1893), 134.

[133]   Mary Bolton, "Living Pictures," *The Children's League of Pity Paper* 2.10 (May 1895), 82.

here the Leaguers entertained our visitors with Japanese songs, fan-drill, and umbrella-drill, all of which seemed to give much pleasure.[134]

Again, the industriousness of these children for the sake of a good cause is portrayed as praiseworthy, as the "willing helpers" who "busied themselves" in staging this event are held up as an example to other Leaguers. For children to perform in the service of a good cause, it would seem, is to be industrious in the proper sphere, and to allow adults to feel unqualified pleasure in watching that performance.

These child performers fail to provoke anxiety, I would argue, because they are, essentially, amateurs. Leaguers were "well-to-do" children, and their performances, though in the service of a good cause, had as much to do with play as they did with labor. Their tableaux and dances, therefore, brought pleasure to their audience in part through the childishness that was displayed within them. Like Collins's Madonna, these child performers were successful because they did not truly perform; instead, they gave the audience the pleasure of seeing a child be a child, because the child appears most child-like when it attempts to play adult roles—such as organizing and staging a performance, or holding a tea and waiting on guests. As Steedman notes, "A middle-class appreciation of the child on the stage was of a miniature participant in adult life, with much delight taken in the contrast .... What is 'priceless' in the child's performance is its attempt to be part of the adult world, and the very uselessness of that attempt."[135] The "uselessness of that attempt" is, in the case of the Leaguers and of other children who participated in amateur performance, dependent upon the fact that the child performer could not jeopardize its own dependence, its own child-like insufficiency, by earning wages.

Though paid child performance elicited concerns because of the "precociousness" of those children who worked in the street, the circus, and the stage, amateur child theatricals confirmed the child's preciousness, its need for imagination and play, and its separation from adult concerns and anxieties. Far from being a danger to the child, amateur theatricals instead celebrated the ideal child, and by transforming seductive, precocious boys and girls into treasured children, such performances sanctioned and sanctified unadulterated adult pleasure in the observation of the child's body on display. Where individuals or troupes benefited from a child's labor, restrictions, licenses, and an audience trained to watch for abuse were considered necessary. Where charitable performances were concerned, no restrictions were imposed. Therefore, it would seem, financial gain was the essential factor in "dangerous" performances for children. As long as a child gained nothing for itself and or for its family, its performance required nothing but applause.

---

[134]   Bolton, "A Branch to Be Copied," *The Children's League of Pity Paper* 6.1 (August 1898), 11.
[135]   Steedman, *Strange Dislocations*, 144.

Chapter 4
"Cannibalism in England": Commerce, Consumption, and Endangered Childhood

In *Past and Present* (1843), Thomas Carlyle tells of a Stockport Mother and Father" who were "found guilty of poisoning three of their children, to defraud a burial-society of some *3 l. 8s.* on the death of each child." Carlyle asserts that such a crime meets only with disgust—"'Brutal savages, degraded Irish,' mutters the idle reader of Newspapers; hardly lingering on this incident"—but argues that it should be, instead, read as a sign of the condition of England, as an act to which the parents have been "driven" by poverty and starvation. Rather than dismissing the parents as mere "savages," then, Carlyle imagines the "committee of ways and means" by which these parents came to their fateful decision:

> Our poor little starveling Tom, who cries all day for victuals, who will see only evil and not good in this world: if he were out of misery at once; he well dead, and the rest of us perhaps kept alive? It is thought, and hinted: at last it is done. And now Tom being killed, and all spent and eaten, Is it poor little starveling Jack that must go, or poor little starveling Will?[1]

This family's wretched preoccupation with "starvation" and with "victuals" translates into a kind of cannibalism, in which the child who cries for food becomes the child murdered so that others might be fed. Though gruesome, however, this choice is one for which Carlyle betrays a kind of sympathy, or at least a recognition of the role that desperation, coupled with temptation in the form of the child's burial insurance, might have played in these parents' decision to kill their children. Such desperation, Carlyle argues, is intimately connected to England's commerce: a commerce that produces "plethoric plenty" while England's people "perish."[2] In such conditions, Carlyle suggests, the starving family has little choice but to engage in a crude commerce of their own, converting their family into a "committee of ways and means" and their children into commodities.

Carlyle's preoccupation with the influence of commerce upon the home and family speaks, I argue, to an anxiety that was continually reiterated in nineteenth-century texts. In particular, as I suggested at the end of the previous chapter, the contamination of the domestic sphere by financial concerns was perceived to be

---

[1]   Thomas Carlyle, *Past and Present* (London: J. M. Dent & Sons, 1960), 4.

[2]   Ibid., 6.

inherently threatening to childhood. This contamination could occur when the home itself became a place of work, when the child was called upon to work to support the home, or when, as in the case of the Stockport family, the child itself had monetary value. As discussed in the introduction, the nineteenth century saw the transition between residual conceptions of the child as a productive, working member of the family (particularly within lower- and working-class homes) and the emergent conception of the child as an economic dependent, both in the family and in society. This transition coincided with constructions of the middle-class home as a separate "sphere," one that was to be set apart from the commercial transactions of the middle-class male, so as to preserve its integrity as a space of morality, security, and comfort. Such a separation was, at best, an imagined one, borne out of the anxiety produced by the actual interdependence of home and commerce in nineteenth-century England,[3] and concerns about the deleterious effects of commerce upon the lives of children, both in the lower- and the middle-class home, demonstrate the extent to which this imagined separation was perceived to be continually at risk. Children who labored, or worse, represented a kind of commodity to their parents, threatened not only the emergent conception of childhood dependence and "freedom" from adult concerns, but also constructions of the home as a space wholly apart from the harmful effects of commercial activity. Certainly, therefore, while narratives that suggested that it was both right and necessary for working-class children to be gainfully employed persisted throughout the nineteenth century, these narratives coincided and competed with representations of the abused and endangered labouring child.

In an analysis of texts that concern themselves with the influence of commerce upon both working-class and middle-class families, and of the NSPCC's involvement in the child-life insurance debates of the late nineteenth century, I argue that narratives about the interconnectedness of home and work, and of family and fortune, anxiously sought to create a balance between what were perceived to be the defining characteristics of England: its industry and wealth, on the one hand, and its domestic virtues, on the other. In seeking to negotiate the relationship between hunger, consumption, and production in the domestic space, such narratives work to redefine not only the nature of child suffering, but also the role of parental responsibility and affection for the child within the home. For if these narratives delineate commerce as a primary cause of child endangerment, as I believe they do, they also displace questions of social and economic imbalance

---

3   Historians such as Amanda Vickery have pointed out the problems with assigning a time frame to the emergence of the ideology of "separate spheres " and with, in fact, the usefulness of it as a description of actual middle-class homes. I certainly agree with Vickery that the middle-class house was not "in any simple sense a private, domestic sphere" and that "the increased harping on the proper female sphere might just as easily demonstrate a concern that more women were seen to be active outside the home rather than proof that they were so confined" (Amanda Vickery, *The Gentleman's Daughter: Women's Lives in Georgian England* [Yale University Press: New Haven & London, 1998] 9, 7).

with narratives of proper affective relationships between parents and children. Love, within these varied texts, serves an important ideological function, as it represents either the means by which families achieve a balance between financial necessity and happy domesticity, or, a crucial lack within the home itself that leads to the commercial use and abuse of its children. In tracing the development of representations of the child as victim of commerce, then, I argue that by the end of the century, this figure becomes read not as a sign of necessity or privation, but of its parents' failure.

Necessity and Tyranny: Child Labor in Early Nineteenth-Century Literature

As Penny Brown points out, "In the late eighteenth century, many writers spoke approvingly of child labour for, at a period of widespread unemployment with the very real threat of starvation for an increasing population, the ability to work was seen as a question of survival."[4] Children of the poor had always been employed, wherever possible, but "the coming of steam power created a great demand for children in textiles in the early nineteenth century." [5] Even as late as 1834, when many in England began to be concerned about the conditions of child labour in the factories, "the unemployment and underemployment of children was perceived … to be as great a problem as the exploitation of their labour."[6] The work of the children of the poor was seen as intimately connected to the lower- and working-class family's well-being, because without that labour, the child, and its parents, might starve.

By the late eighteenth century,[7] however, the child laborer also began to be seen "as a victim and a slave,"[8] a revolution in thinking about childhood that Cunningham links to "debates about slavery and freedom, and the emergence of a romantic conception of the child."[9] But it was only the publication of the reports of the Select Committee on the Labour of Children in the Mills and Factories, and the First Report on the Employment of Children in Factories that marked the "first significant point of successful intervention, leading as [they] did to the Factory

---

[4]   Penny Brown, *The Captured World*, 65.

[5]   Lionel Rose, *The Erosion of Childhood: Child Oppression in Britain 1860–1918* (London and New York: Routledge, 1991), 3.

[6]   Hugh Cunningham, "The Employment and Unemployment of Children in England, c. 1680–1851," *Past and Present: A Journal of Historical Studies* 126 (February 1990), 140.

[7]   Most notable, perhaps, is the work on behalf of chimney-sweeps by Jonas Hanway, who in 1770 "helped set up a Friendly Society of Chimney Sweepers, and then in 1773 … headed a Committee in Behalf of Chimney-Sweepers' Young Apprentices, and wrote a book which highlighted their condition" (Hugh Cunningham, *The Children of the Poor*, 53).

[8]   Ibid., 87.

[9]   Ibid., 50.

Regulation Act of 1833."[10] As a result of these various interventions, some forms of child employment, specifically that in the factories and, later, the mines, went from being considered a boon to poor families and to the domestic economy, to being constructed as one of England's greatest shames: as Catherine Robson notes, "the novel and relatively widespread spectacle of concentrated child labour began to engender concern in a ruling class newly attuned to the idea of childhood's especial claims."[11]

The reports of the Select Committee on Children's Employment of 1831–1832 focus extensively on the exhaustion children faced while working within the factories, particularly in the later hours of the day. As one worker testified, "towards the latter end of the day the children become completely bewildered, and know not what they are doing, so that they spoil their work without knowing,"[12] and recalling his own work, stated, "I sometimes should have slept as I walked if I had not stumbled and started awake again; and so sick often that I could not eat, and what I did eat, I vomited."[13] As well as exhaustion, the children were also injured by the work they performed: as one surgeon witnessed, "I have seen cases in which the arm had been torn off near the shoulder joint; I have seen the upper extremity chopped into small fragments, from the tip of the finger to above the elbow; I have seen every extremity in the body broken ...."[14] Finally, the children at work within the factories and mills were also subject to beatings by their overseers: when asked "Have you recently seen any cruelties in mills?" a witness replied, "Yes; not long since I was in a mill, and I saw a girl severely beaten .... I looked that way, and saw the spinner beating one of the girls severely with a large stick."[15]

Anti–child labor activists were undoubtedly moved by reports of the harsh conditions in which children worked in the factories, but there is evidence to suggest that children were not significantly more endangered by this labour than they were by domestic and cottage-industry work.[16] In the factories, however, children were also believed to be in greater moral and spiritual danger. That is,

---

[10]   Catherine Robson, *Men in Wonderland: The Lost Girlhood of Victorian Gentlemen* (Princeton: Princeton University Press, 2001), 62.

[11]   Ibid., 58.

[12]   British Parliamentary Papers: Report form the Select Committee on the "Bill to Regulate the Labour of Children in the Mills and Factories of the United Kingdom" (Shannon, Ireland: Irish University Press, 1968), 97.

[13]   Ibid., 96.

[14]   Ibid., 503.

[15]   Ibid., 99.

[16]   In *The Erosion of Childhood*, Rose argues that "Under the old cottage system of production, where the children were under parental supervision, conditions were at least as bad; children received no wages, and young hand-loomers might work in cold, damp cellars. There were, it seems, some indications that factory children were in less bad health than child domestic weavers in the 1830s" (8).

while the Children's Employment Commission focused extensively on the broken and exhausted body of the working child, concerns on behalf of children employed in the factories were (in part) motivated by the perception that this kind of work disrupted familial and communal ties. Many families had to move outside of their parish in order to obtain factory employment for their children, and though children were sometimes supervised by family members in their work, representations of the factory child often suggested that this was not the case, and instead often construct the child as alone, laboring under the harsh or inadequate supervision of strangers. One report from the commission highlighted the dangerous influence of factory life upon children, with claims from witnesses that "most of that [the children's bad language and immorality] goes on towards night, when they begin to be drowsy; it is a kind of stimulus which they use to keep themselves from drowsiness, and it generally happens to be obscene language."[17] Robson notes that this inquiry in support of the Ten Hours Movement was "Hugely—and famously—slanted to prove that most of the evils of the factory system could be laid at the door of the overlong working day."[18] Significantly, though, as Robson observes, the evils focused upon are as likely to be moral evils as physical ones; the nature of factory work requires these children to be "stimulated," a highly suggestive word, and the stimulus they have learned emulates those in charge of them, who, as one question put to the witnesses made clear, do not have the children's moral welfare in mind: "Is not conduct grossly indecent often practised by those who have the control over these children in factories?"[19]

As discussed in Chapter 1, the government blue books on children's employment provided the basis for many literary interventions on behalf of the laboring child, including works by writers such as Caroline Norton, Frances Trollope, and Charlotte Elizabeth Tonna. These writers, and later writers of what have come to be known as "social-problem novels," including such works as Dickens's *Hard Times*, Gaskell's *Mary Barton* and *North and South*, and Charles Kingsley's *Alton Locke*, employed fiction and poetry in order to inform their readers of the social problems of the day. What authors such as these could do with the government reports was appeal to idealized constructions of the home and the nation that could not fully be developed or expressed in the interviews and reports themselves. This is not to assert that the reports were "factual," while the literary interpretations were "fictional"—such an easy dichotomy fails to acknowledge the extent to which, as Robson reminds us, "preexisting ideas undoubtedly influenced the ways in which the commissioners conducted their questioning and presented their material."[20] However, as Robson argues in her excellent discussion of Elizabeth Barrett Browning's "The Cry of the Children," "Working within a literary form, Barrett makes creative use of opportunities unavailable to [Richard Henry] Horne in his

---

[17] Qtd. in Robson, 60–61.

[18] Ibid., 60.

[19] Qtd. in Robson, 61.

[20] Robson, 63.

role as subcommissioner."[21] So too were Norton, Trollope, and Tonna, within their own works, able to discuss the extent to which factory labor had an impact on the domestic space, and in particular, on those affective qualities of comfort, love, and care seen as so central to the home. As Ella Dzelzainis notes of Charlotte Elizabeth Tonna's use of Blue Books and testimony, "Her narrative ability enables her to draw together disparate elements from this factual material, recasting the carefully selected details to create coherent, alarming stories of family decline." In so doing, she offered "her readers a family structure as a shared point of identification," and thus "enable[d] them to respond sympathetically to her accounts of domestic disintegration."[22]

Because child labor in the factories was perceived to be harmful not only to the children themselves, but also to their families, literary depictions that engage with the cause of child endangerment in the factories and mills provide insight into early-Victorian constructions of the home. In *A Voice from the Factories*, Caroline Norton depicts the life of a child factory-laborer, whose days are spent surrounded by "sounds of wailing grief and painful blows"[23] and by companions who enjoy only a "base and saddening merriment."[24] Upon returning home, the child is met by "his remorseful Mother"[25] who "tempts in vain / With the best portion of their frugal fare."[26] The mother's remorse makes it evident that this "frugal fare" is bought with her child's labor, but it is food that the child is "Too sick to eat …. He turns him idly from the untasted share, / Slumbering sinks down unfed, and mocks her useless care."[27] This home presents a nightmarish contrast to the ideal home Norton describes immediately prior, in which "the good man goes to seek the twilight rest of home,"[28] and finds refuge from his labors, where he "shut out the world's associate throng, / And closed the busy day's fatiguing hum."[29] Within, he and his wife "*together* pass their happy lives,"[30] while around them "Scattered like flowers, the rosy children play."[31] The focus on the completion of this family, highlighted by the italicized "together," is symbolically linked to nature and plenitude. In this, one of the "happy homes of England,"[32] the burden of labor is borne by the father, who is rewarded for his efforts by the comfort

---

[21]   Ibid., 66.

[22]   Ella Dzelzainis, "Charlotte Elizabeth Tonna, Pre-Millenarianism, and the Formation of Gender Ideology in the Ten Hours Campaign," *Victorian Literature and Culture* (2003), 184.

[23]   Caroline Norton, *A Voice from the Factories*, stanza 47, line 1.

[24]   Ibid., stanza 48, line 2.

[25]   Ibid., stanza 49, line 5.

[26]   Ibid., lines 5–6.

[27]   Ibid., lines 7–9.

[28]   Ibid., stanza 32, line 9.

[29]   Ibid., 5–6.

[30]   Ibid., stanza 34, line 3, italics in original.

[31]   Ibid., stanza 35, line 1.

[32]   Ibid., stanza 32, line 1.

of his family. However, in the working-class home, this "proper" order has been overthrown. Rather than the father enduring labor so as to provide the security of the home for himself and his family, it is the child who must do so, rendering the mother's duty of "care" and "comfort" useless, a hollow mockery of the ideal family relationship.

The damage caused to the poor family's home is the result, Norton argues, of a struggle between two defining qualities of England: its "happy homes" which "have been / A source of triumph, and a theme for song"[33] and "Merchant England's prosperous trade."[34] Although the "ideal" home she describes suggests that a balance can be struck between the two so long as commerce and labor do not infiltrate the familial hearth, Norton argues that in the homes of the industrial laborer, the Merchants of England have taken advantage of necessity, and, as a result, have initiated the contamination of the poor home by economic consideration: "Do not your hearts inquire / Who tempts the parents' penury? They yearn / Toward their offspring with a strong desire, / But those who starve *will* sell, even what they most require." [35] The homes of the factory worker, Norton suggests, have seen the displacement of the parents' natural love for their children by the harsh demands of the market. The parents feel a "strong desire" for their children, they must also "sell" them in order to stave off starvation. Although, Norton submits, these children have an inherent emotional value—they are what their parents "yearn" for, what "they most require"—this value is superseded, because of the family's "penury," by the children's material value. Furthermore, though "in the British senate men rise up"[36] to proclaim that "By *some* employ the poor man's child must earn / Its daily bread,"[37] Norton, by focusing on the laboring child's inability to eat, demonstrates that the child's labor is not providing for his or her own maintenance, but is, in fact consuming the child, while only providing "frugal fare" for the family. That which makes the homes of England a point of pride—the familial bonds of love and affection described in Norton's depiction of the proper home—is therefore destroyed by the reality of starvation and by the "commercial avarice"[38] of the nation.

Although Caroline Norton suggests that the children and families of the factory laborers are damaged by the influence of commerce in the home, she does not question the presence of love and affection in those homes, a stance shared by Frances Trollope in *The Life and History of Michael Armstrong, the Factory Boy* (1840). Michael is sent out to work by his mother in order to support her and his frail brother, but Trollope makes it clear that such a decision is not the result of choice, but of necessity. The mother's "patient suffering" and the family's "extreme poverty"

---

[33]   Ibid., lines 1–2.
[34]   Ibid., stanza 33, line 3.
[35]   Ibid., stanza 20, lines 6–9.
[36]   Ibid., stanza 16, line 1.
[37]   Ibid., stanza 20, lines 2–3, italics in original.
[38]   Ibid., stanza 23, line 6.

make Michael willing to undertake any labor on their behalf, and his work, though exploitative, is therefore also a sign of his filial duty and affection. He asks, "How will you get on without me? … I am sure Teddy can't make your bed as I do—he hasn't the strength in his arms. And who's to fetch water?"[39] Michael's work in the factory is an extension of his work within the home, and because it is motivated by love and duty, his willingness to perform labor is presented as both natural and right; instead, it is his employer's willingness to take advantage of both Michael's family's need and Michael's own desire to be of use to them that is the cause of the family's suffering.

The influence of greed and avarice makes men such as Sir Matthew Dowling (the factory owner) and his overseer, Mr. Parsons, unable to recognize what Trollope presents as the inherent value of children, because such men see children (at least, working-class children) as commodities. The parents of the children themselves, however, do not make the same mistake. When instructing a poor woman—who is in the process of beating her child—on the value of sending children to work in the factories, Mr. Parsons suggests, "And isn't it a comfort now, Mrs. Miller, to get rid of the plague of 'em?" Her response demonstrates the extent to which the overseer has overestimated her compliance with his point of view: "The woman ceased to shake her little boy, and looking for a moment at the clear blue eyes, that, notwithstanding her rough discipline, were very lovingly turned up to her face—something like a shudder passed through her."[40] Here, Trollope refuses to sentimentalize poor families, but also refuses to suggest that they share less affection for their offspring than do their wealthier neighbors. This woman might treat her child roughly, but she cannot bear to be parted from him, and cannot see him either as a "plague" of which to be rid, or as a commodity to be sold.

Although writers such as Norton and Trollope were willing to place the blame for the poor child's suffering not at the feet of its parents, but of the nation's merchants and their employees (such as the overseer), other writers explored the possibility that the poor family itself could be infected with avarice and, as a result, be willing participants in their children's suffering. In *Helen Fleetwood* (1839–1840), for example, Charlotte Elizabeth Tonna tells the story of the Widow Green, her four grandchildren and adopted grandchild Helen, and their migration from their happy, but impoverished, rural home to Manchester. The happiness of the family in their rural home makes evident that it is not poverty itself that is a concern—the children all labor to support the family, but they do so in the context of the idealized country parish, close to their home and to their betters. Lured by the promise of lucrative employment in the factories, this family is severed from its parish ties, a move that, Tonna makes clear, adds to the family's vulnerability. The bonds of religion and duty that hold the family together are further weakened, upon the family's arrival in Manchester, by the separation of the children from

---

[39]   Frances Trollope, *The Life and Adventures of Michael Armstrong, the Factory Boy* (London: Henry Colburn, 1840), 39.

[40]   Ibid., 36.

the moral and spiritual influence of the grandmother, as they are put to work in the factories among those who do not share their strong Christian faith. Though the Widow Green does what she can to care for the children, both physically and spiritually, she is unable to combat the influence of the factories in which the children spend most of their time, and must watch helplessly while the children give in to alcoholism, lose their faith, and become hardened.[41]

Tonna clearly demonstrates the destruction factory work wreaks upon this family despite the virtues of the family itself, but she also carefully depicts the ways in which working-class families themselves contribute to the ruin of their children. The Widow Green's daughter, with whom the family stays upon arriving in Manchester, is one such example of an avaricious parent. Though the Widow Green and her grandchildren are entrapped by the factory system through necessity, her daughter, Mrs. Wright, is moved by a kind of greed, visible in the conspicuous consumption in her dwelling. Though it is filthy, "yet a struggle to look fine was manifest throughout the whole establishment," as evidenced by a "number of the most tawdry prints, evidently quite fresh, and placed there for particular display," and by Mrs. Wright herself, who "though she had not combed out her matted locks, had surmounted them with a cap of unusual form, decorated with showy ribands."[42] This showy but filthy dwelling forms a sharp contrast to the "beloved cottage" in the country of which the Widow Green had been "a wise and faithful steward."[43] That poor home had been, nevertheless, a true home, in comparison to Mrs. Wright's dwelling, in which "Of ornaments there was no lack ... of neatness, comfort, and respectability, nothing relieved the eye."[44]

The description of Mrs. Wright's home and person taps into common nineteenth-century fears about factory employment. Unlike domestic servants, who fell under the influence of their masters and mistresses, and unlike the rural working class, equally "supervised" by the local gentry, factory workers enjoyed a relative independence. As Dorice Williams Elliot observes in "Servants and Hands: Representing the Working Classes in Victorian Factory Novels," "Factory workers ... were supposedly ruled only by what Carlyle called the 'cash nexus'." As a result,

> While they endured killing hours and were treated like machines while at work, whatever leisure hours they had were unsupervised and their dress, recreation, and personal relationships were left to their own discretion. In other words,

---

[41]   Charlotte Elizabeth Tonna, *Helen Fleetwood* (London: R. B. Steeley and W. Burnside, 1841), 288, 320, and 422.

[42]   Ibid., 49.

[43]   Ibid., 12, 9.

[44]   Ibid., 49.

> although industrialism exploited workers and caused many of them immense
> suffering, it also gave them a frightening new kind of freedom.[45]

Divorced from the influence of their "betters," those members of the working class who were supported by factory labor could make their own choices as to how they should comport themselves and order their homes. In her description of Mrs. Wright, Tonna taps into middle-class anxieties that, without the paternalistic influence of the middle and upper classes, the choices of the poor would be influenced solely by materialism. Rather than live in respectable poverty and run a "proper" household, Mrs. Wright instead seeks to ape the upper classes through her displays of "tawdry" finery.

Perhaps more importantly, Mrs. Wright's failure to create a respectable home corresponds to a similar failure to care for her family, for what is represented as most disconcerting about her dwelling is that its scanty material ornaments have been purchased through the labor of her own children. Tonna's description of the eldest daughter, Sarah, reveals the price paid by this family for their precarious material wealth: "it was already apparent to all, that poor Sarah had only one arm, and that one so contracted as to be nearly useless; while her feet were bent in, until she rested on the ankle-bones. 'You see,' said her mother, 'what an object she is. The arm was lost by an accident and all the rest came from convulsions and fits.'"[46] Broken, contracted, and economically useless, Sarah's body is a visible sign of the factory system's consumption of children; she has been used to provide her family with cheap, material luxuries, but once used and thrown away, she becomes merely an "object,' and as such, of no worth to her mother. The treatment of Sarah by the Widow Green and her grandchildren, by contrast, demonstrates how such a child should actually be valued: she is cared for, loved, and most importantly in terms of the novel's evangelical message, "saved" through the religious instruction of her cousins.

Although Mrs. Wright is an entirely unsympathetic character, Tonna suggests that where monetary interest is allowed to overturn proper familial relationships, such a failure to recognize the affective and spiritual value of a child will not be uncommon. Tom South, a friend of the family whose own children work in the factories, acknowledges, unlike Mrs. Wright, the evils of factory employment, and argues that "it's a cannibal sort of life to be eating, as one may say, the flesh off our children's bones, and sucking the young blood out of their veins."[47] The use of the term "cannibal" to describe the parent's relation to his or her child captures not only the fact that these children are consumed by their labor so that others might be fed, but also that such an arrangement breaks a taboo—that it goes against a natural, proper order and as such, threatens society itself. It is a taboo, however,

---

[45]   Dorice Williams Elliot, "Servants and Hands: Representing the Working Classes in Victorian Factory Novels," *Victorian Literature and Culture* (2000), 381.

[46]   Ibid., 75.

[47]   Ibid., 85–6.

that even those as aware of its evils as Tom South are willing to break for the sake of monetary gain. When told of the death of Tom South's daughter, who died as a result of overwork after taking on extra shifts, the Widow assigns blame to the parent as well as to the employer:

> Here was first a lure spread before her by the mill-owner in the shape of additional wages, for which to barter her very life; then most culpable encouragement given by the act of the parents in allowing her to appropriate extra earnings; while they pocketed the fruit of her day-labour—actual encouragement that rendered void whatever they might *say* against the proceeding.[48]

Tom South, moved by concern for her health, spoke out against his daughter's extra work, but his acceptance of her decision, and more damningly, of her wages, "rendered void" both his concern *and* his authority. His complaint to the Widow Green that "Disobedience to parents is one of the first lessons learned in the mill"[49] suggests again that factory labor infects its workers with an unseemly independence, a concern that, given the increasing focus throughout the period on childhood dependence, particularly applied to children. However, it is also Tom's own interest in the "fruit of [his daughter's] day labour" that overturns the rule of authority in his home. His daughter's betrayal of filial duty, her failure to obey, is thus connected to his betrayal of his parental duty through his failure to protect, care for, and ultimately, control his child.

Although Carlyle's cannibalistic parents represent the dangers that must ensue when the familial relationship is replaced, by necessity, with a "committee of ways and means," Tonna's comparison of the actions of the Widow Green, who never fails to work to relieve her grandchildren's distress, with those of Tom South and Mrs. Wright, suggests that greed is as much a factor in the destruction of the poor family as is necessity. Worse even than the family that becomes a "committee" as a result of starvation, or the family that is disrupted by the removal of children from the home, is the family that operates within the confines of the factory itself. That is, while some concerns about the factories focused upon the extent to which children were removed from parental supervision, Tonna suggests that in those cases in which fathers and elder brothers are also employed in the mills tyranny soon replaces duty:

> They are themselves paid by the piece, and consequently it becomes their interest to have the given work completed in the shortest possible time; and if they have young daughters, or little sisters, they of course save or rather gain considerably by employing them: and it is an awful fact, that under the hardening influence of covetousness, or the cravings of wretched want, more barbarous usage awaits the girl at the hand of a father or brother than that of a stranger. No tyranny is

---

[48] Ibid., 202, italics in original.
[49] Ibid., 201.

so dreadful as domestic tyranny: and he who sacrifices natural affection at the shrine of mammon, becomes a monster among God's works.[50]

In the opposition she constructs between "interest" and "natural affection," Tonna argues that the two cannot co-exist: when the familial relationship is infected by the demands of "covetousness," and even "want," which almost always become elided with greed, love and duty will cease to hold sway. Whereas Trollope was able to recognize, in her depiction of Michael's labor on behalf of his family, that labor and love are not necessarily antithetical, even when the labor is paid factory employment, Tonna suggests that factory labor, at least, will always destroy the family. Even the faultless Widow Green, who never fails to care for and love her charges, does fail to save them, and, with the exception of the saintly Helen and the equally virtuous James (both of whom are dead by the novel's end), to meet with respect and love from them. When the home is contaminated by financial interest, rather than honest labor, Tonna suggests, love and affection will be displaced, and when the factory itself becomes the domestic space, the home becomes the site of "hardening" influences, rather than a place of refuge.

In their examination of the effects of factory labor on working-class families, Norton, Trollope, and Tonna therefore express concern about the imposition of the values and concerns of the market economy onto a space that should presumably be ordered by bonds of duty, affection, and responsibility. As such, they suggest that a balance between England's homes and England's commerce can only be achieved through a clear separation between the domestic and the economic spaces, and particularly, through a separation of children from paid extra-familial labor. Even in Trollope's *Michael Armstrong*, it is clear that while Michael's labor might be motivated by love, it nevertheless is a threat to his childhood innocence and helplessness. The assumption that children, and in fact, women, were inherently damaged by factory work, and with them, the heart and soul of the family itself, suggests that to preserve the working-class family, the paid labor of both women and children must be restricted, and it is not surprising that while many texts focused on child labor in the factories, women working in the factories were also a subject of concern. As Deborah Kaplan argues, "Tonna's fictions express a 'myth' of the fall of working women out of the supposedly natural state of feminine domesticity and into industrial capitalism." As with children, women who worked in the factories were perceived as threats to the income of male bread-winners,[51] or as dangerously sexualized by the immoral behavior in the factories.[52] In order to preserve the working-class home, therefore, these texts, and in fact, the legislation

---

[50]   Ibid., 249.

[51]   Deborah Kaplan, "The Woman Worker in Charlotte Elizabeth Tonna's Fiction," *Mosaic* (Spring 1985), 55.

[52]   Robson, 70–71.

passed by the English government, could be viewed as seeking to impose upon working-class families the values of middle-class world.[53]

By focusing upon the effects of commerce upon familial relationships, however, these writers effectively subsume the problem of necessity and starvation within a discourse of domestic ideology. That is, by centering their critique of child labor upon the ways in which such labor contaminates or overthrows feelings of duty and affection as a result of the child's separation from the domestic sphere, these writers displace issues of economic imbalance with issues of domestic and familial imbalance. As such, their texts show similarities to the work of early sociologists such as James Kay Shuttleworth, who, according to Nancy Armstrong, "enclosed a problem of class relations and national proportions within a discrete space divided by streets, homes, and bedrooms." While for Armstrong, this work by early sociologists "translated a political scandal into a sexual one,"[54] I argue that in literary representations of endangered children in the factories such as those discussed here, the political scandal is transformed into a domestic, familial scandal. Political and economic tyranny is, in part, replaced by domestic tyranny, and the tragedy of the home takes precedence over the tragedy of mass starvation, dehumanizing labor, family displacement, and labor unrest caused by the industrialization of England. As Carolyn Betensky persuasively argues, the focus upon middle-class knowledge of working-class suffering in social-problem novels provides a "glorification of the pursuit of knowledge as a (or, for the most part, *the*) middle-class response to social injustice [that] works to displace and to defer other sorts of remediation (such as the redistribution of wealth, for instance)."[55]

Furthermore, in its focus on the child as a subject of concern, anti–child labor discourse successfully transformed "the dangerous hungers of powerful adults into the blameless and pitiable needs of infants."[56] The appeal of the child laborer, as opposed to the potentially violent adult laborer, is made patently obvious in Trollope's Preface to *Michael Armstrong*. She acknowledges her earlier proposal to write a second part to Michael's story (somewhat shockingly, given the length of the part she actually wrote), in which "the hero of the tale, having lived through his toil-

---

[53]   According to Robson, the Factories Legislation Act of 1833 "established a minimum age of nine for all workers in textile mills … and also set a maximum forty-eight-hour working week for children between the ages of nine and twelve, and a sixty-nine-hour week for thirteen- to seventeen-year-olds and women" (62). In response to the Royal Commission on Children's Employment of 1842–1843, legislation was passed in which "girls and women were totally excluded from colliery labor" (73–4), as were boys under the age of ten.

[54]   Nancy Armstrong, *Desire and Domestic Fiction: A Political History of the Novel* (New York and Oxford: Oxford University Press, 1987), 172.

[55]   Carolyn Betensky, "Knowing Too Much and Never Enough: Knowledge and Moral Capital in Frances Trollope's *Life and Adventures of Michael Armstrong, the Factory Boy*," *Novel* 36, no.2 (Fall 2002), 62.

[56]   Laura Berry, *The Child, the State, and the Victorian Novel*, 10.

worn boyhood, should have been seen embarked in those perfectly constitutional struggles for the amelioration of the sufferings of his class." As a result, however, of "scenes of outrage and lawless violence" perpetrated by England's workers, Trollope "determined that the existence of her hero as an operative shall close with his childhood" because "No misconstruction of principles, no misconception of motives can exist with regard to an attempt to ameliorate the lot of infant labourers."[57] Separating domestic concerns from national ones, and infant laborers from adult (male) ones, writers such as Norton, Trollope, and Tonna proposed the abolition of child labor and a "return to paternalism"[58] as the solution to the ills they describe—a solution that did not address the issue of necessity, and that failed to recognize the very different expectations and understanding of home and childhood within the working classes.

Ambition and Endangered Childhood in the Middle-Class Home

The anxieties expressed by writers of social-problem texts such as Norton, Trollope, and Tonna about the lack of separation between home and factory, between familial affection and commercial "interest," also, I argue, reveals an awareness on their part of the extent to which the comforts enjoyed in many middle-class homes, and the luxury of those homes' own separation from non-domestic labor, was dependent on the exploitation of working-class families. As Leonore Davidoff and Catherine Hall observe in *Family Fortunes*, "The overriding objective of pursuing a moral and genteel life made it almost impossible for employers to acknowledge the price paid by their employees and displaced craft workers under capitalist industrial expansion."[59] Although Davidoff and Hall suggest that "the romantic vision"[60] allowed the middle classes to bridge the contradiction between "on the one hand, the disruption and squalor caused by manufacture and urban development which were the bread and butter of the middle class and, on the other, the intense desire for order and moral superiority,"[61] the concerns expressed by Norton, Trollope, and Tonna suggest that "romantic vision" was insufficient to erase feelings of communal responsibility for the suffering of working-class families.

Furthermore, in their depictions of manufacturing families who depend upon the exploitation of the working poor, writers such as Trollope and Tonna suggest

---

[57]   Trollope, iii, iv.

[58]   Betensky, 70.

[59]   Leonore Davidoff and Catherine Hall, *Family Fortunes: Men and Women of the English middle class, 1780–1850* (London: Hutchinson, 1996), 196.

[60]   Ibid., 26. According to Davidoff and Hall, this "romantic vision" consisted of escapes into nature: "Young chemists and attorneys could leave their mundane occupations for walking tours in the mountains, and, more sedately, with their sisters or sweethearts, passionately experience sunsets or seaside vistas" (28).

[61]   Ibid., 27.

that this exploitation cannot fail to harden the factory owners themselves, and thus cause damage to their own homes and families. In *Michael Armstrong*, Trollope describes Sir Matthew Dowling's children as possessing hearts "seared and hardened by the ceaseless operation of opulent self-indulgence." These children have been raised to believe "that not only was it agreeable to enjoy and cherish all good things which wealth can produce, but that it was their bounden and special duty to make it visible before the eyes of all the men that they could."[62] Because this family's concept of "duty" is simply that of making a spectacle of themselves, and of their material wealth purchased by the suffering of child laborers, they obviously do not represent "the right kind of domestic values," "dedicated" as they are "only to dressing well and aping the aristocracy."[63] Like Tonna's Mrs. Wright, the Dowling family gives up domestic virtue in the pursuit of a class above their station, if not above their financial means. And if it is evident from this and other descriptions that Sir Matthew's children have been ruined (in the development of their better natures, at least) by their family's immense wealth, his daughter Martha illustrates the pain that can be caused to a loving child through an awareness of the cruelties exercised by her father. Martha, unlike her siblings, "contained the only spark of refinement of which the Dowling family could boast,"[64] and possessing this "spark of refinement," Martha is pained and horrified to witness her father's cruel treatment of Michael Armstrong.

A similar moment occurs in Tonna's *Helen Fleetwood*. The Widow Green's efforts to ensure proper treatment of the saintly Helen in the mills of Mr. Z. lead her to appeal to him in his home. While Mr. Z. responds only with anger to the widow's concerns, his daughter is moved by them:

> During her appeal for Helen, whose orphan state she briefly, but touchingly described, the young lady frequently suspended the operations of her pencil, and listened with looks of kind commiseration: Mr. Z. was silent, and a gloomy expression gathered on his features, which might, however, result from dissatisfaction at hearing of his people's malpractices. At length, he glanced towards his daughter, and catching one of her compassionate looks directed to the speaker, he abruptly exclaimed, "Amelia, go to your sisters."[65]

Though Amelia, like Martha Dowling, is blessed with kindness and consideration, such kindness becomes distressing to the father when it is aroused by those who labor for him. She is an ideal daughter, as shown by her compassion, but here it is the very fact of her ideal nature that causes her father's discomfort, critiquing as it does his own actions in the public sphere. As a result, the manufacture that supports this family's home is shown to be antithetical to the domestic virtues

---

[62] Trollope, 53.

[63] Elliot, 384.

[64] Trollope, 53.

[65] Tonna, 118.

found within it. Though the very purpose of the separation of the spheres was predicated on the assumption that the public sphere was a place of competition and questionable morality, the collision of the "pure" domestic space, represented by Mr. Z.'s innocent and ignorant daughter, with the market interests of the public sphere, represented by Mr. Z.'s mill, demonstrates the extent to which Tonna felt the division between the two to be critically unstable.

Concerns about the infiltration of market interests into the working-class family can therefore be understood as intimately connected to similar concerns about the middle-class home. Narratives of the separate spheres notwithstanding, it was true that, for many in the middle class, business was a family affair. According to Davidoff and Hall, the middle class was characterized by the "interpenetration of family and production,"[66] because trade relationships, partnerships, and economic connections were negotiated through the "ties of kinship, friendship, and business." Familial relationships were often, therefore, business relationships, and Davidoff and Hall observe that

> Nowhere were the ties of kinship, friendship and business more evident than in the way partnership functioned. By far the most common form of partnership was father and son(s), brothers, uncle and nephew. Sisters married their brothers' partners and sisters' husbands often became partners after marriage thus binding two families into the fortunes of the enterprise.[67]

This connection between "family and fortune" meant that, in the middle-class home, the affective domain was always entangled with the economic: marriage was both an "economic and social building block for the middle class" as well as a spiritual and emotional relationship;[68] children were both treasured members of the family and the future of the family's business endeavors. Any representation of home and business as inherently separate, therefore, was constructed upon a social edifice in which the two were entirely interdependent.

This interdependence of home and business is evident in texts such as Dickens's *Nicholas Nickleby* (1838–1839), in which "Families in the book—the Mantalinis, the Cheerybles, the Crummleses, the Squeerses, the Nicklebys—are also family businesses, where the claims of the domestic and the economic are intimately bound together."[69] As Paul A. Jarvie notes, *"Nickleby* presents a highly commodified world where everything, including children, is assigned an exchange-value and is subject to circulation as an object."[70] This conflation of economic and affective interests

---

[66]   Davidoff and Hall, 196.

[67]   Ibid., 217–18.

[68]   Ibid., 322.

[69]   John Bowen, "Performing Business, Training Ghosts: Transcoding *Nickleby*," *ELH* 63.1 (1996), 154.

[70]   Paul A. Jarvie, "'Ready to Trample on All Human Law': Financial Capitalism in the Fiction of Charles Dickens" (PhD diss., Tufts University, 2004), 95.

is particularly evident in representations of marriage in the novel, in which girl
children play a significant role as objects of exchange. Kate Nickleby's desire to
support her family and to find love and affection, for example, are shown to be
related enterprises. After the death of their father, Kate and Nicholas Nickleby,
along with their mother, are thrown upon the care of their father's brother, Ralph
Nickleby. While Mr. Nickleby finds employment for Nicholas in the odious
Dotheboy's Hall, Kate finds herself unable—due to her exceptional loveliness and
the jealousy it arouses—to keep her employment at Mrs. Mantalini's dress-making
business. However, her uncle invites her to "keep house" for him at a dinner he
is holding for his business associates, an invitation that fills both Kate and her
mother with hope. Her mother declares that "Your uncle has taken a strong fancy
to you, that's quite clear; and if some extraordinary fortune doesn't come to you,
after this, I shall be surprised, that's all." The connection between her uncle's
perceived affection for Kate—his "fancy"—and her hopes for financial security—
"good fortune"—demonstrates the extent to which, for both Kate and her mother,
the idea of love and economic advancement go hand in hand:

> With this [the mother] launched into sundry anecdotes of young ladies, who had
> had thousand pound notes given them in reticules by eccentric uncles; and of
> young ladies who had accidentally met amiable gentlemen of enormous wealth
> at their uncles' houses, and married them, after short but ardent courtships; and
> Kate, listening first in apathy, and afterwards in amusement, felt, as they walked
> home, something of her mother's sanguine complexion gradually awakening in
> her own bosom, and began to think that her prospects might be brightening, and
> that better days might be dawning upon them.[71]

For Kate and her mother, the prospect of marriage is imbued with both romance
and financial security for the family; that a gentleman who is "amiable and ardent"
and also of "enormous wealth" will be moved by Kate's beauty is a "prospect" that
could substantially alter the fortunes of her family. For Kate, therefore, the career
of marriage holds the possibility of serving her emotional and her economic needs,
as well as those of her family.

Although this balance between the affective and the economic domains sought
by Kate and her mother is depicted as both natural and right, the uncle himself
shows no such balance, for it becomes evident that, for him, his niece is important
only insofar as she serves his own business interest. Kate is the only lady present
at the dinner held by her uncle, and while there, she is subjected to the advances
and insults of the libertines her uncle hopes to ensnare through usury. As a result
of her uncles' selfish employment of her, Kate is exposed not to the appropriate
advances of courtship and possible marriage, but to a kind of prostitution, as

---

[71]   Charles Dickens, *The Life and Adventures of Nicholas Nickleby* (Hertfordshire:
Wordsworth Editions Limited, 2000), 210–11.

the men vie for her attentions and even make her the subject of a bet.[72] After she is violently accosted by Sir Mulberry Hawk, her uncle intervenes, much to Mulberry's anger. Mulberry realizes that Kate has been set as bait, not for him, but for the idiotic Lord Verisopht: "You would sell your flesh and blood for money; yourself, if you have not already made a bargain with the devil .... Do you mean to tell me that your pretty niece was not brought here as a decoy for the drunken boy downstairs?" In his acknowledgment that he brought his niece to the supper "as a matter of business,"[73] Mr. Nickleby reveals his failure to respect the duty he owes his niece: the duty to provide for his "flesh and blood" (a duty recognized even by the vicious Sir Mulberry). Instead, Mr. Nickleby chooses to "sell" his niece, violating, as his niece declares, "the memory of one you must have loved in some old time."[74]

Kate's appeal to her uncle's love for his dead brother, her father, is extremely important to the narrative, because it is love that, Dickens suggests, allows for the proper negotiation between business and familial interest, and it is love that should inspire her uncle to protect Kate's interest—that is, to help her to become a commodity in an arrangement that will be more lucrative for her, both emotionally and financially—rather than use her in the service of his own. Later in the novel, after Kate has been forced to endure the continued attentions of Sir Mulberry, her appeal to her uncle makes it clear that she is urging the primacy of an affective relationship over the demands of economic interest: "I have come at last to you, the only friend I have at hand—almost the only friend I have at all—to entreat and implore you to assist me."[75] Her appellation of Ralph Nickleby as "friend" has a double connotation—it suggests an appeal to affection, but also to protection, a role which Ralph Nickleby, as her uncle, should willingly undertake. His response, however, that he cannot take her part because he and Sir Mulberry "are connected in business,"[76] demonstrates that for him the demands of business interests far outweigh the responsibility he bears as her uncle. Kate is endangered, therefore, by the displacement of duty and affection with avarice and ambition.

Dickens also demonstrates, however, through his depiction of Madeline Bray and her father, the ways in which duty and affection can be manipulated in order to serve economic gains. Her selfish, spendthrift father agrees to Madeline's marriage to the aged and repugnant Arthur Gride as a means of buying his "independence" both from penury and the charity of the Cheeryble brothers. Nicholas, who is aware of the nefarious plans behind the marriage,[77] attempts to dissuade Miss Bray

---

[72]   Ibid., 216–18.
[73]   Ibid., 220.
[74]   Ibid., 221.
[75]   Ibid., 331.
[76]   Ibid., 332.
[77]   Although Arthur Gride is undoubtedly attracted to Madeline Bray because she is, as he describes her, "a delicate and beautiful creature" (545), his primary reason for wishing to marry her is so he can take possession of "some little property—very little—to which

by telling her that "You are betrayed and sold for money," but her reply—"You say you have a duty to discharge ... and so have I. And with the help of Heaven I will perform it"[78]—suggests that her duty as a daughter requires her to consent, even to a marriage she knows to be wrong. But Nicholas's appeal to Madeline is, tellingly, based on the importance of love to a marital relationship:

> Reflect, reflect, before it is too late, on the mockery of plighting to him at the altar, faith in which your heart can have no share—of uttering solemn words, against which nature and reason must rebel—of the degradation of yourself in your own esteem, which must ensue, and must be aggravated every day, as his detested character opens upon you more and more. Shrink from the loathsome companionship of this wretch as you would from corruption and disease.[79]

Though Madeline's devotion to her father is depicted as both right and admirable, and in keeping with the patient air of self-sacrifice that makes Nicholas love her, her willingness to follow her father's wishes even so far as to marry where she does not love is shown to be a grave error, particularly when contrasted with Kate's courageous and righteous defiance of her uncle in support of her own right to be free from the marriage proposals of Sir Mulberry. As Jarvie notes, the "opportunistic elision of one relationship (father, or adult) into another (seller, or user)" results in "danger for children and for society itself. As implied in Kate's story, the commodification both young women suffer seems to have affected the order of social and familial relationships in the world of the novel."[80] Because it is the presence of love alone that distinguishes a proper marriage from a kind of prostitution, from the "degradation" and "corruption" of a spousal relationship based purely on avarice and greed, Madeline's acquiescence to a loveless marriage, though motivated by duty, can only contribute to her father's further degradation and her own future unhappiness.

Although Mr. Bray's and Ralph Nickleby's manipulations of Madeline and Kate are exemplary of the dangers to girl-children that occur when avarice, greed, and ambition replace the duty to protect, the Cheeryble brothers serve to demonstrate the positive aspects of the interpenetration of business and family, offering "the Cheeryble's capitalism as a viable alternative to Ralph's."[81] Though unrelated to either the Nicklebys or Madeline Bray, the Cheeryble brothers nevertheless assume responsibility for both. Their relationship to these separate families is ostensibly a business one, because Nicholas is employed by them and they provide charity

---

this pretty chick was entitled; which nobody does or can know of at this time, but which her husband could sweep into his pouch" (547). The property's value, of course, is not "very little."

[78]   Ibid., 618.

[79]   Ibid., 618–19.

[80]   Jarvie, 100, 99.

[81]   Jarvie, 109.

to Madeline under the pretence of "purchasing her little drawings and ornamental work at a high price, and keeping up a constant demand for the same."[82] But where Madeline's father fails to care for her, the Cheeryble brothers find the means to provide that care, and where Ralph Nickleby fails to provide support and protection for his niece and nephew, the Cheeryble brothers vow to do just that: "They shall not hurt a hair of your head, or the boy's head, or your mother's head, or your sister's head …. We have all said it, and we'll all do it."[83] Through their machinations and influence, Madeline is married to Nicholas, and Kate is married to the Cheeryble's nephew, Frank, thus making what had been a business association a family association through marriage. Though Jarvie points out the limitations of this type of "brotherly capitalism," noting both "the Cheeryble's controlling, money-based paternalism" and the relatively "achievable and safe" alternative the Cheerybles present to any other kind of radical social change,[84] the text suggests that a balance between the interests of commerce and the interests of affection can be reached. When family ties are abused in the aims of commerce, duty no longer has any meaning, but when business is informed by and tempered with affection, duty, generosity, and mutual benefit, commercial partnerships have the potential to represent the ideal family. The presence of love and affection in a relationship is therefore shown to be crucial to the middle-class concept of family, replacing even blood ties in importance. Given the interpenetration of family and fortune, Dickens's novel suggests, familial bonds are at risk of serving commercial interest alone, replacing care with tyranny and duty with avarice. Proper feeling, therefore, far from being relegated simply to the sphere of individual emotion, plays an important ideological and social role by representing and ensuring a balance between "interest" and affection.

In homes where a displacement of such feeling has taken place, even the wealthy child is represented as being vulnerable to exploitation and endangerment. They might not be threatened by starvation, but the emotional neglect suffered by both Flora and Paul Dombey in Dickens's *Dombey and Son* (1848) is, nevertheless, presented as both physically and emotionally damaging. Flora and Paul are endangered as a result of their father's failure to distinguish between the commercial "house" of Dombey and Son and the home in which he raises his children. For Mr. Dombey, parenthood contains only the "hope of giving birth to a new partner"[85] and the "perpetuation of the family"[86] business, and childhood, in keeping with his own experience of it, only the promise of one day succeeding in the business: "He had risen, as his father had before him, in the course of life and

---

[82]   Dickens, *Nicholas Nickleby*, 533.

[83]   Ibid., 529.

[84]   Jarvie, 116, 110.

[85]   Charles Dickens, *Dombey and Son* (Harmondsworth, Middlesex: Penguin Books, 1970), 50.

[86]   Ibid., 51.

death, from Son to Dombey."[87] His daughter, because she will play no role in the patriarchal family enterprise, is to him almost non-existent; before the birth of his son, Dombey understood his marriage as having had "no issue": "to speak of; none worth mentioning. There had been a girl some six years before .... But what was a girl to Dombey and Son! In the capital of the House's name and dignity, such a child was merely a piece of base coin that couldn't be invested—a bad Boy—nothing more."[88] The diction of this passage—"capital," "coin," and "invested"—forcefully speaks to the predominance of economic concerns in Dombey's mind, in which children represent either good currency that will produce returns, or bad currency that cannot "be invested." [89]

Dombey's emotional neglect of Flora, particularly after his son's death, is extraordinarily painful to her, and her situation in the home is perceived by those around her to be worse than that of an orphan, for as one character observes, "not an orphan in the wide world can be so deserted as the child who is outcast from a living parent's love."[90] Dombey's behavior towards his daughter is depicted as both unfeeling and unnatural, but if it causes grief and sorrow to Flora, it also, Dickens suggests, does harm to Dombey himself. Flora's "one absorbing wish" is "to be allowed to show him some affection, to be a consolation to him, to win him over to the endurance of some tenderness from her, his solitary child."[91] But in response, Dombey perceives her only as "an aggravation of his bitterness": "Her loving and innocent face rising before him, had no softening or winning influence. He rejected the angel, and took up with the tormenting spirit crouching in his bosom. Her patience, goodness, youth, devotion, love, were as so many atoms in the ashes upon which he set his heel."[92]

Flora's "patience, goodness, youth, devotion" and "love" all speak to the affective capital of the girl-child in the nineteenth century. As Robson observes in *Men in Wonderland: The Lost Girlhood of Victorian Gentleman*, "it is precisely in her role as the affective center of the home that the daughter is of the greatest service to the men of her family." The girl-child "clearly represents the home as a

---

[87] Ibid., 50.

[88] Ibid., 51.

[89] Furthermore, as David W. Toise points out in "'As Good as Nowhere': Dickens *Dombey and Son*, the Contingency of Value, and Theories of Domesticity" (*Criticism* 41, no. 3 [Summer 1999]: 323–48), Dombey's obsession with family and lineage demonstrate the extent to which he represents "an increasingly archaic early modern ideology that was unable to separate the personal from the private. Dombey's obsessions that everyone have "daily practical knowledge of his position in society" (51) is tinged by early modernity's aristocratic ideology and reflects a sense that no relationship is outside the concerns of status" (326).

[90] Dickens, *Dombey and Son*, 423.

[91] Ibid., 320.

[92] Ibid., 356.

realm of emotion worlds away from the maelstrom of competitive commerce,"[93] thus providing a refuge for her father, in which his better self can be restored through the action of love and affection. Moreover, because Victorian childhood was "feminized" as a "time of 'softness,' and 'vulnerability,' requiring 'gentleness' and 'protection,'"[94] the girl-child also served as a memorial of her father's own childhood, thus providing him with a two-fold retreat from the world of commerce and from the world of adulthood. The very thing that makes Flora worthless to her father—her separation from the world of commerce—is, in fact, the very thing that should make her most precious to him. Because Dombey understands his family only in terms of lineage and business, however, and his daughter only in the light of commercial, rather than emotional "investment," he deprives himself, Dickens suggests, of the humanizing influence the child could bestow upon him. In the "House" of Dombey and Son, Flora can be nothing but a "Bad boy," because the role she is most suited for—the center of a home, rather than a "House"—does not effectively exist.

Although Flora's childhood suffering is the result of her lack of worth in her father's unbalanced domestic economy, little Paul Dombey is endangered by virtue of his ultimate value within it. Unlike his sister, Paul is expected to "accomplish a destiny,"[95] a destiny that shapes his father's interactions with him even from the moment of his birth. After his mother's death in childbirth, Paul is put in the care of a wet-nurse, whose dealings with him are strictly controlled by a rhetoric of economic exchange. As Dombey explains to Mrs. Toodles, "When you go away from here, you will have concluded what is a mere matter of bargain and sale, hiring and letting: and will stay away. The child will cease to remember you; and you will cease, if you please, to remember the child."[96] Through his insistence upon the commercial nature of Mrs. Toodles's interactions with his infant son, Dombey seeks to prevent any emotional attachment, any feelings of affection that would allow her to insinuate herself into the "business" of the family. Mrs. Toodles is not to imagine herself playing the role of mother to Paul; instead, she is "literally food for the rich."[97]

Dombey's treatment of Mrs. Toodles suggests that the narrative of cannibalism present in both Carlyle's and Tonna's texts is here displaced from the familial to the social—in that it is the wealthy cannibalizing the lower classes, rather than the parent cannibalizing the child—but it becomes evident that Paul himself is consumed by his father's ambition. Though he is sickly throughout his early childhood (particularly after the dismissal of his nurse), Paul awakens no anxiety in his father, who feels only "Impatience for the time to come, when his visions

---

[93]   Robson, 53.

[94]   Ibid., 4.

[95]   Ibid., 52.

[96]   Ibid., 68.

[97]   Laura Berry, *The Child, the State, and the Victorian Novel*, 74.

of their united consequence and grandeur would be triumphantly realized."[98] Dombey's focus upon Paul's future worth, which blinds him to the child's present precarious physical condition, also blinds him to the child's emotional needs, since Dombey succeeds, after the dismissal of Mrs. Toodles, in finding caregivers who restrict their relationship to mere "hopes and ventures," "plans and speculations."[99] Caring as they do only for the ways in which Paul will benefit them financially, these caregivers fail to see the child's increasing illness. Separated from the love of his sister and from the comforts of a true home, Paul feels "an aching void in his young heart," "as if he had taken life unfurnished, and the upholsterer were never coming."[100] His father's ambition can purchase nourishment, caregivers, and an education for the child, but it cannot provide a home, and it is this absence of a home, captured in the simile likening Paul's aching heart to an unfurnished dwelling, which causes the child's weakness, sickness, and eventual death.

Paul's death means the end of the company's prospects, suggesting that both the child and the business are destroyed by the absence of a proper home. Dickens's portrayal of the fall of Dombey and Son, brought about by the lack of a domestic space in which his child would have, presumably, received both physical and emotional nourishment, makes the connections between a healthy, thriving home and a healthy, thriving business apparent. Dombey's investment in his business is not, therefore, the primary problem in this text: instead, it is his failure to recognize the interdependence of both home and business. The paradox of the text is that it is only in making the home a separate sphere, one in which affective investments take precedence over financial considerations, that the symbiotic relationship between "House" and home can be maintained.

There are similarities in the representations of children as victims of commerce in the depictions of working-class and of middle- and upper-class homes discussed here. In all these texts, an argument is being made for the inherent value of children, for the recognition of their ultimate worth outside systems of economic exchange. Michael Armstrong, Helen Fleetwood, Madeline Bray, and Flora Dombey all have gifts of love, affection, duty, innocence, and virtue to bestow upon their caregivers, gifts that should, these texts suggest, far outweigh these children's value as commodities, laborers, or financial investments. Furthermore, the gifts they possess are "naturally" suited (in terms of domestic ideology) to the home and to the kind of affective (unpaid) labor that makes the home a refuge from the harsh, material, public world. What differs between the situations of working-class and middle-class children in these texts, however, is the relationship between economic and affective endeavors. Though it might be imperative for Kate Nickleby, for example, to make a proper marriage in order to ensure her financial security, all that is required to bring such an arrangement about is for her uncle to assume responsibility for her. Furthermore, the wealth she can acquire

---

[98]   Dickens, *Dombey and Son*, 150.

[99]   Ibid., 148.

[100]   Ibid., 215.

through marriage, and the fortunes she can bring to her family as a result of it, can be achieved through an arrangement that preserves her place within the domestic sphere, a place that reconciles both her affective and her economic worth. Questions of economics become subsumed, in depictions of marriages such as Kate's, in a rhetoric of affect, thus making her value as a commodity effectively invisible (if no less significant). For children who work in the factories, however, such as young Mary Green in Tonna's *Helen Fleetwood*, who is hardened by her labor, economic worth and affective work cannot be reconciled. Only when business and family are intertwined, as in the case of middle- and upper-class homes, and only when a business relationship is a de facto familial relationship, as in the case of the Nicklebys and the Cheerybles, will children be protected, Dickens's texts suggest, from the harmful effects of commercial and financial interest. But where economic necessity removes the child from the space of the home, and where the child's economic worth is visible *as* economic worth, love and duty alone are represented as insufficient to ensure the child's well-being.

Commerce and Child Abuse

Though the linkage between novelistic depictions of emotionally neglected middle-class children to narratives of child abuse in NSPCC discourse of the late nineteenth century is not immediately obvious, it is, nevertheless, significant. The representations of parental love and of children endangered by commerce seen in these texts provide a crucial framework for understanding the NSPCC's own construction of children endangered by commerce. To construct the begging child, or the child "improperly employed" as the abused child requires eliding a parent's use of a child for economic purposes to a failure of affect, wherein labor becomes "cruelty." Obviously, the focus upon the child as a victim of commerce evident in the novels discussed here speaks to the increasingly dominant belief that children who worked outside the domestic space were perceived to be undertaking "adult" responsibilities, and by the end of the nineteenth century, it became more common to believe that any child "whose knowledge and responsibility were 'adult' needed rescue."[101] It is not surprising, therefore, that NSPCC rhetoric echoes many of the same concerns—about the child as commodity, about parental abuse of the child for the sake of financial gain, and about the "cannibalism" that allowed the parent to live off the child's labor—found within these literary texts. What I will suggest, however, is that the NSPCC's construction of child abuse as a classless crime, one connected to individual character flaws rather than economic or social factors, meant that the Society's understanding of children as victims of commerce was particularly influenced by representations, such as those in Dickens's texts, that linked such endangerment to a parent's or guardian's avarice. That is, novelistic representations of endangered childhood allowed for an understanding of cruelty

---

[101]   Anna Davin, *Growing Up Poor*, 4–5.

and abuse that centered on, for lack of a better term, crimes of feeling. Parents or guardians such as Ralph Nickleby cause harm to the children in their care because they fail to demonstrate the proper feeling. Such a failing on the part of Ralph Nickleby may speak to a larger social ill—such as the hypocrisy of the middle classes, or the injustice faced by children within adult society—but it is, nevertheless, his own failing, his own sin for which he must make reparation. The ability of the Victorian novel to recast social problems as domestic problems, to find both the solution and the blame for social ills within the private space of the home and the inner workings of the individual, finds its way, I would argue, into the late-nineteenth century social-scientific narratives of the NSPCC, for in the NSPCC's stories of children as victims of commerce, such victimization is always realized on the level of the individual. That is, where children suffered as a result of either their value or their involvement within economic systems, the NSPCC locates the root cause of this abuse in the abusive parents' failure to feel the proper regard for their children, rather than in the parents' necessity.

According to Benjamin Waugh, financial concerns threatened children in a variety of ways: in the continued employment of children in theatrical work; in the failure of the wealthy families of England to provide support to organizations such as the NSPCC; in the neglect of children that must invariably occur when the "commercial condition" of England was in disarray;[102] and even in "homes" where children were put to work in order to support the institution itself.[103] Where children suffered, financial considerations were often to blame, even, Waugh argued, in the London SPCC's battle to bring about new legislation. In July 1889, the bill before Parliament that would eventually become the "Children's Charter" faced severe opposition on two counts—on its proposed double restriction of the employment of children in theaters and on children trading in the streets—that some members of Parliament felt would represent "a perfectly unnecessary influence with the freedom of trade."[104] Waugh's response to these critics was that their motivation "is not Christian. It is not English. It would be unfair to Paganism to say it was Pagan. It is perhaps commercial."[105]

Waugh's designation of commercial interests as "not English" would seem to suggest that he understood Englishness, and in particular, the proper English home, to be antithetical to the concerns of business and trade. His acknowledgment, however, in an editorial on "The Dawn of Justice to Little Children" in January 1889, that "We are a commercial people,"[106] suggests instead that for Waugh "commercial" is a shifty signifier. When it is used to define financial activities that, in one form or another, threaten children, "commercial" signifies greed, avarice,

---

[102]   Benjamin Waugh, "Notes," *The Child's Guardian*, 7.11 (November 1893), 149.

[103]   Waugh, "Notes," *The Child's Guardian*, 8.5 (May 1894), 66.

[104]   Qtd. in Behlmer, *Child Abuse and Moral Reform*, 103.

[105]   Waugh, "Notes," *The Child's Guardian*, 3.31 (July 1889), 124.

[106]   Waugh, "The Dawn of Justice to Little Children," *The Child's Guardian*, 3.25 (January 1889): 125.

unbridled ambition, and misplaced priorities. In the second instance, however, it signifies a recognized and even, perhaps, admirable aspect of English life and character that is not, in and of itself, evil. As long as English people "draw the line somewhere,"[107] Waugh argues, commercial and social considerations can happily (and prosperously) co-exist. Furthermore, commerce itself is safeguarded in Waugh's and the Society's rhetoric by having its negative effects upon the lives and children constructed as an individual, rather than a systemic problem. For example, in his article on "Cruelty to the High Born," Waugh cautions that

> Long flowing hair combed and crisped, and elegant dress of children, may conceal fatal constitutional mischiefs being deliberately wrought by those who have the custody of the little wearers. If disease will but play its part, monies left to them by a father's will, or coming through a dead mother's marriage settlement, will fall into their guardians' hands.[108]

These children might be threatened by their value within an economic system, by the promise of "monies left to them," but there is no indication here that inheritance itself is a serious social concern. Instead, as in Dickens's novels, it is here the failure of these children's "guardians" to truly undertake that role, to "guard" and protect the children in their charge, that endangers these children, making "Wills and settlements made all honestly enough years ago ... a bonus on what is nothing less than child-murder."[109] The interconnectedness of family and finance, of children and "monies" is understood to be "honest" in and of itself, so long as avarice does not replace affection in the relationship between guardian and child.

This focus on the individual, moral, and criminal failings of parents and guardians in the middle- and upper-class home makes greed the operative motivation, according to Waugh, in the abuse of children as victims of commerce, a motivation that Waugh equally ascribes to the lower classes. While the wealthy child's economic value—in the forms of wills and settlements—is "honest enough," however, child labor that supported working-class homes, though as common to that culture as were wills and supplements to upper-class culture, is depicted as nothing less than unnatural. In his 1891 article in *The Child's Guardian* on "Cannibalism in England," Waugh argues that "From infancy to death it is not possible for any of us to escape the need of something to eat. Life-long the doom of nothing to eat is death, which is first averted by our hunger being supplied by our parents, and in the course of time by our own labour." While these are, he posits, the "general conditions of child and adult life," yet "there are strange and astounding exceptions to them." Until the passage of the "Children's Charter,"

---

[107]   Ibid.

[108]   Waugh, "Cruelty to the High Born," *The Child's Guardian*, 3.25 (January 1889), 131.

[109]   Ibid.

Waugh suggests, "it was lawful to make the baby toil for the man," and "These [toiling] children were regarded as the pantry, yielding the necessaries of adult life. They stood between the idle man and the gnawings of hunger. Their starving bodies were slowly transmuted into the muscles with which he got about."[110]

The cannibalism Waugh describes here is very much akin to that described by Tonna in *Helen Fleetwood*, in that in both instances, the child's labor supports the parent to the detriment of the child's own health and well-being. Although writers such as Norton and Trollope, however, understood—if only partially—that child labor might be motivated by fear of the family's *and* the child's starvation, Waugh sees it only as a reversal of the "general conditions" of life, the word "general" suggesting here that there is no recognition on his part of the fact that "conditions" of life vary greatly from class to class. Any "exception" to these "general conditions" can only, therefore, be understood as "strange and astounding," and as the result of individual, rather than social, failings. The "gnawings of hunger," that is, become constructed through Waugh's rhetoric not as the result of serious social imbalance, but of "idleness," a moral flaw. Murdering (by neglect) a child for its insurance money, and living off a child's labor are crimes that share, in other words, the same root cause. In both cases, the child is abused as a result of the parent's or guardian's failure to recognize his or her own duties and responsibilities towards the child, and his or her desire to benefit financially from the child. Such a stance succeeds in constructing child abuse as a crime that shares universal—i.e., non-class-specific—motivations, but it also succeeds in portraying choices imposed by poverty and necessity as evidence of, at best, a lack of affect and, at worst, greed.

The NSPCC and Child-Life Insurance

Nowhere, however, were issues of class, commerce, and child abuse more clearly entangled than in the debate over child-life insurance. Such insurance allowed parents to receive money on the death of a child, ostensibly for the purposes of providing a decent burial. This practice, however, met with criticism on two major counts. The publication of Edwin Chadwick's "A Supplementary Report on the Results of a Special Inquiry into the Practice of Interment in Towns" in 1843 "set the pattern for bourgeois criticism of the working-class celebration of death," suggesting as it did that "the poor ... spent far too much on their funerals."[111] Such a criticism speaks to both the desire of middle-class commentators to impose models of frugality and respectability onto working-class homes, and the failure of these same commentators to recognize the motivations behind such a seemingly wasteful practice as the decent burial of a child. As Ellen Ross observes, "The careful adherence to the rules of etiquette with respect to the dead child, sometimes

---

[110]   Waugh, "Cannibalism in England," *The Child's Guardian*, 5.2 (February 1891): 9.

[111]   Behlmer, *Child Abuse and Moral Reform*, 120.

against all reason and economy, reveals the same determination to do one's duty" that was a key aspect of working-class family life in the nineteenth century.[112] The middle-class fear that the money lower-class families spent on child-life insurance could have been better spent, then, demonstrates the distance between middle-class and working-class perceptions and understanding of how a parent should care for its child.

As stories such as that of Carlyle's Stockport parents suggest, however, child-life insurance aroused an even greater concern than the expense of child funerals. As Behlmer notes,

> the notorious financial instability of these clubs encouraged parents to buy multiple policies, particularly on the young, for whom insurance premiums might run as low as a penny per week. To Edwin Chadwick and many social critics after him, it seemed that duplicate policies on the lives of children earned reimbursements that were greater than the actual cost of a funeral, thereby sweetening the "temptation for evil." In extreme cases—for example, the Manchester man who enrolled his baby in nineteen different burial societies— Chadwick cautioned that the reward for a child's death could serve as "a bounty on neglectual infanticide."[113]

Concerns such as this were raised over the next twelve years in England, but although a variety of measures were undertaken by the government in response to these concerns, a lack of evidence that child-life insurance was in fact tempting parents to murder their children meant that no serious legal restrictions were put in place.[114]

The issue of child-life insurance continued to resurface, however, particularly after the emergence of large life-insurance companies, such as the Prudential. Earlier burial clubs were often run by working-men's associations based within the community, but larger insurance companies had no ties to the parents they represented other than a business relationship. "As a result," Behlmer argues,

---

[112]   Ellen Ross, *Love and Toil: Motherhood in Outcast London, 1870–1918* (Oxford: Oxford University Press, 1993), 193.

[113]   Behlmer, 121.

[114]   Behlmer notes that in August 1850, "Parliament passed legislation (13 & 14 Vic., c. 115) that prohibited insurance in excess of £3 on any child under the age of ten. More importantly, the Act stipulated that all death benefits be paid directly to the undertaker" (123). However, this legislation was "experimental, intended to stay in force for one year only" and when "in 1854 the House of Commons requested a list of persons tried during the previous decade for the murder of children who were members of burial societies, MPs found that neither the Record of Trials nor the Clerks of Assize could supply the desired information" (ibid). Opponents to restrictions on burial insurance argued that £3 was not enough to decently bury a child, and that "Legislation that barred the poor from conducting the last rites for their own children was insulting" (Behlmer, 124).

"mid-Victorian England witnessed the rise of burial societies wherein the mutual aid ideal gave way to an obsession with growth and profit."[115] Concerns about the influence of "profit" in a field in which money benefits accrued after the death of a child led to the appointment of a Royal Commission on Friendly Societies in 1870.[116] The findings of the commission were such that the commissioners urged the prohibition of insurance of children, but "largely because of renewed pressure from burial societies, this guideline emerged in the Friendly Societies Act of 1875 ... as ceilings of £10 and £6 on the lives of children under ten and five respectively."[117] These ceilings were felt to be insufficient to protect the lives of the children of the poor, and throughout the late 1870s and 1880s, child-life insurance continued to draw criticism. But with the emergence of child-protection in the 1880s, a new way of attacking the practice presented itself: that of depicting it as a form of cruelty to children.

The London SPCC felt that child-life insurance encouraged unprincipled parents to neglect or even murder their offspring, and made a point of mentioning, in *The Child's Guardian*, those cases in which abused children were also insured children. Although insuring a child was not a crime, claims made within the journal such as "fourteen of these 100 suffocated children were admittedly insured"[118] sought to make the practice seem so, and the Society was "sufficiently impressed with the strength of public sentiment that it announced in October 1888 its commitment to the total abolition of insurance on young lives."[119] After its success bringing about the "Children's Charter" in 1889, and its reconstitution as the NSPCC in that same year, the Society seemed poised to take on what it perceived to be a grave threat to children in England, and by 1890, the NSPCC had prepared a bill for Parliament, proposing to restrict the size of payments for children, and to make all monies payable only to the undertaker, rather than the parents.[120]

The NSPCC's involvement in the debate over child-life insurance, however, damaged the Society's claim that its work was "no class work."[121] Child-life insurance was purchased primarily by those who had little to no savings and insufficient income to pay for a funeral, and as such, any attack upon the practice was perceived to be an attack upon the working classes. Insurance journals (however self-servingly) accused the NSPCC of slandering the poor in its opposition to

---

[115]   Ibid., 125.

[116]   As Behlmer notes, "That the mortality rate for children in heavily insured Liverpool jumped inexplicably during the second year of life, 'precisely within the year when infants first come into full insurance benefits,' thus impressed the commissioners as strong circumstantial evidence against such policies" (126).

[117]   Ibid.

[118]   "Insurance and Suffocation in Liverpool," *The Child's Guardian*, 2.22 (October 1888), 93.

[119]   Behlmer, 128.

[120]   Ibid., 129.

[121]   Waugh, "Notes," *The Child's Guardian*, 3.36 (February 1889): 224.

child-life insurance, claiming that "Baby is [the poor woman's] only treasure, and on it she lavishes a wealth of affection that is a beautiful illustration of the finer emotions."[122] The language employed here suggests that the companies sought to reframe the terms of the debate, arguing that the only "treasure" and "wealth" to be found in the relationship between the working-class mother and child was that of affection, and that any suggestion that such "treasure" could be displaced by financial gain was nothing less than an assault on the working-class home. Waugh became, if his many "Notes" and articles on the subject are any indication, extraordinarily frustrated with such accusations. In a July 1890 article on "The Rights of the Working Man," Waugh argues that the suggestion that the NSPCC's bill "proposes to interfere with the working-man's rights" is "false in sentiment and in fact," because "A right to do wrongs belongs to no man, whether conferred by Parliament or custom or brute force." He continues, "'The rights of the working man!' The working man has neither more nor less rights than any other man."[123] According to Waugh, therefore, the NSPCC's attack upon child-life insurance is nothing less than positive evidence of the NSPCC's classless stance. "Wrongs" against children, regardless of who perpetrated them, and whatever custom they might have represented, could not be tolerated.

Although Waugh's reply to accusations of class bias leveled against the NSPCC suggests, in part, a failure to recognize the extent to which applying universal standards based upon middle-class values might itself be a form of class bias, there is much to suggest in his writings on the subject of child-life insurance that this opposition to the practice went beyond a middle-class inability to respect working-class customs. Instead, Waugh's rhetoric on the subject of child-life insurance reveals a great anxiety about the influence of commerce on the working-class home, and about the lack of proper domestic virtues within that home. In articles such as "Child-Life Insurance," published in the *Contemporary Review* in July 1890, Waugh disputes the charge that "to lay the responsibility for the death of so many children at the door of child-life insurance societies is a slander on the working class" by arguing that "the class that is charged is all who worship a pound they have not got but want, more than a child they have got and do not want."[124] Much like the insurance companies themselves, Waugh seeks to recast the terms of the debate by referring to class not as something that is defined by economics or social status, but by moral standards and levels of care. Such a "class," of course, could include the rich as well as the poor, and Waugh's rhetoric is meant to suggest that it does indeed encompass both the guardians of well-endowed children and parents of well-insured children alike. These are parents, Waugh argues, to whom "a child

---

[122]   Qtd. in Behlmer, 128.

[123]   Waugh, "The Rights of the Working Man," *The Child's Guardian*, 4.8 (July 1890), 81.

[124]   Waugh, "Child-Life Insurance," *Contemporary Review* 58 (July 1890), 41.

presents greater attractions dead than alive, especially if alive it costs sixpence and dead it is worth six shillings," and most importantly, "they exist in every rank."[125]

When Waugh says, however, that the "class" he is referring to is not the "respectable poor" but, instead, "that inglorious herd of people who are everywhere the perplexity of our police,"[126] it becomes obvious that he is speaking primarily of parents of the lower- and working-classes, utilizing language that works within classed discourses of criminality and the "lower orders" current at the end of the nineteenth century. Such rhetoric depicted "the 'laboring and dangerous classes' as a separate race, primitive, animal-like and threatening," and as an "atavistic resurgence of 'prehistoric man.'"[127] Representations of the criminal dovetailed with that of the pauper in this discourse, who was constructed as "defective, lazy, and unintelligent."[128] Waugh's depictions of abusive parents, throughout his writings, share these qualities: they are described as "big-limbed, arbitrary,"[129] "reckless men,"[130] "impecunious, idle people,"[131] "lazy as sloths, lustful as monkeys, crafty as serpents, savage as tigers,"[132] and mere "she-things."[133] Such representations of abusive parents serve to emphasize the separation between them and the "genuine British mother and father,"[134] and consequently, to mark these brutal parents as a distinct social class, one whose ills are "considered signs of moral weakness rather than economic struggles."[135] In his desire to assert, therefore, that the class he accuses of child murder for profit is distinguished by its immorality rather than its poverty, Waugh does not challenge classed rhetoric: instead, he operates firmly within it.

But what is particularly frightening to Waugh about these parents is that this "herd of reckless married and unmarried creatures with maternal organism," with "males to match them," "have babies."[136] Waugh's language suggests that though these parents "have babies," they are not truly "mothers" or "fathers," but instead only "creatures with maternal organism." Such female creatures might be able to procreate, that is, but they are not able (or willing) to fulfill the affective role that "mother" suggests. Furthermore, Waugh's focus on the "gnawings of hungers" in the lower-class home, as described in "Cannibalism in England," betrays anxieties

---

[125]   Ibid., 53.

[126]   Ibid., 52.

[127]   Marie-Christine Leps, *Apprehending the Criminal: The Production of Deviance in Nineteenth-Century Discourse* (Durham and London: Duke University Press, 1992), 5.

[128]   Ibid., 4.

[129]   Waugh, "Street Children," *Contemporary Review* 53 (June 1888), 827.

[130]   Manning and Waugh, "The Child of the English Savage," 699.

[131]   Waugh, "Child-Life Insurance," 41.

[132]   Ibid., 53.

[133]   Waugh, "Baby Farming," *Contemporary Review* 58 (May 1890), 705.

[134]   Waugh, "Child-Life Insurance," 52.

[135]   Leps, 26.

[136]   Waugh, "Child-Life Insurance," 53.

about the presence of hungry, starving adult bodies, an anxiety that is particularly evident in his writings on child-life insurance, for while the NSPCC's depiction of the abused child as innocent and helpless might suggest that Waugh's fear of the English savage is expressed on behalf of their offspring, his rhetoric in "Child-Life Insurance" suggests also that it is the ability to the savage to reproduce that is of grave concern. The "inglorious herd," according to Waugh, is made up of strong "hardy folks" of the "stolid Amazon type," and they give birth to children who "are hardy themselves," and therefore hard to kill."[137] Despite the professed fear that the practice might lead to countless death of insured children, therefore, the central anxiety these images express is that this group has the capacity to replicate itself. Considering that London at the end of the nineteenth century "was a city of children, and its poor districts contained the greatest number of them,"[138] and that discourses about the urban slums depicted them as "symptoms of a physical and moral deterioration of society,"[139] it becomes clear that Waugh's images of savage fertility tapped into common fears about the growth of the lower classes. The hungry and starving of England evoke fear in Waugh's rhetoric, not pity, because of the perceived strength of those who seek to satisfy that hunger.

Waugh's article connects these hungry bodies that can reproduce to the growth of corrupt business practices in the insurance industry. Waugh argues that the incentive of the insurance agent to sell as many policies as possible is that "Offices must have increase."[140] The necessity and capacity of insurance business to "increase" is a source of concern, according to Waugh, because these businesses, like their clients, tend to spread contamination and death while they do so. Waugh focuses particularly on the touts, the paid agents of insurance companies who sold policies door to door who, he argues, are "silently teaching strong lessons on a vast scale."[141] These lessons, Waugh suggests, result in child murder in "vast numbers."[142] The growth of the insurance industry is therefore depicted as directly connected to a perceived increase in the starvation of children, children of whom there is, because of their parents' ability to "have babies," an endless supply. Both the insurer and the client benefit from the "increase" of the child population (and from the death of those children), making them both "cannibals" upon England's children, much as the factory owners and parents of child laborers were believed to have done earlier in the period.

---

[137]   Ibid., 52, 50, 51, 50.

[138]   Ross, *Love and Toil*, 13. According to Ross, "In 1871, 43 percent of the population [of London] were aged fifteen or younger. By 1901, despite a birthrate that had been declining for four decades and the continuing influx of single adults, London's population was still nearly a third children" (ibid.).

[139]   Leps, 23.

[140]   Waugh, "Child-Life Insurance," 54.

[141]   Ibid., 52.

[142]   Ibid., 42.

The alliance between the insurance companies and the savage (lower-class) parent is therefore appalling to Waugh because it teaches the parent to be the wrong kind of "productive" member of society. That is, the lessons the touts teach the parents is how to put their reproductive powers to work for them, to transform their children into food and drink. The business in which the insurance company and the abusive parent are engaged is that of "the making of 30s. on starved [children] for the churchyard,"[143] money which can then be spent by "the drinking, gambling, impure" and "idle" as they see fit.[144] This system of money-benefit, according to Waugh, "incites such to change the child for the pound," a system of exchange which perverts the proper parental role of caring for and nurturing the child.[145] Instead, the "effect of the policy on the matter of which the child is composed tends not to the preservation but to the waste of it, and to the rate and certainty with which infantile disease becomes fatal to it."[146] Child-life insurance here represents, again, a form of economic cannibalism, as the parents reap financial benefits through a process that consumes the flesh and blood of their children. Furthermore, the appetites that are fed by this process of altering "the matter of which the child is composed" go beyond those of mere physical hunger, as seen in Waugh's example of insuring parents who feel "a strong animal affection for one another."[147] The waste and starvation of the child produces further reproduction, reproduction that will support the "impure" pursuits of the parents and the increase of insurance offices alike.

Although Waugh's depiction of child-life insurance seems to suggest a closed circuit, in which savage parents satisfy their appetites through the continual production of offspring for the graveyards, he is careful to point out the ways in which such production can and will infect the body of the nation itself. Towards the goal of increased benefit, according to Waugh, insurance companies and their agents seek to convert "impecunious, idle people into crafty murderers. It teaches the drunkard that to face his son's death is the way to drown his raging thirst."[148] In order to do these things, of course, the "impecunious" and "idle" had to be taught how to cheat the legal system, something that Waugh believed the insurance industry well-suited to teach. According to Waugh, touts (by their actions, if not by their words) suggest to their clients that "You may go to the inquest, and because two of you were in the room, neither of you being able to give evidence against the other; you may escape by the skin of your teeth; you may be called by the court 'a disgrace to humanity;' only pay me your pennies, and when denounced

[143] Waugh, "Children as Articles of Commerce," *The Child's Guardian*, 4.10 (October 1890), 122.
[144] Waugh, "Notes," *The Child's Guardian*, 4.8 (August 1890), 91.
[145] Waugh, "Child-Life Insurance," 41.
[146] Ibid., 58.
[147] Ibid., 49.
[148] Ibid., 41.

you leave the court, I will give you my pounds."[149] The touts instruct the avaricious parent, Waugh argues, that the denunciation of those in authority means nothing, and that money—however gained—means everything. With this instruction, the parent goes on to dupe those in power, and Waugh marvels at "the crafty practices whereby child-killing is accomplished and yet inquests are escaped" and laments that "defrauding the coroner of his case is the rule, not the exception."[150] The fear elicited by the alliance between the money-loving parent and the money-loving tout is not just, therefore, on behalf of the child, but on behalf of the rule of law. The failure of these parents to respect the natural order, that is, to feel "natural affection" for their child,[151] or to obey "the general conditions of child and adult life"[152] by providing for those children threatens English society itself.

What might appear to be a domestic scandal becomes in Waugh's article a national shame, one which must be addressed "for the sake of England's children and the morals and interests of their homes."[153] Because the alliance between the lower classes and the insurance industry perverts the home itself, it degrades the community. The "moral sense of the nation," that is, depends upon "the convenience of commerce" being made "to bend to the comfort and safety of our children,"[154] for, as Waugh asserts, "A child dishonoured is a nation's bane."[155] These pronouncements serve to underline a perceived connection between home and nation, wherein the failure to uphold the natural order within one leads to the destruction of the other. These sentiments do not, of course, displace responsibility for the child's suffering from the abusive, neglectful parent, but they do place the imperative to address that suffering on the national level. The failure to intercede on behalf of the child is a failure not only to protect that child, but also to uphold the laws of England. Child-life insurance, then, "Whether it be by societies, their agents, the undertakers, or the parents ... must be treated as a serious crime, against both the bodies of children and the welfare of the State."[156]

Waugh and the NSPCC believed that the only way to address the threat of child-life insurance was through "the abolition of all child death-money payments."[157] Such an aim, however, was never to be achieved. Though the NSPCC published a special issue of *The Child's Guardian* in August 1890 that included condemnations of child-life insurance from doctors, police, and coroners, such testimony "offered

---

[149]   Ibid., 52.

[150]   Ibid., 43.

[151]   Waugh, "Doing Children to Death for Money," *The Child's Guardian*, 4.8 (August 1890), 85.

[152]   Waugh, "Cannibalism in England," 9.

[153]   Waugh, "Child-Life Insurance," 63.

[154]   Ibid.

[155]   Ibid., 59.

[156]   Ibid., 63.

[157]   Ibid., 62.

impressions rather than facts."[158] Even the case studies provided by the NSPCC failed to offer conclusive evidence that parents were "doing children to death for money" (as the opening editorial proclaimed); although the NSPCC gave these narratives such titles as "The Way to £20" and "A £5 Prize for Killing a Baby," the cases themselves contained the same stories of neglect and abuse that could be found in any of the NSPCC's cases. In one entitled, "£17 7s. 0d.: Bonuses on Neglect," for example, the description of the family and their home simply underlines their desperate poverty. The house is described as being "in a shockingly neglected condition, very filthy. The bed-room in which the prisoners and their family slept measured 14ft. by 12ft., the height being 9ft. …. The heads of the [six] children were covered with sores, and full of vermin; in fact, they were generally in a disgraceful condition."[159] The article provides in great detail the cross-examination of the parents' insurance agent, but the parents themselves are given no voice: instead, the reader is provided with the instructions they receive at the end of the trial for neglect, in which it is hoped that "the prisoners would consider the responsibilities devolving upon them as parents—a responsibility they could not get rid of so long as the children were dependent upon them."[160]

Although this case is indicative of the kinds of cases the NSPCC investigated and prosecuted under "The Children's Charter," it does not provide, in its details, any solid evidence to suggest that these children were, in fact, neglected for their insurance money. The shocking condition of the home could indicate that the parents might have spent their pennies on their children, rather than on insurance, but the case also points out that the mother had failed to make payments on the insurance, and could not pay the arrears of 1s. 3d.[161] Clearly, the parents not only failed to feed their children, they also failed to meet the demands of insurance agents. Therefore, other than its title, this narrative does not support the NSPCC's argument against child-life insurance, and in fact, the extreme similarity of this case to the many other cases of neglect published in the journal calls into question *any* causal connection between the condition of the home and the insurance of the children. Instead, as Behlmer observes, Waugh's attacks upon the practice could be read as signs of the extent to which he "overestimated the ease with which working-class mothers and fathers might be tempted to barbarism."[162] As a result of a lack of factual evidence, the NSPCC's bill to abolish child-life insurance failed, as did every measure against the practice brought before parliament in the following years.[163]

The lack of any persuasive support for his attacks was a point on which Waugh expressed great frustration. As he complains in "Child-Life Insurance,"

---

[158]   Behlmer, 132.

[159]   "£17 7s. 0d.: Bonuses on Neglect," *The Child's Guardian*, 4.8 (August 1890): 88.

[160]   Ibid., 89.

[161]   Ibid.

[162]   Behlmer, 136.

[163]   Ibid., 135.

> I am at a loss to understand the state of mind which excludes all the merely
> probable, however highly probable, from consideration, where all that happens
> happens to a little invalid in the sole charge of a drunken nurse, who has £6
> coming at that little invalid's death; where, whatever moral certainty there may
> be in the doctor and amongst the neighbours, based on however many outside
> facts, as to what happened in the sickroom, is of no assize value; where, the child
> once dead, neither of its parents can give evidence as to what the other did.[164]

The problem Waugh identifies here is that of *access* to the lower- and working-
class home, of ascertaining what goes on within it. The gap between the "moral
certainty" of commentators such as Waugh and any actual evidence of wrongdoing
within the working-class home underlines the extent to which ideological
constructions of the lower classes provided the primary impetus behind attacks
upon the practice of child-life insurance. For Waugh, however, this gap is merely
a sign of the need for greater intervention. Until child-protection workers, he
suggests, can move beyond simply asserting the "highly probable," the problem
itself "cannot be approached."[165]

Or, to be more precise, it cannot be approached by the right people. Waugh
laments that "It is miserable to a patriot to think how many of these collectors of
premiums upon child death policies openly, week by week, call at doors within
which, the neighbours believe, a child is being slowly neglected to death,—a fact,
by the way, with which the canvassers have no concerns."[166] The home might
be closed to those—such as neighbors, doctors, or coroners—who are most
invested, according to Waugh, in the child's well-being, but it is open only to
those who "have no concerns" for that same child. The working-class home is
therefore permeable by those who will have no positive effect upon it: who will
not support or instruct the parents in their proper responsibilities and duties, but
will instead teach the parents "lessons" that will lead to the degradation of that
home. Although, Waugh argues, the tout may have "eyes in his head to see what
he was doing" to the children in the home, he has "orders" to continue his work.[167]
Under the system of child-life insurance, then, those who are privileged to see
what others can only "believe" to be happening, are bound, by their love of money
and the demands of commerce, to not intervene. As long as those who have no
investment in supporting proper parental care and affection in the home have the
most access to it, Waugh suggests, the children of the poor will be at risk, and, as
Waugh's appeal to "patriots" makes apparent, so too will the nation itself. Waugh's
battle against child-life insurance, then, is as much a battle for influence within the
working-class home as it is an attack on the practice itself.

---

[164]   Waugh, "Child-Life Insurance," 60.
[165]   Ibid., 60.
[166]   Ibid., 49.
[167]   Ibid.

It is also, however, a battle on behalf of the nation's commerce. For though children might die for many reasons, Waugh argues, "whatever these may be, if money benefit does not arise, the commerce of the country may wash its hands of all complicity. Till then, child-blood is on them."[168] As long as the spirit of commercial competition overrides the dictates of domestic ideology, as in the alliance between the working-class parent and the insurance tout, Waugh argues, both of England's attributes—its homes and its commerce—will be soiled. Insurance companies, motivated as they are by competition and avarice, cannot care about the "children of unnatural mothers and fathers,"[169] nor can their standard of commerce be allowed to hold sway. The nation's commercial spirit can only be healthily sustained, Waugh therefore suggests, when it is balanced by an awareness of the importance of love and care within the home—affective qualities that served to, symbolically at least, deny the extent to which home and commerce were inextricably linked.

The implicit contrast to the influence of the insurance company upon the working-class home provided by Waugh is, of course, the NSPCC, whose sole interest in that home is in its reform, its sole desire to transform "parents, who are absolutely indifferent to their children's necessities and welfare, who even hate their children and see in their helplessness inducement to tyranny" into parents who "treat them with care, with even affection."[170] Where the bad influence of commerce degrades the home, the NSPCC's influence can restore its proper order:

> By the Society's treatment, and in a way little short of amazing to the ordinary mind, in ten thousand bad parents' conduct care has taken the place of hate. Under the means the Society employs, natural feelings have proven to be hidden, and those feelings have had the opportunity given to them to arise, have of themselves arisen, have been cultivated and strengthened, and have become in the strictest sense the feelings generally operating between the human race and its offspring.[171]

Again, Waugh asserts here the existence of universal laws governing the parent-child relationship. In the home of the English savage, he attests, these laws have been overthrown, but through the intercession of the NSPCC, such laws can once again take hold. The insurance agent, on the other hand, might have "eyes in his head," but he does not have the will or desire to see the true potential of the lower- and working-class parent. The NSPCC *can* see that potential, Waugh's discourse promises, and if given more influence upon the home than that of commerce,

---

[168]   Ibid., 59.

[169]   "Doing Children to Death for Money," 85.

[170]   Waugh, "Emancipation—Child and Parent; or, Can Bad Homes be Reformed?" *The Child's Guardian*, 10.3 (March 1896), 33.

[171]   Ibid.

will bring about reformation within it by attacking "unnatural habits and tastes which prevent natural parental feeling arising."[172] Necessity and starvation are not, therefore, what primarily threatens poor children and poor families; instead, it is the fact that the "old kindly affections of our race for its young have lapsed."[173] Those kindly feelings can be rekindled, but only through the proper guidance, and the proper education. In order for the homes of England to be saved, according to Waugh, they must be open not to commerce, but to intervention, not to the tout, but to the inspector.

Waugh's focus on production and commercial exchange allows him and the Society to avoid accusations of class bias and to answer charges that the NSPCC's work criminalized poor and starving parents. His representation of the problem of child-life insurance, however, reveals the extent to which the practice did, in fact, tap into deep-rooted fears about the lower classes, and, for that matter, about commerce. What ostensibly originates with a concern for abused and starving children expands into a critique of the role of lower-class families and children in England's commercial economy, and of the role of commerce within those families. While it might be difficult to comprehend how the purchase of life insurance could be perceived as a business venture—and a corruptive one at that—the fact that Waugh does construct it as such suggests that it is the possibility of a kind of alliance between the lower classes and commerce that is a significant source of fear here. Such a fear might speak to, in part, a more widespread recognition that the growth of England's economy had significantly altered the relationship between the higher and the lower classes, displacing an earlier paternalism that the NSPCC here seeks to reassert. I believe it also, however, speaks to a fear of the lower-class child. For while that child is represented as an object of pity, the many images of productivity and consumption link the child as commodity to the child as future producer and consumer. The attack upon child-life insurance might be on behalf of the child, but it is also, in the end, on behalf of an England that is threatened by that child, and by what that child might become.

---

[172]   Ibid.

[173]   Ibid.

Chapter 5
The Dangerous Child: Juvenile Delinquents, Criminality, and the NSPCC

As indicated throughout this text, a central aspect of child protection in the nineteenth century was that of childhood innocence; that is, the child deserved and required the assistance of parents, guardians, public and private charities, and the government itself primarily because of the child's helplessness, and because of the innocence signified by that very helplessness. James Kincaid has argued, however, that constructions of the innocent child of the Victorian period have been overstated—that our own present-day reading of this figure "express[es] and expos[es] a need of our own,"[1] more than it necessarily reflects a Victorian investment in childhood innocence. Readings about the juvenile delinquent in the nineteenth century certainly support this claim, for with that figure we are presented with a child that is, as Mary Carpenter states, "positively ... *dangerous*."[2] While one could suggest that the proper normative child was, in fact, innocent, and that the juvenile delinquent represented a child made wrong, a blameless child perverted by its environment that could only, through proper intervention, be made childlike again, there is much to suggest that this narrative was not the sole, or even the dominant narrative in the nineteenth century. For while representations of the pure and helpless child abound in nineteenth-century discourse, there were as many representations of the precocious, the violent, and the sadistic child as there were of the former. For every Oliver Twist there is a Noah Claypole, and for every child that saves a suffering animal, there is a child inflicting that suffering.

The juvenile delinquent was therefore a key figure in Victorian narratives of child endangerment precisely because the issue of that child's endangerment could not be easily ascertained. Was the child a criminal because of nurture, because that child had been reared in a lawless culture or, worse, a culture that had laws entirely opposed to those of normative Victorian society? Or were some children simply "born bad," destined from the cradle for a life of crime? Questions raised by the juvenile delinquent, that is, got at the very heart of childhood itself as either a socially contingent state of being or as a God-given right that should be shared by all. Because the very act of committing a crime, an act that was constructed, inherently, as the act of an adult, called into question the boundary between supposed childhood dependence and adult independence, the child criminal

---

[1]   James Kincaid, *Child-Loving*, 72.
[2]   Mary Carpenter, *Juvenile Delinquents*, 15.

threatened emergent constructions of children as inherently other than and outside of adult society.

I would therefore like to conclude my examination of the endangered child by examining juvenile delinquency as a test case for the limitations of "cruelty to children." This is not to suggest that criminal children could not also be classified as abused children; as George K. Behlmer notes of mid-Victorian legal reformists, "Many of those who urged Parliament to save young offenders from mixing with adult criminals believed that the working-class home was becoming a cauldron of cruelty,"[3] and he further records that the NSPCC believed that the "delinquencies of children should be regarded ... as the delinquencies of their parents."[4] Nevertheless, children who committed crimes also threatened the narrative of the endangered child as inherently innocent, blameless, and helpless. As such, I would argue, the juvenile delinquent remains to this day a figure of great complexity—one who continually challenges both narratives about the nature of childhood and about social concern on behalf of that child. Heather Shore has argued that the juvenile delinquent of the nineteenth century "provoked both despair and expectation. Such children and youths could be saved and reincorporated into respectable society, or they could fall, and be absorbed, into the life of the hardened criminal."[5] In an examination of Dickens's *Oliver Twist* (1837–1839), Mary Carpenter's *Juvenile Delinquents* (1851), W. T. Stead's *The Maiden Tribute of Modern Babylon* (1885), and selected articles from *The Child's Guardian*, I argue that the delinquent child disrupts binary oppositions between child and adult, between child independence and child dependence, and between the child as salvageable and the child as lost. The "fall" Shore refers to is not just, I assert, a fall from respectability into lawlessness, but a fall from childhood into a kind of adulthood. As such, the figure of the juvenile delinquent in nineteenth-century discourse—and in current attacks upon separate punishments for child criminals—reminds us that it is not, perhaps, the child itself that Victorian child-savers, or even our own culture, wants to save, but rather that constructed figure of the ideal victim — helpless, innocent, malleable, and eminently "worthy" of intervention. When the child fails to be that figure, child protection itself often proves insufficient to account for or save that child.

---

[3]   George K. Behlmer, *Friends of the Family: The English Home and its Guardians, 1850–1940* (Stanford University Press, Stanford, 1998), 233.

[4]   NSPCC, *Seventh Annual Report* (1891), pp. 52–3; qtd. in Behlmer, *Friends of the Family*, 242.

[5]   Heather Shore, *Artful Dodgers: Youth and Crime in Early Nineteenth-Century London* (Woodbridge: The Royal Historical Society, 1999), 1.

The Juvenile Delinquent in Nineteenth-Century England

As Marie-Christine Leps describes in *Apprehending the Criminal: The Production of Deviance in Nineteenth-Century Discourse*, the late eighteenth and early nineteenth centuries saw the rise of a form of criminality that was based, ostensibly, on issues of equality: "one of the most important functions of the new legal discourse was to erase all class divisions by establishing a blind social *process* in which position and wealth—but also starvation and misery—played no role."[6] In practice, however, this equality before the law held real benefits for the middle classes: they both "profited from the abolition of aristocratic privilege," and from the new justice system that "gave considerable powers to the middle classes, whose members acted as J.P.s, jurors, and M.P.s to enact new laws as dictated by (their) changing needs."[7] Empowered by a law that sought to erase the significance of social inequality as a factor in the commission of crimes, middle- and upper-class lawmakers could institute constructions of criminality that, while purporting to be classless, in fact solidified classed values that targeted the poor and working classes:

> Fines, demotions, or dismissals were judged punishment enough for what has come to be known as white-collar crime, while prison sentences, often qualified with hard labor, were considered necessary for the repression of "ordinary crime" (such as vagrancy, thefts, minor assaults, drunkenness, and disorderly conduct), the infractions of the "lower classes," which were processed without jury in the special circuits of police courts and the summary justice of the Petty Sessions.[8]

However, though the law assigned responsibility for the crime to the perpetrator and determined punishment for the crime by the offence, there were real points of disagreement as to how such a thing as criminal responsibility should be determined. Lisa Rodensky notes that "disagreement there was, particularly around questions pertaining to criminal states of mind and to the relations between states of mind and acts."[9] As Leps and others have explained, the desire to ascertain the "criminal state of mind" contributed to the rise of criminology in the late nineteenth century, represented by such figures as Italian psychiatrist Cesare Lombroso and Alexandre Lacassagne, doctor of forensic medicine,[10] figures who certainly disagreed on the extent to which criminality was either innate or socially constructed.

---

[6]   Marie-Christine Leps, *Apprehending the Criminal*, 18.

[7]   Ibid.

[8]   Ibid.

[9]   Lisa Rodensky, *The Crime in Mind: Criminal Responsibility and the Victorian Novel* (Oxford: Oxford University Press, 2003), 3.

[10]   Leps, 32–3.

But it was the juvenile delinquent, I argue, that most clearly exemplified the problematic nature of criminal responsibility and of criminality itself. Child criminals "formed a large portion of the criminal class in England in the first half of the nineteenth century,"[11] and this fact alone challenged fledgling constructions of the child as innately innocent. Even as early as 1828, child criminality was attributed "not merely to unemployment and distress but to the collapse of family discipline under the impact of economic stress,"[12] and while the focus on "unemployment and distress" suggests a social cause for the crimes, the stress upon a lack of "discipline" nevertheless indicates a bad tendency within the children themselves that is only exacerbated and allowed because of poor social conditions and inadequate parenting.

It is well known that children did not receive special privileges under the law in the early part of the nineteenth century,[13] and in fact, were even sentenced to the harshest punishment the law allowed:

> In 1800 when a boy of ten was sentenced to death the judge refused to respite the sentence, because of 'the infinite danger of it getting about that a child might commit such a crime with impunity,' and many judges of the day still really believed that this was a danger. In 1801 a boy of thirteen was hanged for breaking into a house and stealing a spoon; two sisters aged eight and eleven were hanged at Lynn in 1808; in 1831 a boy of nine was hanged at Chelmsford for setting fire to a house and in 1833 another nine year old was sentenced to death at the Old Bailey for pushing a stick through a cracked shop window and taking twopennyworth of printer's colour.[14]

By mid-century, however, "a new system to cope with juveniles had started to evolve."[15] This movement to judge children differently than adults sought to distinguish between child criminals according to the extent to which some juvenile delinquents were "hardened" and some were "salvageable." As Shore notes, "the degree to which a child was 'hardened' dictated his or her responsiveness

---

[11]   Jeannie Duckworth, *Fagin's Children: Criminal Children in Victorian England* (London and New York: Hambledon and London, 2002), 5.

[12]   Ibid., 10–11.

[13]   With the exception of children under the age of seven; between 7 and 14, if they were held to be *doli incapax* (lacking in understanding and judgment) they also could not be hanged (Uwe Böker, "Childhood and Juvenile Delinquency in Eighteenth-Century *Newgate Calendars*," in *Fashioning Childhood in the Eighteenth Century: Age and Identity* [Burlington, VT: Ashgate, 2006], 135. However, for the most part, prior to 1847, "Children were generally sentenced to the same retributive punishment as adults, grade by statute and judicial precedence according to the magnitude of the offence. Age by itself gave no right to special treatment and children were tried with the full publicity and formality of judge and jury or magistrate" (Duckworth, 50).

[14]   Ibid., 40.

[15]   Shore, 2.

to, or eligibility for, reformation."[16] Though I agree with Shore that "Criminal responsibility rested less on age or gender than on this conflict between innocence and experience," I would argue that the very presence of "innocence and experience" as key elements in a child's reformation speaks to the extent to which narratives *about* childhood set the terms of the debate, even while some children, based on their "experience," were denied the designation of childhood itself.

Charles Dickens's *Oliver Twist* is an important text in the construction of the child criminal in the early nineteenth century, and provides an excellent example of the distinction between childhood innocence and childhood responsibility and experience. Oliver, neglected and abused, finds himself caught up in the criminal underworld of pick-pocketing and robbing, lured by the Artful Dodger into Fagin's gang of child criminals. Throughout the novel, Oliver is presented as essentially innocent and good, and his immersion into criminal life is as much about the threat it poses to that childhood innocence as it is about the actual dangers he faces within it. Oliver should be, given the life he leads in the early part of the novel, well on his way to being "fallen," for "As far as the world is concerned, Oliver has no identity other than the one imposed on him by external circumstances: he is illegitimate, illiterate, and impoverished, just another 'item of mortality,' a member of the vast Victorian underclass of the disenfranchised and marginalized."[17] Yet despite his harsh upbringing, Oliver is unstained—one has only to look upon his face to see the "truth of infancy" written upon it: "the old gentleman looked somewhat sternly in Oliver's face. It was impossible to doubt him; there was truth in every one of its thin and sharpened lineaments."[18]

This innate goodness is deeply seated within Oliver, making him impervious to Fagin's assaults upon his innocence, despite his work to corrupt Oliver as he has corrupted other children before him. Leaving Oliver with *The Newgate Calendar* to read, Fagin obviously hopes to inspire his young charge with the lives of criminals, much as critics of the time felt publications of this type corrupted the minds of their readers.[19] The book, however, has the opposite effect upon Oliver: "In a paroxysm of fear the boy closed the book and thrust it from him. Then falling upon his knees, he prayed Heaven to spare him from such deeds, and rather to will that he should die at once, than be reserved for crimes so fearful and appalling."[20] Oliver's countenance is not a counterfeit, for the purity that the paternal and charitable Mr. Brownlow sees there is a true record of Oliver's soul and conscience. Oliver is as incapable of committing crimes as he is of guile, and even though he is instructed in crime in such a way that he perceives it as an

[16] Ibid., 3.
[17] Goldie Morgentaler, *Dickens and Heredity: When Like Begets Like* (London: Macmillan, 2000), 37.
[18] Charles Dickens, *Oliver Twist* (London: Penguin Books, 2002), 93.
[19] See p. xxx of Philip Horne's "Introduction" in *Oliver Twist*.
[20] Ibid., 164.

amusing game,[21] yet in the actual commission of it, his conscience does not fail him: "In one instant the whole mystery of the handkerchiefs, and the watches, and the jewels, and the Jew, rushed upon the boy's mind. He stood for a moment with the blood tingling so through all his veins from terror, that he felt as if he were in a burning fire...."[22] In Oliver's particular case, it is evident that upbringing and training alone do not a criminal make.

Other characters in the novel, of course, make the argument for upbringing and environment as causes of delinquency and crime, particularly the tragic Nancy, who blames her life as a prostitute upon Fagin: "I thieved for you when I was a child not half as old as this (pointing to Oliver). I have been in the same trade, and in the same service, for twelve years since; don't you know it? ... It is my living, and the cold, wet, dirty streets are my home; and you're the wretch that drove me to them long ago ...."[23] Nancy's claim that Fagin "drove" her to the life she leads assigns criminal responsibility at least partially to him, yet Oliver's own ability to refuse to participate in crimes suggests that even as a child Nancy herself must have had some agency. But Oliver's very rejection of criminal life remains a problem in the text, because it cannot merely be an innate childhood goodness that sustains him, as other children are shown to fall where he does not.

The obvious answer to the anomaly that is Oliver is, of course, that he is "well-born," and though he is illegitimate, he nevertheless sustains a native virtue that is the result of heredity. As Goldie Morgentaler notes,

> The Victorians assumed that such matters as the state of mind of the parents and the degree of their affection for one another at the time of conception had a bearing on the personality of the engendered child. The fact that Oliver's parents loved each other makes their son a love child in the full sense of the word, with the result that, shielded by the grace of his heredity, Oliver emerges from the near-starvation and brutalization of the workhouse, from the miserliness and mistreatment of his employers, and from the company of thieves, prostitutes and murderers, unscathed and unscarred.

But if Oliver's innate goodness is the result of heredity, it is nevertheless also inherently classed, for "What Oliver inherits from his parents is more than just their moral essence, it is their moral essence as defined by their social class. Virtue in *Oliver Twist* is a middle-class characteristic, bound up with such traits as respectability, honesty, hard work, personal honor and a good command of English."[24] In the end, Oliver's story "will entitle him to what his Standard English already anticipates, a full integration into middle-class respectability."[25]

---

[21]   Ibid., 71.

[22]   Ibid., 76.

[23]   Ibid., 133.

[24]   Morgentaler, 39.

[25]   D. A. Miller, *The Novel and the Police* (Berkeley: University of California Press, 1988), 9.

Though it is in part his heredity and his class that safeguard young Oliver, rather than simply his youth, it is clear from those children who are not as lucky as him that constructions of childhood do play a central role in the text. The quintessential "hardened" child who can neither be saved nor rehabilitated is, of course, the Artful Dodger. From the moment of his introduction, the Dodger clearly represents a child who is not a child:

> The boy who addressed this inquiry to the young wayfarer was about his own age, but one of the queerest-looking boys that Oliver had ever seen. He was a snub-nosed, flat-browed, common-faced boy enough, and as dirty a juvenile as one would wish to see; but he had got about him all the airs and manners of a man .... He wore a man's coat, which reached nearly to his heels .... He was altogether as roistering and swaggering a young gentleman as ever stood three feet six, or something less, in his bluchers.[26]

This description of the Dodger carefully indicates his youth, from the detail that he is the same age as Oliver, to the "man's coat" which swathes his young figure. The Dodger is not so much adult as *playing* adult, and such play is both what makes him an essentially charming figure, despite his delinquency, and what marks him off as inherently fallen, for the Dodger's adult-like characteristics go beyond clothing and "manners" to a decided independence of spirit that sets him apart from the essentially helpless and dependent Oliver. When Oliver expresses a wish to be released by Fagin, the Dodger exclaims, "'Go!' ... 'Why, where's your spirit? Don't you take any pride out of yourself? Would you go and be dependent on your friends, eh?'"[27] The Dodger's words ironically reflect a disdain for those who "cadge" off others, rather than attain the very middle-class aim of, as Charley Bates describes, being able "to retire on your property, and do the genteel...."[28] The problem is, of course, that while the trajectory the boys map out for themselves is an emulation of proper society, the "work" they do is a direct affront to it. Furthermore, because they are still, despite their actions and their aims, children, such independence of spirit makes them problematic figures of social concern.

This is not to say that the Dodger's independence is essentially un-child-like, for though a child, he is also a boy (unlike the extremely feminized Oliver), and his spirited defense of himself at his trial is, though foolhardy, yet still in its way attractive: "'I'm an Englishman, an't I?' rejoined the Dodger. 'Where are my priwileges? .... 'Now then, wot is this here business?—I shall thank the madg'strates to dispose of this here little affair, and not to keep me while they read the paper, for I've got an appointment with a genelman in the city ....'"[29] The Dodger's trial is meant to be comical, in the same way that a child playing

---

[26]   Dickens, *Oliver Twist*, 60.
[27]   Ibid., 149.
[28]   Ibid.
[29]   Ibid., 367.

an adult elicits laughs from an adult audience. But though played for laughs, the moment is essentially tragic—a child in an adult world, the Dodger has no real means of representing himself, and is sentenced to the very adult punishment of transportation. His play-acting, because it carries over into actions, and thoughts, and feeling, has essentially made the Dodger—in the eyes of the court—an adult, entirely separate from Oliver who is unable to leave his own "childishness" behind: "There was a still greater obstacle in Oliver's youth and childishness. He only cried bitterly all day; and when the long, dismal night came on, he spread his little hands before his eyes to shut out the darkness, and crouching in the corner, tried to sleep ...."[30] Oliver cannot, and the text makes clear, *should not*, leave behind the "obstacle" of his childishness, as it is that which makes him an object of sympathy and compassion to the right-minded Mr. Brownlow and Rose Maylie.

In the end, though *Oliver Twist* demonstrates that not all children are alike, and that not all children can be saved to childish dependence, it also implicitly argues the virtues and attractions of one particular kind of child. That is, while Oliver is saved because of a nature that is hereditary and a character that is essentially middle class, his nature and character are nevertheless representative of the *ideal* childhood. Not having those characteristics, the Artful Dodger is not simply lower class; he is also not easily a child. And what is significant about representations of children throughout the nineteenth century is that the kind of classed child Oliver represents comes to be constructed as the kind of child *every* child should be. Therefore, though Shore is right that questions of innocence versus experience structure discussions surrounding the child far more than simple questions of age or youth, yet narratives of childhood itself are key elements in the debate surrounding juvenile delinquency, so much so that the child criminal comes to be represented as a figure that should be separated and distinguished from the adult criminal.

Special Measures for the Child Criminal

From the 1830s on, England saw changes in the way that child criminals were dealt with by the legal system. In part, such changes speak to an overall shift in the way that crime and criminality were perceived; in the early eighteenth century, criminality was believed to be innate, a moral flaw in the individual: "From the point of view of the industrious middle sections of society, deviant individuals, irrespective of gender, were accused of self-induced intemperance and lack of moral restraint, of diverging from the path of religion and what their parents had told them to follow."[31] But "from the 1780s onward a change took place, and it involved the construction of the concept of juvenile delinquency and an

---

[30]   Ibid., 17–18.
[31]   Böker, "Childhood and Juvenile Delinquency in Eighteenth-Century *Newgate Calendars*," 139.

emphasis on the guardians' responsibility."[32] Such a shift forecast the growth of environmentalism as a perceived cause of social deviancy, a belief that especially took hold in the early to mid-nineteenth century, in which "The distribution of 'health and virtue' was said to depend on the influences of the physical and moral environment."[33] The combination of an emergent construction of the child, with the development of constructions of criminality that focused on the extent to which young criminals were shaped, rather than born, led to the rise of the "juvenile delinquent" as a distinct kind of criminal. While it would be easy to read the emergence of this figure as evidence of a growing compassion towards children, Behlmer argues that this "unproblematic reading of legal history" fails to take into account the extent to which fears of the working-class home inspired legal reforms:

> The logic for criminologists, as it had been for the advocates of district visiting, seemed self-evident. Since the urban working-class home had been allowed to turn increasingly violent, and since children were 'copyists' whose habits formed through imitating those around them, the next generation of city-bred poor would grow up still more brutal. Somehow this cycle of savagery had to be broken.[34]

Furthermore, the emergence of the juvenile delinquent also coincided with fears about the perceived increase of youth crime. Whether or not youth crime actually increased in the early nineteenth century, it can be said that "the growth of a new set of discourses about juvenile delinquency and its 'alarming increase' in the 1810s, which was rooted in the interactions between broader social anxieties, penal reform, changing attitudes to childhood and the growing urge to discipline the poor, had a vital impact on the number of juveniles indicted for felony," if the "incredibly rapid rises in the proportion of indicted offenders who were juveniles that occurred in London and Manchester in the 1810s"[35] are any indication.

According to Jeannie Duckworth, the ideas of "social reformers, like Mary Carpenter and James Greenwood ... on saving children from vice and a life enmeshed in crime struck a responsive chord in the Victorian consciousness."[36] Because the primary fear surrounding child criminals was that they would become "hardened," the practice of housing children with adult criminals was a great concern as it was

---

[32]   Ibid., 141.

[33]   Felix Driver, "Moral Geographies: Social Science and the Urban Environment in Mid-Nineteenth Century England," *Transactions of the Institute of British Geographers* 13, no. 3 (1988), 277.

[34]   Behlmer, *Friends of the Family: The English Home and its Guardians, 1850–1940* (Stanford University Press, Stanford, 1998), 233, 234.

[35]   Peter King, "The Rise of Juvenile Delinquency in England 1780–1840: Changing Patterns of Perception and Prosecution," *Past and Present* 160 (August 1998), 161.

[36]   Duckworth, *Fagin's Children*, 135.

believed to exacerbate this problem: as a case from Mary Carpenter's *Reformatory Schools for the Children of the Perishing and Dangerous Classes* (1851) records, "Of the 24 boys who were in prison during 1850, 12 have become *decidedly more hardened and reckless* since their imprisonment."[37] Carpenter relates one case in particular in which the child's history is presented as ample evidence of the extent to which the English justice system itself has worked to corrupt the child. Starting from his first imprisonment at the age of seven for begging, the child moves on to larger crimes, encountering only a smattering of education while within the prison system. After his sixth imprisonment "for stealing a cocoa-nut" the boy is "induced to go into the Ragged Industrial School ... *but the School authorities having no legal right to keep the lad against his will*, being either tempted by others, or impatient of control, or the vagrant life having taken too deep a hold of his mind."[38] Like the Artful Dodger, this child's independence contributes to both his endangerment and his criminality, as his ninth committal, for felony, makes clear: "*His prison life has made him bold and insolent*. He bounds into the dock, casts his eyes round the Court, and with a nod places his head erect, and says 'Not Guilty!' With a knowing look he asks with insolent pride of the witnesses one or two questions."[39] The child's precocity, his pride, and his "insolence" are as much indications of his fallenness as are the records of his crimes, but for Carpenter, they are the results not just of his life of crime, but also of English society's supposed solution to them.

Reformatory schools for juvenile delinquents were proposed as a better solution than imprisonment to the problem of child crime. Asylums and homes for child criminals had been in place since the 1790s,[40] but it was in the 1830s that they began to take hold as the primary means of dealing with delinquents, a part of what Hugh Cunningham identifies as "an intensified phase of institution building, catering for children of all kinds thought to be in need."[41] Mary Carpenter was a key figure in the reformatory movement. After founding a Ragged School in Bristol in 1846, Carpenter's "day-to-day experience in the slums turned her attention to government blue books and the law, and like other reformers of her generation

---

[37]   Carpenter, *Reformatory Schools for the Children of the Perishing and Dangerous Classes* (New York: Augustus M. Kelley Publishers, 1969), 273, italics in original.

[38]   Ibid., 278, italics in original.

[39]   Ibid.

[40]   Duckworth mentions "the asylum in the village of Stretton-on-Dunsmore," established in 1818 (143), but notes that it "was not the first institution of its kind. That honour goes to the refuge of the Philanthropic Society founded in 1790 for children of criminals who had been hanged or transported"; the same society founded "an establishment in St George's Fields, Southwark" in the early nineteenth century that had "a 'place' for very criminal boys" (144). She also mentions the Children's Friend Society, founded in 1830 (147), and Elizabeth Fry's "asylum for criminal girls," founded in 1825 (150).

[41]   Hugh Cunningham, *Children and Childhood in Western Society since 1500* (Harlow, Essex: Pearson Education Limited, 1995), 146.

she began to compile data on social conditions."[42] According to Frank Prochaska, "As a humanitarian Carpenter took exception to the harshness of the penalties applied to children .... In her opinion, unusual at the time, a child in trouble was still a child and must be treated as such."[43] She brought such attitudes to her testimony for a Commons Select Committee in 1852, at which she argued that "she considered 'the nature of the child, *as a child*,'" further declaring, "I would in the case of the child merely refer to the spirit of the English law, that a child should be *treated as a child*."[44] Hugh Cunningham notes that Mary Carpenter's agenda goes one step further, however; rather than seeing it as one in which the juvenile delinquent is simply recognized "as a child," he argues that her solution was that "the delinquent 'has to be turned again into a child.'"[45] The distinction is important, working as it does within Shore's caveat that special measures for child criminals were motivated not by age alone, but by issues of innocence and experience. The juvenile delinquent does not deserve special treatment, in Carpenter's works, simply because of its tender years, but because it may (or may not) be *restored* to childhood: to a condition that is about the child conforming to increasingly dominant constructions of what a child should be. Cunningham notes that "This was not simply sentimentalism .... It was also the outcome of an internalization of the romantic belief that the enjoyment of a proper childhood was the only foundation for a tolerable adult life. And that childhood must be one of dependence and protection within the bounds of family, or a substitute family."[46] The juvenile delinquent, that is, had to be transformed from the Dodger into Oliver.

In her influential *Reformatory Schools for the Children of the Perishing and Dangerous Classes*, Carpenter works within the "humanitarian narrative," for, insofar as that narrative operates by making "bodies the common ground of humanitarian sensibility and explicat[ing] their human suffering,"[47] Carpenter uses the body of the juvenile delinquent, rendered as a type that stands in for the whole, in order to recreate the criminal child as suffering subject, rather than simply dangerous other. Carpenter notes that

> the external aspect of these poor children is calculated to excite compassion
> in any heart not rendered callous by absorption in the world's selfish interests;
> — their tattered garments, their bare feet, their starved look, their mean and

---

[42]   Frank Prochaska, "Mary Carpenter," *Oxford Dictionary of National Biography*.

[43]   Ibid.

[44]   Qtd. in John Springhall, *Coming of Age: Adolescence in Britain, 1860–1960* (Dublin: Gill and Macmillan, 1986), 164.

[45]   Cunningham, *Children and Childhood*, 146.

[46]   Ibid.

[47]   Thomas Laqueur, "Bodies, Details, and the Humanitarian Narrative," 182.

degraded aspect … must touch even those who regard them only as young beings, susceptible as our own children of privation and suffering.[48]

Laura Berry asserts that the child in the nineteenth century "homogenized" the community because, as Berry notes, "everyone can lay claim to membership, at least for a time, in the community of children,"[49] and thus, Carpenter's juvenile delinquents can be seen to elicit sympathy because they work to remind her readers of the child they once were. However, Carpenter's children are also explicitly linked to the proper middle-class child—the ideal child who is, presumably, cared for and loved. Just like that ideal child, Carpenter attests, this child is "susceptible" to "privation and suffering," and its juxtaposition with what it should be—much "as our own children"—with what it is—ragged and "starved"—lends weight to her argument that the juvenile delinquent must be separated from the adult criminal. That is, the juvenile delinquent's "mean and degraded aspect" should call for amelioration, rather than punishment, because of the potential the criminal child represents.

More importantly, however, there is another possibility for this child. Children such as this can be saved to a life of proper, cared-for childhood, or they can be left as is, taking part as "future actors in the world's theatre, destined to increase the vast amount of evil now existing if their course is not arrested."[50] Carpenter's narrative here works within what Harry Hendrick identifies as one of the defining dualisms of child welfare, that of endangered children as either "victims or threats": "The child victim was nearly always seen as harbouring the possibility of another condition, one that was sensed to be threatening to moral fibre, sexual propriety, the sanctity of the family, the preservation of the race, law and order, and the wider reaches of citizenship."[51] Carpenter's narratives of juvenile delinquents do not so much, therefore, leave behind earlier constructions of them as dangers to the social body, as they work to incorporate those residual narratives into ones that support the reformation, rather than simply the punishment, of the child criminal. She further supports this agenda by reminding her readers that the child is not simply a body, but also an immortal soul in need of salvation: "the painful external aspect loses its horrors in comparison with the infinitely greater dangers which attack the immortal spirits of these young creatures."[52] The body of the child, therefore, takes on significance not simply as the means of connection between the reader and the object of pity, but as a signifier of the "immortal spirit" that resides within. Focusing on the body and spirit of the child, as well as the cost the fallen child

48   Carpenter, *Reformatory Schools*, 58.
49   Laura Berry, *The Child, the State, and the Victorian Novel*, 4.
50   Ibid.
51   Harry Hendrick, *Child Welfare: Historical Dimenstions, Cotemporary Debate* (Bristol: The Policy Press, 2003), 7.
52   Carpenter, *Reformatory Schools*, 59.

represents to society, Carpenter makes the care of this child a humanitarian, social, financial, and divine injunction.

All criminal children are not, however, alike, and as with many of her contemporaries, Carpenter utilized systems of classification to distinguish between "'good' boys, who had fallen into trouble as a result of external factors, such as peer pressure, or simply temptation; and 'bad boys,' who were seen as confirmed, and 'hardened' delinquents."[53] Such rhetoric was not separate from divisions used for the poor in general, as Carpenter "was enunciating a two-tiered model of 'perishing' and 'dangerous' juveniles, again echoing the rhetoric of provision for the 'deserving' and 'undeserving' poor."[54] In her *Juvenile Delinquents: Their Condition and Treatment* (1853), Carpenter claims that the term "juvenile delinquent" "is an anomaly, and should startle us as something monstrous and fearful; something which should lead us to think, 'How can this be? And if it be so, what can each one of us do to remove so dreadful an evil?' For we are speaking of children ...."[55] Yet though she relies on the assumption that children are something inherently other than "monstrous," "fearful," and "evil," and that it is an "anomaly" for a child to be otherwise, her text also makes clear that not all children are equally worthy. Interestingly enough, in Carpenter's text it is sometimes the child's clothing that works to separate the dangerous from the merely fallen. Rather than simply classifying the delinquents according to crimes committed, Carpenter also focuses on the extent to which some "classes" of juveniles possess the ability to pass in society. She observes that

> many fine open-looking boys who really belong to the felon class, as the law now stands, would pass without suspicion, while many half-starved creatures, who would naturally be placed in it by most, may prove to have committed no greater offence than seeking, in ways which to their view were quite innocent, to obtain their daily bread by mendicancy.[56]

Both groups of children are guilty of crimes, but Carpenter distinguishes between those who pass, and are guilty of what she labels as "fraud," and those whose ragged attire and starved appearance would seem to suggest their actual innocence: though *technically* guilty of the crime of begging, these children, she asserts, do not recognize or understand it as a crime.

By contrast, those children engaged in thievery, pickpocketing, and coining are "more dangerous" because "often less distinguishable by their external appearance and manner."[57] Focusing on one "well-dressed youth," Carpenter

---

[53]   Shore, *Artful Dodgers*, 6.

[54]   Ibid., 7.

[55]   Carpenter, *Juvenile Delinquents: Their Condition and Treatment* (Patterson Smith: Montclair, 1970), 15.

[56]   Ibid., 20.

[57]   Ibid., 24.

refers to the "class" as a whole as "not unfrequently" having "the semblance of young gentlemen."[58] In this case, the clothing of the child stands in for the crime he is committing: fraudulent in aspect, he is fraudulent in behavior, and his fine attire bespeaks a desire for easy work and a dislike of "an honest livelihood" more befitting one of his class.[59] Such children, Carpenter attests, are "likely to become even more injurious to society ... because practising dishonesty in a way which can be less guarded against."[60] Their ability to pass, in other words, is both the tool of their trade and the sign of their crime: their transgression of class and social boundaries is achieved through their transgression of legal ones. Unlike "A.," who, Carpenter attests, has crime "written on his countenance," and whose "miserable, ragged, barefooted aspect shows that he is not reaping ... the reward of his iniquity,"[61] pickpockets conceal their fraudulence behind a finery they have not earned the right to wear, and which must, as a result, be nothing more than a deceptive costume.

Carpenter's use of the children's fraudulent outward aspect signifies that, while she asserts an essential childhood to which all children have a right, she also operates firmly within classed constructions of the children she encounters. Though an idealized childhood remains the model against which these dangerous and perishing children are compared, Carpenter here indicates that respectable poverty, modeled after but not confused with proper middle-classness, is that to which she aims to save these children. Just as the Artful Dodger is dangerous in his precocious challenging of the boundaries between childhood and adulthood, so too these pickpockets and frauds are dangerous, in part, because they blur the lines between the poor and their betters.

But it is in the blurring of these lines that Carpenter herself gains her authority. Carpenter's text is a case study, a genre that, as I have discussed, privileges the authority of the investigator, the expert, and the eyewitness. Carpenter's focus on the ability of the dangerous juvenile delinquent to pass without suspicion makes her reading audience aware of the extent to which they require a trained eye to discern between the classes of criminals, and even between those children who are in fact "young gentleman" and those who only have the "semblance" of them. Carpenter notes that distinguishing between the "two great classes, those who live, or profess to live, under regard to law ... and those who do not," can, in fact, be achieved—but only by some: "There are, indeed, certain outward and visible signs of the inward condition, whereby the two classes are distinctly indicated to the experienced eye."[62] Her eye, of course, is "experienced," and as such, her classifications and suggestions for amelioration are meant to hold great authority to the reading audience.

---

[58] Ibid.
[59] Ibid.
[60] Ibid., 24–5.
[61] Ibid., 22.
[62] Ibid., 1.

There are moments in Carpenter's text, however, where her careful classifications break down, particularly in a narrative she supplies of a boy "doomed almost from infancy to be a convict."[63] The predetermination of the boy's fate springs from, in this case, the horrendous abuse he suffered primarily at the hands of his father, which Carpenter describes as "surpass[ing] any that we have heard of":

> ... the father making his two little boys get out of bed, to come with him to be murdered; his wife standing by, and instead of a word of expostulation at so unnatural a purpose, desiring with a cool selfishness, which manifests a full realization of his intentions, that he would leave the shoes; the unresisting obedience of the poor boys to their unnatural parent, their going with him to death, (what, indeed, was life to them?) the fiendlike man leading his own children to the brink of the canal, and, not even then relenting, throwing the eldest in with violence, as if he were drowning a dog; all this may seem incredible to some, too revolting to human nature to be true.[64]

This narrative is presented as an *extreme* example of abuse—as a horrific incident that is recognized as such not only by Carpenter herself, but also by other characters within the narrative, such as a boatman and the children's neighbors.[65] However, while the story is presented as virtually unique, it also forms a part of Carpenter's case study of the juvenile delinquent, and as such, is presented as "only a solitary instance of the too common domestic condition from which much juvenile crime springs."[66] Carpenter's text works, in other words, by presenting exemplary individuals who stand in for the whole. She acknowledges, in her opening to the text, that the juvenile delinquent itself is an "anomaly,"[67] and stresses the necessity of distinct classifications, because "Juvenile thieves must not ... all be classed together, any more than all those patients who are brought within the walls of the infirmary."[68] As representatives of a sickness that, unchecked, threatens the whole social body, juvenile delinquents must be classified so that their individual "cures" can be ascertained.

Nevertheless, Carpenter's assertion that the child's situation, though it "surpasses" others, is yet "common," speaks to the necessity of these individual cases to serve an illustrative purpose. This child is both "an anomaly" and a commonality, both an extreme case, and simply a "solitary instance." In part, the contradictions inherent in this story and its use as an exemplary case speak to problems in the genre of the case study itself. As Laqueur notes, case studies make use of dominant "social narratives" that give the cases meaning: "they gain power

---

[63] Ibid., 59.

[64] Ibid., 61–2.

[65] Ibid., 60, 63.

[66] Ibid., 63.

[67] Ibid., 15.

[68] Ibid., 20.

precisely because they are repeated in so many different contexts and become ... the means for comprehending the actions of others."[69] For the most part, Carpenter's stories of juvenile delinquents do just this; relying on typical narratives of the progress of the child criminal, the story related in her text of "A Single Captive," for example, works because that progress is so utterly familiar: "The youth went home, got into work, but was thrown out of it by his master's breaking; his parents refused to maintain him; he went marauding expeditions, and fell in with poachers; was taken up, but let off on condition of turning evidence against the others; he proved treacherous in this ...."[70] The narratives within Carpenter's text make sense precisely because they "all present the same features,"[71] and in so doing, provide the means for producing blanket "cures" to the social ills they describe.

As Shore notes, however, such sources as Carpenter's "bend" the child criminals into "the desirable shape": "Sources that record criminals, examine them, question them, are shaped by the agenda of the creator—the social investigator, the prison chaplain, the philanthropist and the magistrate. These authorities present a particular construction of criminality, dependent on time and place...." As a result, "Both statistics and public debates have reduced historical juvenile offenders to a social problem; hence the individuality of children ... is lost in the mire of numbers and rhetoric."[72] At times, however, the individuality of, at least, the children's circumstances do emerge, and while Carpenter attempts to integrate the case of the child thrown into the canal into her larger argument, yet her own rhetoric when describing it makes it stand out. In this particular case, importantly, the uniqueness of the children's circumstances allows Carpenter to gesture to that which is not entirely within the purview of her text: the role that parental abuse plays in the molding of child criminals. It is this story that Carpenter uses to call for child protection beyond that currently existing in England: "society will continue to endure such shameful violation of the laws of nature and abuse of parental authority ... until some undertake the cause of oppressed children."[73] Though not perhaps an exemplary story of a juvenile delinquent, this incident provides an exemplary narrative of child abuse, containing many of the elements—the helplessness of the child, the brutality of the father, the neglect of the mother—that would become common in later NSPCC narratives.

In Carpenter's text, therefore, this case represents somewhat of an anomaly, but its forecasting of later child-protection discourse provides an important bridge between work on behalf of juvenile delinquents and later work on behalf of abused children. The boys in this story do become delinquents, but their past experience also clearly constructs them as victims. As a result, the amelioration their story calls for falls outside of Carpenter's expertise, and outside of the current laws

---

[69]   Laqueur, "Bodies, Details, and the Humanitarian Narrative," 187.

[70]   Carpenter, *Juvenile Delinquents*, 70.

[71]   Ibid., 39.

[72]   Shore, *Artful Dodgers*, 12, 16.

[73]   Carpenter, *Juvenile Delinquents*, 64–5.

of England. Nevertheless, the abused or endangered child and the criminal child are clearly linked, the first always containing the possibility of becoming the other. As Linda Mahood notes,

> The juvenile reformatory experiment first removed convicted children from the adult prison system; the influence of mass industrialization, urbanization and environmentalist philosophy then created another category of child, the child in danger. The focus of this discourse was the large group of orphan, semi-orphan and destitute children who, though not technically law-breakers, shared their characteristics, for example, working-class background, bad housing conditions and poverty. This was a category of children who, through no fault of their own, were seen as being in moral and physical danger of falling into criminal habits.[74]

Clearly, then, the neglected or abused child was not inherently separate from the dangerous child criminal. Yet, as I will argue, their status as delinquents also made them problematic figures of child protection.

Gender and Youth Crime

Another category of child criminal that uneasily straddled the line between victim and threat was the girl criminal. Nowhere else in terms of delinquency, perhaps, did social narratives hold as much power as they did in the gendered construction of child criminality, in which a tacit blindness came into play in the association of boys with thievery and girls with prostitution. Shore notes that "One of the perennial features of all juvenile offending is its overwhelmingly masculine character,"[75] and Carpenter's texts, with their parade of boy thieves, beggars, and coiners, certainly upholds that character. "When females had a strong presence in these narratives," Shore observes, "it was in the standard role of the prostitute or criminal moll."[76] In "'The Boys are Pickpockets, and the Girl is a Prostitute,'" Larry Wolff argues that such binary constructions of child criminals "reveal important aspects of Victorian culture. One discovers, in fact, the same strategic agenda, the same emphatic gendering of prostitution and juvenile crime, in the celebrated social reports of Henry Mayhew and William Acton."[77] Such an agenda, Wolff argues, allows Dickens in *Oliver Twist* to "tame and contain the text's almost explosive sexual and criminal energies, and permit to emerge

---

[74] Linda Mahood, *Policing Gender, Class, and Family: Britain, 1850–1940* (London: UCL Press Limited, 1995), 36.

[75] Shore, 9.

[76] Ibid., 10.

[77] Larry Wolff, "'The Boys are Pickpockets, and the Girl is a Prostitute': Gender and Juvenile Criminality in Early Victorian England from *Oliver Twist* to *London Labour*," *New Literary History* 27.2 (1996), 229.

out of representational chaos and crisis Dicken's most delicately contrived, tautly balanced, and ambivalently inflected ideological contribution to Victorian culture: the innocence of childhood."[78]

Focusing on the ways in which inference and suggestion in the text leave open the possibility for Oliver as both future pickpocket and child prostitute—Nancy's accusations that Fagin has ruined her through a process of criminality that leads, eventually, to prostitution, makes the reader aware, Wolff notes, that Fagin "recruits not only pickpockets, but also prostitutes, and he recruits them as children"[79]— Wolff argues that Dickens's later assertion that "the boys are pickpockets, and the girl is a prostitute," "was essential to an innocent reading of the novel's complex encounters between old gentlemen and young boys."[80] In order to safeguard not simply Oliver's innocence, but also the pure intentions of the male guardians who save him, that is, Dickens had to belatedly attempt to close off the indeterminacy in his text that allowed for a different reading of the threat to Oliver's childhood.

Though Dickens sought to clearly indicate that Mr. Brownlow's attraction to Oliver was entirely innocent in its own right—an attraction to the truth of his infancy, rather than to the beauty or eroticism of the child himself—Seth Koven argues that nineteenth-century philanthropy on behalf of the poor was inherently tied to sexuality and sexual politics: "when elites wrote about slums, they tended to romanticize and eroticize them as sites of spectacular brutality and sexual degradation to which they were compulsively drawn."[81] This was no less true of London's street Arabs, who, as discussed in Chapter 3, held as much fascination for what they could do with their bodies as did the prostitutes with whom they associated (but, as in Mayhew's text, from whom they were carefully differentiated). In his discussions of Dr. Barnardo's famous "before and after" photographs,[82] Koven notes that

---

[78]   Ibid.

[79]   Ibid.

[80]   Ibid., 241.

[81]   Seth Koven, *Slumming: Sexual and Social Politics in Victorian London* (Princeton: Princeton University Press, 2004).

[82]   Dr. Barnardo was one of the premiere child-savers of Victorian England. His homes for children are still in existence today, but he is perhaps best known for his innovative use of "before and after" pictures that purported to record the change in children from when they were first found to their eventual transformation after having been "saved." In 1877, he faced "a sensational mix of charges .... These included misappropriating funds to enrich himself; physically abusing the children he rescued from the streets by cruel punishment and inadequate attention to their religious, dietary, and medical needs; falsely assuming the title of Doctor without completing his qualifying examinations; and engaging in immoral relations with a prostitute. Finally, Barnardo was charged with producing and distributing falsified photographs of his ragged children that purported to show them exactly as he found them but actually depicted them in artificially staged poses" (Seth Koven, *Slumming*, 91). See also Lindsay Smith, "The Shoe-Black to the Crossing Sweeper: Victorian Street Arabs

Rumours about sexual misconduct at Barnardo's institutions may well have encouraged some of his critics to suspect that his images of children were not only deceitful but indecent .... Barnardo's photographs and his graphic images intentionally underscored the raggedness of the children's clothing. Raggedness — ripped and torn clothing which exposed bodies and extremities of children — was not only an effective visual marker of poverty but could also be a disturbingly erotic sign.[83]

In terms of his depictions of ragged girls, Koven argues, this eroticism was deliberate: "The tension between sexual innocence and sexual experience lay at the heart of the urgent appeal he evoked in his images of ragged girls."[84] But in terms of the boy children, such eroticism "was neither explicit nor intentional ... Despite the existence of a lucrative 'rough trade' in boy prostitutes and soldiers in Victorian London, Barnardo never acknowledged that life on the streets posed sexual dangers for boys as well as girls."[85] Lydia Murdoch's readings of images used by Barnardo suggests that this might be an overstatement; she writes that

> Boys as well as girls were described in a state of semi-nakedness, as reformers implied, albeit in more veiled terms, that they too were in danger of sexual exploitation and corruption. The typical male child in need of rescue was a boy 'without shoes or stockings, his nakedness scarcely covered by a few wretched rags.' Homeless and friendless, these children were clearly vulnerable to sexual exploitation on the streets of London.[86]

The proximity and shared labor of Mayhew's boy tumblers and girl prostitutes certainly supports Murdoch's assertion that narratives of sexual danger applied to boys as well as girls, suggesting that the careful and persistent connection of boys to thieving and girls to prostitution represented a deliberately gendered separation of deviancy and criminality, even in the face of "veiled" acknowledgments that such a separation was essentially unstable.

Though I agree with Wolff that part of the veiling of the male child prostitute had to do with safeguarding the male user of such boys, I also believe, following Louise Jackson, that the gendering of child crime was coincident with larger narratives about sexual roles in Victorian society. According to Jackson,

---

and Photography," *Textual Practice* 10.1 (1996), 29–55, and Lydia Murdoch, *Imagined Orphans: Poor Families, Child Welfare, and Contested Citizenship in London.*

[83]   Koven, 118.

[84]   Ibid., 130.

[85]   Ibid., 130, 132.

[86]   Murdoch, *Imagined Orphans: Poor Families, Child Welfare, and Contested Citizenship in London* (Rutgers University Press: New Brunswick, New Jersey, and London, 2006), 20.

The reason for the invisibility of boys (despite police knowledge of a market for adolescent boy prostitutes) lies in the emergence of the issue from the social purity and rescue societies' preoccupation with 'fallen' women and young female prostitutes. A woman's character, unlike a man's, was judged in relation to her sexual reputation.

As a result, "Girls and women could 'fall' but boys could not, according to the Victorian sexual schema."[87] If boys who became criminals were both victims and threats because of their economic cost and danger they represented to society, girls who became prostitutes were both victims of rapacious sexual predators, and, as the Contagious Diseases Acts affirmed, threats to the English social body through the diseases they were believed to carry.[88] Therefore, "The sexually abused girl was seen as a polluting presence, and was a particular danger to other children."[89]

Louise Jackson argues that, in fact, "the term 'juvenile prostitution' had become, by the late Victorian period, yet another euphemism—along with those of 'moral outrage,' 'corruption,' and 'immorality'—to refer to what we now describe as child sexual abuse."[90] Such an elision clearly indicates the extent to which the sexually abused girl was perceived as both criminal and victim simultaneously, a perception that leant weight to the social purity movements of late nineteenth-century England. According to Judith Walkowitz, "This loose network of campaigning groups, populist, feminist, and nationalist in their political zeal, was dedicated to eradicating vice and imposing a single standard of chastity on men and women."[91] Believing that raising the age of consent would go a long way to addressing this issue, such groups campaigned heavily for new laws in parliament. A key figure in this movement was, of course, W. T. Stead, whose pioneering "New Journalism" sought to create "an emotional bond" between himself and a new mixed-class public ...."[92] Given the highly attractive mix of vice, childhood ruin and victimization, and female "purity" (or lack thereof) found in narratives of juvenile prostitution, it is hardly surprising that Stead's "Maiden Tribute of Modern Babylon," which sought to provide lurid details of the "white slave trade" in London, "had an electrifying effect."[93]

Published in his own *Pall Mall Gazette*, Stead's "Maiden Tribute" dramatically enacted the entrapment of juvenile prostitutes through Stead's description of

---

[87]   Louise Jackson, *Child Sexual Abuse in Victorian England*, 5.

[88]   The Contagious Diseases Acts, passed in 1864, 1866, and 1869, sought to control venereal disease through the examination and detention of prostitutes. Due to opposition led by figures such as Josephine Butler, the Acts were repealed in 1886.

[89]   Jackson, 6.

[90]   Ibid., 16.

[91]   Judith R. Walkowitz, *City of Dreadful Delight: Narratives of Sexual Danger in Late-Victorian London* (Chicago: University of Chicago Press, 1992), 82.

[92]   Ibid.

[93]   Ibid., 81.

his own "purchase" of a young girl. Aimed as it was at supporting the Criminal Amendment Act raising the age of sexual consent, the "Maiden Tribute" sought to make sexually abused girls and child prostitutes visible *as* children, and as such, deserving of the protection of the law. Echoing in part the rhetoric of child-labor activists such as Elizabeth Barrett Browning, Stead claimed that young girls were victims of the rich, and that their own youth and helplessness made them ill-equipped to protect themselves:

> I do ask that those doomed to the house of evil fame shall not be trapped into it unwillingly, and that none shall be beguiled into the chamber of death before they are of an age to read the inscription above the portal—"All hope abandon ye who enter here."—If the daughters of the people must be served up as dainty morsels to minister to the passions of the rich, let them at least attain an age when they can understand the nature of the sacrifice which they are asked to make.[94]

Stead's language here makes the implicit connection between sexual knowledge and the "death" of childhood innocence very clear: these girls are "sacrificed" in a "chamber of death," wherein their loss of virginity is equal to the death of their childhood. He is clear, however, that this fall is orchestrated, rather than chosen, as the girls are "beguiled," and "trapped," all "unwillingly." This is not to say, however, that he does not acknowledge the possibility of choice for young girls, for he proclaims, "let us at least see to it that they assent to their own immolation, and are not unwilling sacrifices procured by force and fraud."[95] As in Carpenter's text, and in Dickens's, for that matter, there are two types of children present in Stead's text: those that are innocent, yet trapped and defiled through the actions of others, and those that choose their "own immolation."

But are those who choose their vices actually children? Much as the Artful Dodger is set apart from Oliver by his adult manners and clothing, so too are young girls in Stead's text differentiated by the extent to which they perform child-like innocence. In his description of his encounter with two young girls, Stead is careful, like commentators before him, to distinguish between the innocent and the "hardened":

> But at one villa in the north of London I found through the assistance of a friend a lovely child between fourteen and fifteen, tall for her age, but singularly attractive in her childish innocence .... There was another girl in the house — a brazen-faced harlot, whose flaunting vice served as a foil to set off the childlike, spirituelle beauty of the other baby's face. It was cruel to see the poor wee

---

[94]   W. T. Stead, "The Maiden Tribute of Modern Babylon I: The Report of Our Secret Commission," *The Pall Mall Gazette* (July 6, 1885), 9.

[95]   Ibid.

features, not much larger than those of a doll, of the delicately nurtured girl …. It seemed a profanation to touch her, she was so young and baby-like.[96]

These are both "girls," but only one actually possesses the right, according to Stead's discourse, to be called a child. Interestingly enough, it is the contrast between the two that makes the "childish innocence" of the one visible: rather than comparing her to an adult, that is, Stead compares one child to another in order to ascertain which one is *actually* a child. Such a distinction makes clear that childishness and innocence are not synonymous with age, but are instead markers of both a supposedly innate quality— suggested by the girl's "spirituelle beauty"— and a proper upbringing, as he is careful to point out that she has been "delicately nurtured." Stead's combination of both the innate and the cultivated speaks to the constant contradiction present in narratives of childhood innocence that seek both to assert its naturalness and to recognize its fragility. Furthermore, in his description of young children who "although they have not technically fallen, are little better than animals possessed by an unclean spirit, for the law of heredity is as terribly true in the brothel as elsewhere,"[97] Stead clearly operates within narratives of delinquency that elide some of the endangered with the already fallen.

As much as Stead claims that it seems "a profanation to touch" the child-like girl, however, his own language clearly identifies her as the attractive one, even "singularly attractive." In so doing, Stead makes clear the reason behind the traffic in young girls he critiques as a "monstrous evil."[98] As Walkowitz notes, "The 'Maiden Tribute' set into motion a movement to repress the obscene, yet it incorporated the entire repertoire of late-nineteenth-century pornography."[99] A major criticism he faced, then,[100] was that in publicizing the sex trade in London, he also proliferated narratives of sexual danger and defilement: "for a mere penny he had put into circulation lurid images and narratives that were usually restricted to readers of three-guinea volumes."[101] But Stead's discourse reveals that it is not just the lurid that is sexually exciting, but also the chaste and the innocent. His invocation of "profanity" in terms of defiling this innocence seeks to create the proper subjective reaction to this girl-child, but the very weight of his claims—that the "veritable slave trade" of girls in London is a "magnitude of misery"[102]—

---

[96]   Stead, "The Maiden Tribute of Modern Babylon III: The Report of our Secret Commission," *The Pall Mall Gazette* (Wednesday, July 8, 1885), 31.

[97]   Ibid., 30.

[98]   Stead, "We bid you be of hope," *The Pall Mall Gazette* (July 6, 1885), 7

[99]   Walkowitz, *City of Dreadful Delight*, 122.

[100]   Aside from, of course, the *primary* criticism he faced, which was that he had behaved unlawfully in his decision to purchase a girl, something Stead had done in order to prove it *could* be done. For more details on the charges laid against him, on his trial, and on his imprisonment, see Walkowitz.

[101]   Walkowitz, 124.

[102]   Stead, "We bid you be of hope," 7.

suggests that the attraction to youthful innocence, though constructed as evil and perverse, is nevertheless not uncommon. The girl's innocence here represents something always at risk of being lost, requiring the kinds of laws and restrictions Stead wishes to see put in place. As James R. Kincaid notes,

> These well-meaning (maybe) protectors often adopt the line that the innocence needing protection is so feeble and is beset by forces so numerous and wily that any measures are justified, including putting innocence into protective custody or solitary confinement. Innocence is always seen as being defiled, slipping away, not what it used to be.[103]

Kincaid's tone is deliberately cheeky, but his point is well-made—namely, that childish innocence is, in part, attractive because it allows the adult protector to claim some right of control over that child. This particular attraction is not entirely separate, I would argue, from the kind of sexual attraction Stead attacks; instead, as with Mr. Brownlow and his attraction to little Oliver Twist, the protective mode allows for an "appropriate" response to the threat represented by an always eroticized child innocence. The "singularly attractive" young girl-child must be protected from becoming the "brazen-faced harlot," but such protection also safeguards and sanctifies the adult interest and investment in her "spirituelle beauty."

As with Dickens and Mr. Brownlow, Stead's text seeks to carefully construct the difference between the right-minded adult male who seeks to protect young girls and the predatory "minotaur" who seeks to defile them, yet his own role as both protector and purchaser clearly blurs those distinctions. This blurring is the result, in part, of the actual eroticization of the innocent, helpless child, and the London SPCC, though linked to the social purity campaign, sought to carefully distance the sexualized child from the victimized child. Certainly, Benjamin Waugh and the Society were involved in the campaign to raise the age of consent, and Stead's article makes specific mention of "our excellent Society for the Protection of Children" in his recounting of the rape of a five-year-old girl.[104] Despite such clear connections, and Waugh's own personal relationship with Stead and his support of him through the scandal that followed the "Maiden Tribute," yet the Society carefully chose to reconstruct the issue away from questions of sexuality. Waugh explained that "the society viewed indecent assaults on the young 'not as a question of morality, but [as a question] of protecting weak and little children.'"[105] Such a stance protected the Society from accusations of invasions into the private lives and morality of English citizens, but it also worked to differentiate the abused child from the criminal and the prostitute.

---

[103] Kincaid, *Child-Loving*, 73.

[104] Stead, "The Maiden Tribute of Modern Babylon III: The Ruin of the Very Young," 30.

[105] Behlmer, *Child Abuse and Moral Reform*, 76.

Child Protection and Child Criminality

The connections Carpenter makes between childhood suffering and childhood crime, and that Stead makes between child sexual abuse and prostitution, clearly indicate the overlap that existed between discussions of juvenile delinquency and of cruelty to children. For the most part, such overlaps speak to the perception that parents, rather than the children themselves, were more responsible for the criminality of their children; as early as 1816, a study paid "close attention" to "the role of parental neglect in fostering criminal behaviour among children."[106] It is not surprising, then, that in the public debates surrounding the proposed "Children's Charter" in the late 1880s linkages were made between juvenile delinquents and other endangered children. Behlmer records that in 1888,

> An Alfred Mager of Manchester called for a new Shaftesbury to wage a parliamentary war on the 'selfish *laissez-faire*" theory of parental power. Ultimately, Mager admitted, an evil of the magnitude and complexity of child neglect required the intervention of state officials. He envisioned the creation of local tribunals similar to school boards, composed of wise and humane men, to deal with both juvenile delinquency and child abuse.[107]

Certainly, Waugh agreed that juvenile delinquency was, in many ways, a child-protection issue. His book, *The Gaol Cradle, Who Rocks It?* (1873), argued vehemently against the imprisonment of young offenders, and "his proposal for children's courts presupposed state action on a massive scale."[108] The 1854 Reformatory Schools Act "gave power to the court convicting a juvenile offender under sixteen, to sentence him to detention in a reformatory for not less than two or more than five years," but this was "in addition to imprisonment in a gaol for not less than fourteen days."[109] This mandatory 14-day sentence to jail was not done away with until the Reformatory Schools Amendment Act of 1893,[110] and it would be 1908 before the first children's courts were established in England.[111]

Recognizing that juvenile crime might have its roots in the way in which the child was raised did not, however, mean that child criminals had a special place in the Children's Charter. Instead, what the London SPCC aimed to provide was the means of addressing problems in the home presumably before the children within could be damaged beyond repair. As the philanthropist Baroness Burdett-Coutts asserted in her article, "Our Object," in the first issue of *The Child's Guardian*:

---

[106]   Ibid., 9.
[107]   Ibid., 97.
[108]   Ibid., 63.
[109]   William Clarke Hall, *The Queen's Reign for Children*, 95.
[110]   Ibid., 98.
[111]   Behlmer, 221.

> It [the London SPCC] seeks, by speedy succour, to rescue its children from the degradation of mind and body which vice and cruelty inflict on the helpless, and which must — and that in no short space of years — produce a generation of men and women rendered, from the earliest dawn of their existence, incapable of health, honour, chastity, or courage: plague spots which will shrink up the pith and marrow of the country, and drain the life-blood out of a large proportion of the population.[112]

Burdett-Coutts's language here clearly places children within the binary of victims/threats, making an argument similar to Carpenter's, and in fact, similar to the majority of social texts focusing on endangered childhood in the nineteenth century. "Vice and cruelty" are not wrong simply in and of themselves, but also because of the damage they inflict, the marks they leave upon their helpless victims. The humane impulse to halt cruelty, then, is essentially tied to an environmental concern about the social costs of that cruelty to the whole of society.

Importantly, though, Burdett-Coutts does not focus on the "hardened" child that is produced by cruelty, but rather on the "men and women rendered" at some future time, even if it be "no short space of years." By drawing the readers' attention to the adults the children will become, rather than to the perhaps less-than-innocent children they might already be, Burdett-Coutts reserves some space for rescuing those abused and endangered children. This distinction allows her article to construct the suffering child as salvageable, with its innocence and helplessness still intact, a construction very much in keeping with the London SPCC's representation of the abused child. In order to make its rehabilitation *as* a child possible, the abused child had to be shown to have innate goodness, inherent "child-like" qualities that were simply waiting to be discovered and nurtured by those suited for the work. Waugh himself acknowledged that some of the children in the London SPCC's shelter had "been sunk" to a "frightful depth of degradation."[113] However, in answer to the question, "What is the good of it?" he also argued that the conception most people would form about the children rescued by the Society, by "failing to take account of the winning ways, and the obscured but real sensibilities to good found in many of the children," would be incorrect. Waugh here asserts that these children are not lost, are not irretrievable — instead, "They give evidence of local attachment, personal affection, a child-like religious sense, unexpected, and therefore more touching." He goes on to assert that

> In some instances, habits and thoughts of good are awakened, which have long lain dormant — crushed down by cruelty and neglect, following upon some earlier happy stage of life. In other cases it is the budding forth *for the first time* of seeds which were apparently non-existent, but which were, in fact, only

---

[112]   Angela Burdett-Coutts, "Our Object," *The Child's Guardian* 1, no. 1 (January 1887), 5.

[113]   Waugh, "Cui Bono?" *The Child's Guardian* 1, no. 9 (September 1887), 67.

waiting the opportunity — the congenial soil, and the atmosphere — wherein to grow.[114]

While some adults who suffered as children might be hardened, Waugh's language here suggests that no *child* can be wholly so, for the very fact of them being children means some "seeds," some "child-like sense" remains intact. As discussed in Chapter One, however, Waugh makes clear that it requires the special sight of the SPCC to see this potential and the special skills to bring it out, because he argues that even the reader who "thoughtfully and carefully" makes the effort to "imagine the kind of child received into the Shelter" will be "wrong."[115] The bulk of the article is, in fact, on the second topic of the subtitle, "What good can your Society do?" followed only by a short paragraph on the *last* question in the subtitle, "What good can I do?" The only good the reader can do, Waugh asserts, is to, aside from donating money, "further the interests of the Society."[116]

"Furthering the interests of the Society," according to Waugh, meant that all children, in every stage of life and of every background, would receive the benefit of the Society's care and vision. After the passage of the "Children's Charter," Waugh wrote that "Wherever the Crown rules, there, now, the child is protected — in city slums, travelling show, or mountain cottage," because the Act was "for *all* children."[117] Importantly, however, Waugh's description of "*all* children" speaks not to all *types* of children, but to all *ranks* of children. This distinction is important, I assert, because the Society usually only acknowledged one type of child in whose interest they fought: the helpless, the victimized, and the inherently good child. As a result, when speaking of children who committed crimes, the Society paid more attention to those children whose crimes could be seen as evidence of that helplessness. Because the Society asserted that abuse of children was motivated not by the badness of the child, or by any bad acts the child committed, but instead by the perversity of the adult abuser, it had to carefully negotiate those situations in which children themselves were charged with crimes.

Some crimes, such as that of attempted suicide, of course easily lent themselves to the child protection agenda. Waugh argued that "When children attempt suicide … much more ought to be done than to treat the despairing child as a criminal." Relating the story of Lizzie Wilson, who, "In consequence of punishments inflicted by her parents … first threatened to poison herself, and punishment being renewed … carried out her threat by taking some liniment labelled poison," Waugh asks, "All that our law requires is that she be put on her trial for attempting suicide. What of the people who drove her to do so? Should she be the only criminal?"[118]

---

[114]   Ibid.

[115]   Ibid.

[116]   Ibid., 68.

[117]   Waugh, "Prevention of Cruelty to Children," *The Child's Guardian* 3, no. 31 (August 1889), 133.

[118]   Waugh, "Notes," *The Child's Guardian* 2, no. 23 (November 1888), 107.

Though Waugh's language does not absolve Wilson of her own criminality, he does suggest that the responsibility for her actions lies squarely with her parents. In a similar case, a sexually abused girl is turned away by her mother, who "wishing her in her coffin," Waugh suggests, drives the girl to end her own life. Rescued by the society "from Holloway Prison, where she had been sent for trying to drown herself,"[119] the girl in the narrative is transformed from criminal to abused child, a category, Waugh's narrative suggests, she should have been recognized as belonging to in the first place. The choice of the crime here, attempted suicide, matched with both the crime committed against her and the rejection of her own mother, clearly places any and all blame for the situation on the adults. And though Waugh acknowledges that the "wrong of the kind perpetrated on this innocent child can never be redressed," he also claims for her a new life among "friends … who will care for her, and protect her, and guide into safe ways her poor little slipping feet."[120] The reference to the girl's "slipping feet," dramatically recalls her own descent into the river, as well as referencing the inevitable descent into other forms of crimes dominant social narratives predicted for children such as her, had the girl not been rescued by the Society. Far more sinned against than sinning, this girl is relatively easily assimilated into the Society's narratives of suffering and endangered children.

The same did not necessarily hold true for children who were caught begging or were arrested for vagrancy. The Vagrancy Acts of 1824 made it illegal to beg or even to "wander abroad and lodge in barns, tents, the open air, &c, not having any visible means of subsistence and not giving a good account of oneself,"[121] and children who begged in the streets were perceived to be a serious problem throughout the nineteenth century. Again, the NSPCC sought to make the actions of the child in this case, though illegal, yet still the responsibility of the parent, claiming that "the disease, of which child-begging and hawking [was] but merely the symptom,"[122] was in fact a lack of proper parental care and responsibility. The "Children's Charter" therefore sought to impose parental responsibility in begging cases, and where before "it had been the custom to deal with cases of this kind by arresting the child and bringing him before the magistrate," the new law "made it punishable with three months' hard labour for any person to cause or procure any child, being a boy under the age of fourteen years, or being a girl under the age of sixteen years … for the purpose of begging or receiving alms…."[123] Waugh asserted that with the passage of the new law, "The little beggars of the street, guilty under the Vagrant Act, are to be placed in our care …. After now, they will be arrested and charged, and we shall become bail for them." The purpose of this change was to keep the children from the toxic influence of the jail, but also

---

[119]   Waugh, "Changed Children," *The Child's Guardian* 6, no. 9 (September 1892), 118.
[120]   Ibid.
[121]   Qtd. in Behlmer, 200.
[122]   Hall, *The Queen's Reign for Children*, 74.
[123]   Ibid., 78–9.

to allow the Society to discover "whether it is not their parents who are guilty; whether they are starved and assaulted, and to change the charge into one against their parents." He acknowledges that they will still be "her Majesty's prisoners," but his description of them as "pitiable little creatures" works to construct them as victims, rather than threats.[124]

The Society did not necessarily see begging itself as imposed cruelty, but instead focused on cases in which children were abused, and it is in this distinction that the Society's construction of childhood innocence becomes more complicated. Waugh asserted in 1891 that it was not the job of the NSPCC to act as "street scavengers, whose business it is to clear the public ways of beggars, street arabs, and small vendors," but instead that of the police "to deal with these young law breakers."[125] These children deserve the label of criminality, Waugh suggests, because "in very many cases of the sort referred to children are neither the victims of cruelty nor neglect, but are little folks who, having had a good tea to warm them, and who with warm comforter round their neck, [and] a pair of strong boots on their feet ... set off to ply an uninjuring though it may be an illegal trade...."[126] Waugh's labeling of the children as "little folks" immediately separates them from the "pitiable little creatures" forced to beg under threat of violence—these children, it is suggested, "ply" their own "trade," and as such, are not in need of protection. Nevertheless, the stipulations of the "Children's Charter" make their parents liable, suggesting that the law itself, though focused on ending cruelty, was as much about enforcing parental responsibility as it was about protecting children.

And where the children themselves were in need of being schooled, as were, one presumes, these "little folks" with their "illegal trade," the Society was firmly in the camp of parental discipline, even when that discipline included pain. Though the Society virtually without exception constructed the abused child as a creature without fault, it also safeguarded the right of the parent to "correct" the child that went astray. The NSPCC was adamant that it did not seek to interfere with "proper" parental authority, and asserted that "So long as the punishment is for real evil in a child and with a reasonable instrument, and for an endurable time, did we wish it, we have no power to stop it, and had we power we have no will to do so."[127] The Society is not here working within the discourse that the innocent child is truly a child while the violent or criminal child is not, but rather within the equally dominant narrative of the naughty child in need of instruction. Children are capable, Waugh asserts, of having "real evil" within them, and when such evil is made evident, it is the parents' responsibility to "correct evil habits." In fact, "To neglect" to do so is to do harm to the child, for "Much of the happiness of youthful

---

[124]   Waugh, "The Police and Ill-Used Children," *The Child's Guardian* 3, no. 28 (April 1889), 54.

[125]   Waugh, "Children and Street Begging," *The Child's Guardian* 5, no. 12 (December 1891), 130.

[126]   Ibid.

[127]   Waugh, "Punishments," *The Child's Guardian* 6, no. 7 (July 1892), 94.

life, and much of the good character of adult life, is due to the sincere, reluctant, and reasonable infliction of pain for evil."[128] "Pain" and "neglect," the key words of so much of the Society's narratives of cruelty to children, are here reversed in order to support the beating of children for their own good. To "neglect" to give "pain" is to fail as a parent and to take away the child's right to "happiness" through that failure. In relating the case of a mother who wanted to "thrash" her lazy son, and who was threatened by him of being reported to the Society, it is related that she asked, "Now, what I want to know ... is, will you lock me up if I thrash him?" to which the Secretary of the Society replied, "No ... I'll send the officer, if you like, to see it done."[129] Here, the cruelty man of NSPCC discourse becomes the enforcer of the child rather than the protector of the child, and it is the child's own bad nature that makes such a reversal necessary.

In an article entitled, "Rod-pain as educator," the NSPCC made clear its stance on why pain inflicted as a means of discipline was a necessity: "Both the duties and prize of life lie beyond the virtue of youthful obedience. Skin-pain, even where to an unnecessary degree, is as nothing compared with the evils of disrespect and insubordination."[130] Though the earlier article is careful to point out that punishment should be "reasonable," this article asserts that even an "unnecessary degree" of pain is in fact preferable to a child's disobedience. The greatest threat to a child, therefore, is not the cruelty that child might face, but is in fact the child's own bad nature, and the "disobedience" that might result from it. Unsurprisingly, such an attitude carried over into the NSPCC's views on child criminality, in which the Society supported "whipping as an alternative to jail terms for juvenile delinquents."[131] Though such a stance left the Society open to charges of "'cruel, barbarous, and retrogressive' thinking," the belief was that the children were far more endangered associating with adult criminals than they were by suffering "controlled corporal punishment."[132] Again, what such a belief suggests is that the child's own proper and child-like nature—dependent, and even more important, perhaps, obedient—whether protected from the influence of hardened criminals, or enforced with parental and school discipline, was of greater concern than the child's own experience of pain.

In cases of sexual misconduct, the Society could be equally "unsentimental" in its treatment of children and in its refusal to call certain children "victims."[133] In a case in which a boy was charged with "outrageous conduct," the Society also pressed charges against the 13-year-old girl who "incited it," claiming that

---

[128]   Ibid.

[129]   Waugh, "School Teachers and the Society," *The Child's Guardian* 7, no. 2 (February 1893), 16.

[130]   Waugh, "Rod-pain as Educator," *The Child's Guardian* 10, no. 10 (October 1896), 134.

[131]   Behlmer, *Child Abuse and Moral Reform*, 197.

[132]   Ibid.

[133]   Waugh, "The Morals of the Young—A New Departure," *The Child's Guardian* 7, no. 10 (October 1893), 134.

"The boy committed a serious crime. The girl led him into committing that crime, and had led dozens of other boys into committing the same crime."[134] As is so frustratingly the case with many of the sex crimes reported in *The Child's Guardian*,[135] it is unclear what the crime committed actually was: the article simply reports that "whilst there are unwilling female victims of juvenile masculine vice, there are also willing victims of it, nay, there are those who are not victims of it but ringleaders in it." The age of the girl suggests that the crime the boy had been charged with is statutory rape, but that the girl herself instigated it, being not just "willing victim" but "ringleader." The detail included that she had "led dozens of other boys into committing the same crime" suggests that she has had multiple partners, and in the end she herself is charged with inciting outrageous conduct. Importantly, there is no question of this girl being a child, and being under the age of consent—instead, what is important to the NSPCC is that she is not a "victim." As such, she is not deserving of protection, but is instead deserving of punishment, as "One of the Society's objects is to prevent the corruption of the young."[136] The girl may be a child, but her actions threaten the innocence of other children, and as such, she falls outside of the Society's care.

What results from the Society's construction of the abused child as inherently innocent, and of the angry, the disobedient, the slatternly, or the criminal child as not "victims" and therefore worthy of punishment and violence, is that cruelty against children is not, *in and of itself*, presented as a social evil. Instead, hurting or harming an "innocent" child is represented as the true evil. Such a construction of violence against children allows the Society to encompass narratives of both the helpless child and the naughty and violent child, but it also safeguards parental and social violence towards children who are seen as stepping outside of the very restrictive role constructed for them. Where the child corresponds to the Society's narrative of the child victim—forgiving, helpless, loving, and undeserving of ill-treatment—it merits the protection of the law. But where it does not, it might be a child, but it is not necessarily a victim. Children, therefore, are allowed to show independence, to make choices, even bad ones, and to commit criminal acts, at which point they are being written off as naughty, fallen, or hardened. But in order to be protected, it seems, they had to be ignorant, dependent, and seemingly without fault. This is not to say that only blameless children actually received the help of the NSPCC, but rather, that their own discourse continually constructed the children who received their help as such.

One result of this stance is that it allowed the NSPCC to, in part, ignore the role played by past violence and neglect in its construction of adult perpetrators of child abuse. That is, a potential contradiction occurs in NSPCC discourse between

---

[134]   Ibid.

[135]   Louise Jackson notes that "Victorians used a wide collection of euphemisms ... to refer to sexual assault" (2), and in many of its sexual abuse cases, the language of NSPCC is euphemistic to the point of obscurity.

[136]   Waugh, "The Morals of the Young," 134.

the blameless, salvageable child victim and the child who becomes hardened as a result of abuse. Because adults obviously had more power in society and in the courts than did children, the NSPCC was, understandably, entirely committed to making clear to the public that abuse of a child was unrelated to the child's own actions. Claiming that

> After 400 wronged children have spent two, three, four, and six months in our Society's Shelter whilst their maligners were in prison, speaking generally, I may say that charges pleaded in excuse, and accepted in extenuation of outrages, have proved to be mere inventions of cowardly malice. When the grave, frightened little looks with which they came had passed away, they were full of the ways of sunny childhood. More pleasant docile children, or children more ready to twine their arms around your neck, you seldom find, than have been some little people who had been called liars, thieves, vixens …and the like ….[137]

Separating the abused child from the naughty child, the Society focused intensely on the child's forgiving and loving nature, a nature it claimed was firmly in place even in the face of cruelty. Commenting on the "instinctive loyalty of abused children to their parents," Waugh argued that "Children are of the kingdom of heaven, in this matter of forgiveness to savage parents at least…."[138] Naturally "sunny" and "docile," the abused child of the Society's narrative is also, it seems, incapable of anger or retribution, returning only love and forgiveness, if also fear, for the violence inflicted upon it.

And because the proper abused child of NSPCC discourse does not respond with violence, a space is opened up in that discourse to blame parental (and sibling) failings not on upbringing or environment, but on the individual. In "The Child of the English Savage," Manning and Waugh relate how social attitudes condoning the excessive beating of children have made such behavior tacitly acceptable:

> "My father did it to me, and nothing was done to him," jerked in a fine young fellow, almost in tears, as his case proceeded, and the magistrates rebuked his unspeakable savagery towards quite a little boy. They themselves are magistrates of a terrible kind, yet they will sometimes cry at the announcement of "three months imprisonment" ….[139]

The point of this anecdote is to make evident the reigning attitude in England towards cruelty to children, yet Manning and Waugh, while acknowledging this sentiment, do not in any way recognize the validity of the man's claim as an excuse. His past abuse does not make him a sympathetic character, and he is, in

---

[137] Waugh, "Some Conditions of Child Life in England," National Society for the Prevention of Cruelty to Children, 1889, 9.

[138] Waugh, "Child Forgiveness," *The Child's Guardian* 2, no. 14 (February 1888), 15.

[139] Manning and Waugh, "The Child of the English Savage," 690.

fact, derided for his tears. We are asked, as readers, to despise both the prevailing narrative of how one should discipline one's children, and the actions of one who has, perhaps, abided by them.

Another case that demonstrates the blindness of the Society to the role played by upbringing and environment in cases of cruelty is that of a father and a daughter who were both convicted of neglect. The daughter "was eighteen years of age, and she had to look after the house and children, her mother being dead," but "It was partly the business of the father to look after the children, he being at home once a week, and sometimes twice." The father drank, and the daughter claimed that "her father had never given her any money."[140] The neglected children in question are referred to in the case as "their children," however, and both the father and the daughter were committed for two months each. Obviously, the eldest daughter was also this man's child, and one could argue that she was in an equally neglected condition, having had to take care of the others without any means of doing so. However, "being over sixteen years old," the defendant was charged under the Prevention of Cruelty to Children Act. Had she been three years younger, she would have been one of these abused children, but being 18, she is, instead, an abuser. No mention is made of her physical condition, and while the case places the blame primarily on the father, she receives an equal amount of time in prison. Such a case demonstrates, again, the complete lack of consideration paid by the law or the NSPCC to the etiology of neglect and abuse. Because "cruelty to children" is not constructed as something that is the result of one's environment, notwithstanding the fear expressed by Baroness Burdett-Coutts on behalf of abused children who might become problematic "men and women" in the future, adult abusers who were neglected and abused themselves receive no sympathy, be they only two years past their own childhood neglect.

Yet the contradiction remains between the blameless child victim and the violent child produced by cruelty and neglect. For if children are indeed born innocent, as "The Child of the English Savage," at least, firmly attests, then only the environment can be blamed as the source of adult corruption. The NSPCC was obviously not entirely unaware of the role played by past abuse in the commission of present or future acts of violence, as Burdett-Coutts's very early article for the Society makes clear. It was an issue, however, that clearly problematized the Society's construction of abuse as a moral flaw, and as such, it could not easily be assimilated into the NSPCC's narratives, even when, perhaps *especially* when, it was children who were the perpetrators of that violence. In "Boy Murderers," printed in *The Child's Guardian* in 1895, the NSPCC grapples with the case of a boy's murder of his mother. The evidence put forward in the case is surprisingly similar to that suggested in contemporary child murder cases: the boy is found to be insane, but a series of "penny dreadfuls" read by the boy are also put into evidence, causing the Society to comment, "We do not allow children under a

[140]   "Neglect and Blindness—A Father and His Daughter Convicted," *The Child's Guardian*, 7, no. 7 (July 1893), 93.

given age to sell newspapers in our streets, but we allow children of any age to read the Paradise of Burglars and the apotheosis of murderers. In view of this fact, we ask, is the boy murderer the only person in England for whom a plea of insanity is merciful?"[141] The suggestion is, of course, that "penny dreadfuls" and, as the article goes on to suggest, newspapers, bear some of the responsibility for this boy's actions through their glorification of crime. As a result, the question of criminal responsibility becomes clouded—did this boy receive mercy, a "mitigation of sentence" to confinement in an asylum, because of his age? Was his responsibility for the crime inevitably the fault of another, even so amorphous an "other" as the printed word?

The Society certainly offers this suggestion, but it also pursues another. This boy apparently did not propose the idea of killing his mother; instead, it originated with his younger brother. The act that incited the murder was, apparently, the "hiding" of the younger brother by the mother, soon to be followed by a punishment to the older brother. Because "The idea of the terrible deed occurred first to the younger boy," the Society asks, "Was he, too, insane?" Evidently, what the article seeks to suggest is that the murder was motivated by an abusive parent. It acknowledges that "Of the dead, in this particular case, we know no ill to speak, but we are of opinion that it is of great public concern to know what were the relations of the dead mother and her murderous child."[142] What fascinates me here is the phrase, "great public concern." Why is the etiology of this particular crime "of great public concern?" Certainly, if the boys were in some way driven to the act that the one actually committed, the mother's conduct towards the boy would be important in determining the boy's criminal responsibility. Yet, in this case, the law has obviously already been at pains to be as merciful to the boy as possible.

What is at stake here that makes the circumstances of this crime "of great public concern," then, is not just one boy's future, or even an understanding of that boy's past, but instead the very nature of childhood itself. Though earlier NSPCC documents had asserted both the innocence and the forgiving nature of childhood, making their rescued children truly salvageable objects, this article raises a different question:

> To what extent are the deeds of such parents followed by their children's moral degradation as well as physical suffering? That degradation may not result in such horrible cases to a mother or father in one case in a thousand …. But how many of the outrages upon persons of no relationship to the perpetrator are a consequence of the degradation of moral sentiments by the cruelties of those who by nature are the highest ideal of child-life, and whose tuition is almost wholly the unconscious tuition of example?

---

[141] "Boy Murderers," *The Child's Guardian* 9, no. 10 (October 1895), 134.
[142] Ibid.

The blame here lies firmly on the parents' heads, and there is some recourse to narratives of the "nature" of the child, who cannot help, it seems, but follow their parents' example. This suggests, of course, a kind of filial devotion that is very much in keeping with the Society's construction of the child; nevertheless, these children are yet capable of "moral degradation" that threatens society beyond their home.

However, the article does not firmly resolve this issue. Instead, while hinting toward an explanation of the boy's murder, it also firmly constructs such crimes as inexplicable. The article claims "That we shall ever get at the moral explanation of this outrage upon a mother, and still great outrage on sonship, is not likely," and goes on to state that "Every consideration of humanity, every instinct of nature, every condition of age, makes the crime astounding and incredible."[143] The determination of this crime as inexplicable, mysterious, and astounding serves to leave the nature of childhood violence undecidable. This is not an undecidable that is particularly productive, however; rather, the indeterminacy of this child's crime speaks to the irresolvable contradiction between the innocent child victim, and the aggressive child produced by violence. The two are essentially irreconcilable, and so other explanations—insanity, the influence of the press, parental responsibility—are all called to somewhat mitigate the fear at the heart of this article: that a child could commit a murder that was "planned and carried out in cold blood."[144] What haunts this article, that is, is the spectre of the child who is not helpless—who responds, perhaps, *with* violence *to* violence.

Though this murdering child, therefore, makes an important point for the Society about the necessity of intervention, particularly since, the article argues, "Youthful brutality and ruffianism [are] the curse of the land,"[145] he is still not an attractive object of social concern. There is no home to which this child can be saved, only an asylum that will keep him from society. The asylum becomes a poignant symbol of the place such a child holds in a society that has no explanation for him: not easily a victim and not entirely a monster, he can only be categorized as insane. What the juvenile delinquent therefore tells us about endangered children is that the "innocent" child so common to Victorian discourse was not, as Kincaid has persuasively argued, the only child or even the dominant construction of the child in the nineteenth century. It was simply the most worthy child.

---

[143]   Ibid.
[144]   Ibid.
[145]   Ibid.

Conclusion
Inspector Stories:
The Inspector's Directory
and the Cruelty Man

By the beginning of the twentieth century, I have argued, the story of the endangered child had become the story of the child as institutional subject: of the child represented and caught up within, and finding amelioration as a result of, institutions such as the NSPCC and legislation such as the "Children's Charter." As Laura Berry argues, "it might be said that, at about the time of the passage of the Elementary Education Act, the story of the child in danger was deployed in a more narrow sphere and toward more narrow and explicitly ideological (and state-sanctioned) ends" (164). In this new "state-sanctioned" narrative of the endangered child, the child is no longer, necessarily, the central figure. Instead, its story comes to be shared with newly emergent figures, the most important of which, I would like to suggest, is the Inspector.

Although Benjamin Waugh had been the defining figure of the NSPCC throughout the 1890s, by 1904 he was forced to take an extended leave for health reasons, and by 1905, he had resigned his position.[1] Robert J. Parr, who, according to Behlmer, "relied more heavily on precision than on emotion," was appointed to head the NSPCC, and a result, "the tone of the Society's propaganda ... softened from acerbic to merely assertive."[2] Waugh's fiery, if somewhat controversial, style had been the voice of the NSPCC throughout the 1890s, and with his passage and the appointment of Parr, the tone of the NSPCC's propaganda became far more institutional, and far less individualistic. But if the voice and tone of *The Child's Guardian* became less personal, its institutional rhetoric was balanced by the emergence of the Inspector as the individual face of the NSPCC. The figure of the Inspector had gained prominence in NSPCC narratives by the end of the nineteenth century; whereas early NSPCC casework had focused solely on the Inspector's role in finding abuse and bringing about punishment, by the end of the century, the NSPCC instead began to focus much more closely upon the positive changes brought about in abusive homes through the intervention of NSPCC "cruelty men."[3] In texts such as *The Cruelty Man: Actual Experiences of*

---

[1]   George K. Behlmer, *Child Abuse and Moral Reform*, 207.

[2]   Ibid., 27.

[3]   NSPCC inspectors were male. The first female inspector was hired in 1915 (NSPCC, *A History of the NSPCC: Protecting Children from Cruelty since 1884* [2000], 4); many of

an Inspector of the N.S.P.C.C. Graphically Told by Himself (1912), the Inspector emerges as a fully developed character in NSPCC propaganda and in the emergent narrative of the child and the state.

There is much to suggest that the Society's inspectors did in fact play a significant role in the organization, particularly in terms of the NSPCC's changing construction of child abuse. For example, the Society's *Inspector's Directory* of 1901 clearly indicates the extent to which the inspectors' firsthand experiences were taken into account in the lobbying for new legislation:

> If you want to learn what can be got out of an Act of Parliament, you must give yourself no rest till you learn what is necessary to get out of it for the child's sake
> …. If you can in no way get it out, then make a note of the fact and why it is so, and the suffering the child has endured in consequence, with a view to amending the Act when the opportunity comes, remembering that the Act was made for the child, not the child for the Act.[4]

These instructions empower the inspector not just to make the law work for him and his charges, but also to use his experiences in the field to possibly influence future legislation. Therefore, if the first "Children's Charter" had been brought about, in large part, through the work of Benjamin Waugh and *The Child's Guardian*, instructions such as these in the *Inspector's Directory* suggest that the following Prevention of Cruelty to Children Acts (in 1894 and 1904) can be attributed at least as much to the Society's inspectors, and to the casework they meticulously prepared. And what these Acts demonstrate, particularly that of 1894, is that the NSPCC, no doubt as a result of its inspectors' experiences, had moved away from its definition of child abuse as a classless crime motivated solely by pathological impulses, to a recognition of the role that environment could play in the endangerment of children. According to Behlmer, "If the Children's Charter made cruelty to the young a crime, the 1894 Act established it as a positively hazardous practice,"[5] and the sweeping provisions of the Act, and the relative ease with which it was passed, demonstrate the extent to which the NSPCC had succeeded in making its case for legislation against cruelty to children. Under this Act, parents could receive a prison sentence of up to six months; "habitual drunkards" who abused or neglected their children had to consent to treatment; parents were required to call a doctor when a child was ill; and workhouses were compelled to accept children of parents who could not afford to care for them.[6] The provisions relating to parental drunkenness and to the greater responsibility

---

the NSPCC's inspectors were called to serve during World War I, and "Their wives, who had traditionally supported the Inspectors from behind the scenes, stepped in to fill vacant posts" (4).

[4]   NSPCC, *Inspector's Directory*, 7–8.

[5]   Behlmer, *Child Abuse and Moral Reform*, 159.

[6]   Ibid.

of the workhouse in relieving poor parents of responsibility for starving children speak to the fact that the Society's own statistics made it difficult to argue that social conditions did not play a role in child abuse and neglect.

If it is true that the NSPCC's inspectors, and the information they provided from their investigations, played a significant role in changing the Society's conception of abuse, it is also nevertheless true that the Inspector was, like the concept of cruelty to children and the abused child, created. That is, the Inspector was both an important player in the NSPCC as an institution, and a symbolic construction of NSPCC propaganda. The "cruelty man" of NSPCC rhetoric serves a very specific purpose: that of embodying the Society's ideology and method and of presenting an individual (yet always consistent) face to the public, thus depicting the NSPCC's delicate interventions into the home as far less intrusive. The Inspector as NSPCC employee, and the Inspector as NSPCC representative, however, always overlapped, and texts such as the *Inspector's Directory* and memoirs such as *The Cruelty Man*, sought to demonstrate the ways in which the two could not be separated. The individual Inspector, in these texts, is distinguished by his discipline, by his adherence to a particular "type" that had come to define the NSPCC as an institution, and Inspector stories vividly realize the Society's interactions with children, with parents, and with the law. Representations of the Inspector clearly demonstrate, therefore, both the ways in which the Society perceived itself, and the ways in which it wished to be perceived by the public.

Furthermore, such narratives added an important character to narratives of child endangerment. While stories of child peril throughout the nineteenth century might have included characters who had saved endangered children, such as Mary Brotherton, Mr. Brownlow, Valentine Blyth, and the Cheerybles, such benefactors are represented as taking on the role of parent in the absence of those able or willing to undertake that responsibility. With the emergence of the NSPCC and, in particular, with the social acceptance of the project of child protection in the early twentieth century, the Inspector emerges as the figure who not only fills the absence of protector in the abused child's life, but who also succeeds in making the parent *be* a parent, "parent" of course referring to a very specific role. Rather than a child's protection being left to the arbitrariness of fate or circumstance (little Dicky in *Oliver Twist* being nowhere near as lucky as Oliver), it was instead entrusted, through the work of the NSPCC, to legally sanctioned and specially trained officers of the Society. Nevertheless, the residue of earlier, almost fairy-godmother elements of literary "protectors" of the child remain within the nascent construction of the institutional inspector of early twentieth-century NSPCC discourse.

The NSPCC was very careful about who it picked to be an inspector. According to Behlmer, "For its community militia the NSPCC preferred men who had been trained to follow orders."[7] Drawing from the NSPCC *Record Book of Inspectors* (1889–1910), Behlmer records that the great majority of cruelty men were

---

[7]   Ibid., 162.

policemen before taking up their posts with the Society.[8] Furthermore, "When the Society found a promising 'children's servant,' it subjected him to a rigorous training in law and public relations."[9] The 1901 *Inspector's Directory* includes detailed instructions on every aspect of the inspector's life and work, including his life insurance, his uniform, and his "removal expenses."[10] It provides information on how to go about collecting and writing up witness statements, how to photograph children, what kind of action to take on complaints, and when to talk to the press (never).[11] But perhaps more importantly, in a section entitled the "Inspector's Habit of Mind," the inspector is instructed as to what kind of man he had to be in order to carry out his work. This section includes such subjects as "What Eyes should see," "What a Child knows," "What it Means," and "Why it did Things," all of which detail the "habit of mind" needed in order to discover cruelty towards and abuse of children. For example, the section entitled, "A Traitor's Ways," clearly demarcates the difference between a "cruelty man" and a mere hired investigator:

> The way for a man employed by this Society to be a traitor to a child is *not* to give his heart to the child. When a child's pains are not his, he abandons hope of delivering it …. No genuine pain is felt by heartless men at having to give up a case. It makes no impression on them. Not having an interest in improving an unhappy child's condition, they have no disappointment in failure. They are "hirelings, whose own the sheep are not."[12]

If the abused child is defined by its innocence and helplessness, the cruelty man is constituted by his love for that child. Those who see their work for the Society merely as work are "traitors," "hirelings," and "heartless men," suggesting that the NSPCC Inspector is not constituted merely by his training, but by the kind of man he is, by his character.

As the section on "What Eyes should see" goes on to suggest, however, "Good servants are both born and made, but they are more made than born."[13] That is, although the *Inspector's Directory* suggests that the cruelty man must be a particular kind of man, it also suggests that the work of the directory and of the NSPCC's training is to create these "good servants" who will see children "before everything else," and who will give their hearts "to the child."[14] To be a proper cruelty man, according to the directory, demands a transformation from the inside out, and instructions as to method and as to proper manliness are represented as one and the same: "Stand well up to the child. Keep your heart well to the front.

[8]   Ibid., 163.
[9]   Ibid., 164.
[10] NSPCC, *Inspector's Directory*, 14–15.
[11] Ibid., 36–7, 27, 29–30.
[12] Ibid., 8–9, italics in original.
[13] Ibid., 9.
[14] Ibid., 9, 8.

Don't seem official to it; be nothing but a man—a strong, tender man."[15] Here, instructions on approach, stance, and posture are combined with instructions on personal character, indicating that only a combination of the two can truly elicit the necessary responses from frightened children. And again, in the injunction that "What is going on in the house to a child there may be seen by intenseness of anxiety in a man of trained common sense,"[16] emotion and education go hand in hand. Training in manliness and in proper care and "anxiety" for the child are not separate from training in procedure and method. Instead, the two are shown to be mutually supportive, and mutually necessary: a man who is a "good servant" of children will be both a "strong, tender man" and a disciplined adherent of NSPCC method.

The "Inspector's Directory" makes it very clear, therefore, that the NSPCC perceived the work of the Inspector to be more than a job, more even than a vocation: it is a calling to which one must give one's whole heart and mind, because "everything depends upon the disposition and bent of your life."[17] Throughout the directory, the Inspector is exhorted to *feel* above all, to be motivated by restlessness and anxiety for the child's welfare. He is told that "The best exponent of an Act is not a lawyer, but your own restless, patient, tenacious, intelligent love of a child," and that "Nervous anxiety to get at the whole case—not simply to get up a case— is the first condition of true, complete success for the child."[18] How the Inspector feels about a case is at least as important as how he goes about constructing it, as he must have "anxiety as to detail," but more importantly, "passion" for the child's well-being.[19] And at all times, even when confronted and opposed, he must "practice all the arts of a pure and high intention."[20] Again, the combination of training, suggested by the word "practice," and of inherent qualities of mind, "a pure and high intention," suggests that, indeed, the cruelty man must be *both* "born" and "made," both called to his position and rigorously trained to undertake it. Given that these instructions appear at the very beginning of the directory, before the "General Information for Inspectors" which records the actual details of the inspector's investigative work, it is clear that the NSPCC perceived these instructions regarding the proper feelings and motivations of an Inspector as the primary lessons to be learned. Such instructions suggest that the Inspector is meant to internalize the NSPCC's training, to make himself into a product of that training to the extent that it becomes second nature, and training and feeling become one and the same.

The moral character of the Inspector was therefore a crucial component of the position. Given the rigors of the job, and the lack of material benefits that went

---

[15]   Ibid., 9–10.
[16]   Ibid., 12.
[17]   Ibid., 7.
[18]   Ibid., 8, 11.
[19]   Ibid., 11.
[20]   Ibid., 12.

with it, however, the NSPCC's acknowledged desire for "candidates in whom 'tenderness' was tempered by a 'righteous' anger over misuse of the young" is hardly surprising.[21] NSPCC inspectors in 1901 were paid only 30s. a week (with a possibility of merit increases up to 50s. a week), and although such wages did not put them in the ranks of the desperately poor, they also did not make the position a particularly remunerative one.[22] Furthermore, inspectors were expected to work "occasional Sunday and night duty with extra remuneration" and the Society did not "recognise overtime."[23] Finally, although the Society acknowledged that the "difficult and trying character of an Inspector's work" should earn him "great sympathy generally," it also warned that "Habits about which ordinary employers might be indifferent the Society considers grounds for dismissal."[24] The ideological capital imbued in the position of Inspector, the manliness that such a position was meant to entail and represent, may have served to offset the sheer difficulty of the job itself, replacing material rewards with the "nobleness of [the Inspector's] calling."[25]

Noble though the Inspector's calling might be, it was a position that entailed both an exhausting number of homes for which he was responsible,[26] and voluminous amounts of paper work that had to be carefully and meticulously prepared. That is, while the handbook opens by carefully stressing the quality of mind and nobility of manner required for the position, the remainder of the directory makes very clear that the position is strictly constituted by the Society, and by the regulations pertaining to it. The Inspector is instructed that he is required "to enter daily in his Diary the duties upon which he has been engaged" and that "The Diary is intended to be a minute record of an Officer's doings, and must be regularly kept, and produced for the Hon. Secretary's examination and signature at least once in every week."[27] As well, the Inspector "must always carry a pocket-book, and must be very careful to enter all facts elicited in connection with enquiries, and conversations with different witnesses, with their names and addresses. A well-kept note-book will ensure a well-written report."[28] There are detailed instructions

---

[21]   Behlmer, *Child Abuse and Moral Reform*, 164.

[22]   As Behlmer notes, however, "The job carried other compensations …. At the turn of the century between 80 and 90 percent of the agents and their families lived in the NSPCC's local offices. Resident inspectors sometimes paid no rent, though more often they contributed five shillings a week for their rooms and in return got a weekly allowance of one shilling and sixpence for coals, gas light, and a charwoman" (164).

[23]   NSPCC, *Inspector's Directory*, 13.

[24]   Ibid. These "grounds for dismissal" could pertain to an injunction within the *Inspector's Directory* that "Inspectors must not frequent public-houses, or bad company, or bet, or gamble" (13).

[25]   Ibid., 12.

[26]   See Behlmer, *Child Abuse and Moral Reform*, 166.

[27]   NSPCC, *Inspector's Directory*, 17, underscore in original.

[28]   Ibid., 18, underscore in original.

as to how to go about writing reports, such as "A general statement, 'that the child is much neglected and dirty,' *is bad*. State specifically in what manner the child is neglected or dirty—whether superficially dirty or verminous."[29]

I mention these detailed instructions (which were to become even more detailed in the 1914 *Inspector's Directory*. While the 1901 edition consists of 50 pages, the 1914 edition is 110 pages, of which more than 50 pages alone is dedicated to "Inquiries and Reports"), not because such instructions are surprising, in and of themselves, but because no such details find a place within Walter Payne's *The Cruelty Man: Actual Experiences of an NSPCC Inspector, Graphically Told by Himself*.[30] In the "Foreword," Payne argues that "a generous and confiding public still knows little or nothing of the work they have set in motion, or the difficulties and dangers which beset those who engage actively in the work of social reformation."[31] This disclaimer is, of course, very much in keeping with the NSPCC party line, as evidenced by Robert J. Parr's "Preface," in which he states that "Misconception as to method and motive are met with every day by one or other of the Society's workers." As a result of such misconceptions, Parr welcomes Payne's memoir, because "If what is being done for [children] by the Society's representatives became common knowledge, there would be little need to plead for further support for the Society."[32] Both Payne's and Parr's words suggest that this text will provide the reader with a detailed account of the "method and motive" of the Society, with a glimpse of "the work they have set in motion." Payne, in turn, promises his reader that this "peep behind the scenes" of NSPCC work will be authoritative and true, and he will "attempt in the following pages to tell what I know and have seen. In those pages be it remembered nothing is recorded but *actual fact*" and that "There has been no attempt to colour up the incidents up to the point of the picturesque."[33]

Such statements and claims bear a great similarity, and indeed, debt, to the kinds of claims about the Society's singular vision that Waugh had made throughout his work in *The Child's Guardian*. What is different about Payne's memoir, however, is that his stories are, as the opening chapter is titled, "Strictly Personal." That is, while Waugh always spoke on behalf of the NSPCC as an organization, Payne speaks from his own experience, and his stories are about him, his wife, "Mrs. Inspector," and the various children and parents he encounters in his work. Payne tells the reader about his background as "the son of a Sanitary Surveyor," about his previous job experiences, and about moving his "wife, son and two daughters" to "an Assize town in Cobbleshire" for his first position as an NSPCC Inspector.[34]

---

[29]   Ibid., 36.

[30]   Originally published anonymously.

[31]   Walter Payne, *The Cruelty Man: Actual Experiences of an Inspector of the N.S.P.C.C. Graphically Told by Himself*, by Walter Payne (London: NSPCC, 1912), 8–9.

[32]   Robert Parr, preface to *The Cruelty Man*, 7.

[33]   Payne, *The Cruelty Man*, 9–10.

[34]   Ibid., 11–12.

These details about Payne's personal life make him appear quite ordinary, so that he seems first to be simply a man, rather than a representative of an institution. But more importantly, Payne focuses, in the opening pages, upon his own naïveté, saying that "I used to flatter myself that as a man of the world I knew most things worth knowing," and that "I had preached the 'uplifting of the people' quite glibly; never dreaming … what a horrible stratum of misery there was below the surface of our much-vaunted civilization."[35] At the beginning of his narrative, Payne is as ignorant of the conditions of child-life in England as is (presumably) his reader, and his education as an NSPCC inspector, as related in the following chapters, promises also to be the education of his readers, who are given access (the narrative suggests) to what he sees, and thus able to learn as he himself learns.

Payne's stories, in other words, promise to narrativize the NSPCC as institution, converting statistics, classifications, and case papers, the means by which the Society operates, into individual stories. The first episode, "The Cottage at the End," does this most clearly. When setting out to investigate what has been reported to him as an emergency, Payne informs the reader that

> One must—while exerting all speed, and prepared for any emergency—still preserve that open mind which is so necessary if one would get at the facts, and nothing but the facts, of the matter under enquiry. I was going to find out what had been done? Who did it? Why? Who saw it done? And after all this had been discovered, it was my duty still to preserve the balance between offender and child.[36]

Here, and at other points in his narrative,[37] Payne directly echoes the *Inspector's Directory*, which instructs inspectors to ask,

> What was done?
> Who did it?
> Who to?
> When?
> Why?
> Who saw it done?[38]

Furthermore, the narrative that follows Payne's explanation of the steps he is expected to undertake dramatizes the way in which the Inspector goes about his work, as Payne details his efforts to gather a "chain of evidence" against an abusive

---

[35]   Ibid.

[36]   Ibid., 15.

[37]   In "The Collier's Little Housekeeper," for example, Payne writes that "Emergencies are superior to all rules" (127), a direct paraphrase from the directory: "As to 'emergencies,' in all cases the interests of a child are superior to rules" (21).

[38]   NSPCC, *Inspector's Directory*, 15.

mother, his success in finding a "possible reason" for the child's ill-treatment, and the instrument that caused the injuries.[39] This story operates almost as an example of detective fiction, because it clearly demonstrates how the Inspector goes about finding evidence and interrogating witnesses and suspects so as to build a case. In a narrative such as this, the *Inspector's Directory* comes to life, and is transformed from a series of rules and regulations to a series of actions and interactions between inspector, child, and suspect.

After this story, however, method and procedure largely disappear from Payne's narratives. Instead, the work that Payne undertakes is always represented as that of exerting influence on those around him through the strength of his character, and through the persuasiveness of his manner. The reader is given the impression throughout of Payne as a stalwart, practical, stout-hearted veteran, who can speak to abusive parents in a language they will understand, and who will win the confidences of the most terrorized and wary child. When confronted by a violent father, for example, Payne confides to the reader that "I was somewhat taken aback, and quite unprepared for this."[40] Payne decides, however, that

> for an officer to show the white feather in such an emergency would never do. So I raked up some of my past, and served it up for the benefit of my intending assailant:
> "Nothing I should enjoy so much, Jack! Since I had the gloves on with old Jem Mace, in 'seventy-nine—"
> "Jem Mace! Hev you had the gloves on wi' him, Inspector?"
> "Oh, yes! You see, I was going in for the Army middle weights at the time—"
> "You've been in the Army, and you've boxed."
> "Oh, yes! I used to love it as a youngster."
> "Then I'm noan feightin' thee, mister! You'd be too good for me!"
> I was very glad he thought so, and that we were able to talk over matters without resort to fisticuffs.[41]

Tales such as this are meant to win over the Inspector's reading audience, as we share in his anxiety at the prospect of a fight, and admire the craftiness of the Inspector (and deride the cowardice of the father) in the conversation that ensues. Furthermore, as a result of his courage, resourcefulness, and straight-talking manner, Payne claims he wins over the great majority of parents in these stories: for example, he relates at the conclusion of one episode, "'Funny bloke, that Inspector,' the plumber said to a friend, after I'd gone away. 'He talks to a fellow like a pal, he do, and not like a bloomin' body-snatcher trying to get yer in quod!'"[42] Inspector Payne, rather than the representing the fearful cruelty man of

---

[39]   Payne, *The Cruelty Man*, 18–20.

[40]   Ibid., 125.

[41]   Ibid., 126.

[42]   Ibid., 154.

early NSPCC rhetoric, is instead a "pal," one who manages confrontation through the strength of his character, rather than through the force of law.

The parents are also given distinct personalities in these stories, in a way they never are in the NSPCC's sample cases of the 1890s in *The Child's Guardian*. The reader meets bullies, slatterns, drunkards, cowards, coal-miners, a dentist, and a prostitute, most of whom are given voices, names, and individual characteristics. Some of the parents are irredeemable, but most are capable of reform, and as a result, the most common ending to these stories is that of the parents' conversion. For example, Payne is forced to give a warning to two habitual drunkards who are abusing their children, instructing them to "Work! until the reek of the filth is off your belongings, and the reek of the beer is off your own body! Then you needn't slink away when I call."[43] The threat Payne levels against these parents, rather than imprisonment, is that of continued shame. His admonition suggests instead that, through his influence, these parents could themselves become worthy of respect, and the effect of his admonition is proved by the father coming to "report another case": "'It's Billy Jones,' he said, 'my stall-mate at the pit, and one of those chaps I was boozing with that day. Put the fear o' God into him, sir! like you did into me—and he'll be a better father.'"[44] Because the parents in Payne's text are capable of reformation, of becoming true and loving mothers and fathers, they are not flattened in the way that the "English savage" of early NSPCC rhetoric had been. They are given motivations (if poor ones) for their neglect of their children, and they are therefore comprehensible, rather than purely pathological. But more importantly, they are shown to be persuaded by the notion of respectability. This story is meant to represent, quite clearly, the power of the Inspector not simply as a figure of authority, as one that parents fear, but also as one by whom they wish to be respected.

Because both he and those he comes into contact with are fully drawn characters, Payne's interactions with parents and children have the appearance of a series of relationships, of personal conversations between neighbors, rather than institutional interventions. Payne seems throughout, except when threatened or faced with unrepentant abusers, to be a kind-hearted father figure, who effects change in the lives of abusive parents by virtue of his charismatic presence and by the power of example. Rather than violently accosting parents, he instead models proper discipline: "I 'persuaded' him off the drink first. A severe shaking up—verbal, of course—effected that."[45] By using words instead of violence, Inspector Payne provides an example to these parents of the proper exertion of authority, an example very much meant to be in contrast to the violence these parents use against their children. Furthermore, Payne always represents himself as behaving respectfully towards others, even abusive others, because "It does

---

43   Ibid., 86.
44   Ibid., 87.
45   Ibid., 33.

not do to kick people too much when they are down."[46] And finally, he always takes full responsibility for the families he has had dealings with, taking an almost familial interest in, particularly, the marriages of abusive parents. One abusive father, fearing a reunion with the wife and children he had terrorized before his imprisonment for abuse, says to Payne: "I've been waiting for a chance—to— to—ask if you'd be so good as to go with me on that errand."[47] While the wife's more-than-frosty greeting of her husband makes Payne question "whether the experiment would work for good or evil," he still comments to the reader that "separations are bad things at best," and when the wife asks him, "What do you say, Mr. Inspector," he declares, "I'd try him, this once!"[48] The wife's appeal to the Inspector, and her immediate acceptance of his decision, are meant to demonstrate that he has won over the respect of his clients, and that the relationship he has with them is a personal one, built by and through his actions and interactions with them. Payne's details of his interactions with parents and children throughout the narrative serve not only to elucidate the strengths of the Society's inspectorate, but also to model proper fatherhood, proper manliness, and proper working-class respectability. Payne is not just a model inspector; he is a model of what the NSPCC endeavors to create within the abusive home.

This text is more than a memoir, of course; it is also a deliberate and conscious work of propaganda. Payne's narrative, with its first-person perspective, seems to offer the reader the kind of access that had been a feature of early London SPCC child abuse narratives, such as "The Story of the Shrewsbury Case": whereas that story, however, used fictional techniques to place the reader in the abusive home as witness, Payne's memoir provides the reader with the perspective of the Inspector. As such, his stories never challenge the authority of the NSPCC's sight, nor suggest that anyone but an NSPCC inspector can truly access or comprehend abuse. In fact, both Payne and Parr clearly state in their introductions to the text that these stories "are silhouettes, mere outlines; behind each there is pathos, drama, tragedy" that is, presumably, beyond the reach of the common reader.[49] Moreover, while each family appears individually drawn, Payne acknowledges that they are, in fact, "types": "Too much detail would doubtless weary the reader, so I have tried to make each story and each character a 'type.'"[50] Payne's words here are revealing, because they disclose the extent to which his own experiences have been constructed for his audience. The word "type" is particularly important, because it suggests not just embellishment or edition for the sake of an audience, "weary" or otherwise, but instead a desire to make visible the scope of the Society's work, and illustrate through example the classes of abuse and abusers the Society regularly encounters.

[46] Ibid., 85–6.
[47] Ibid., 111.
[48] Ibid.
[49] Parr, preface to *The Cruelty Man*, 7.
[50] Payne, *The Cruelty Man*, 155.

But if the parents are "types," it is also true that Payne is himself a "type." That is, the kind of man Payne represents himself to be is exactly the kind of man constructed by the *Inspector's Directory*. He is exemplary of the "strong, tender man"[51] of the directory, who has given his whole heart "to the child."[52] When one boy protects his sisters by placing them behind him, Payne comments that "I shall always love little Billy (aged nine) for the manly way in which he stood up to me," and after escorting a crippled child to the train-station to be sent to her new home, he remarks that Mrs. Inspector "declares I was sniveling too."[53] Payne might be a strong man who knows how to box, but he also is not afraid to cry and to be moved by the children with whom he comes into contact. Furthermore, in his interactions with parents, in which he always demonstrates his respectful manner toward them, Payne puts into action the NSPCC's instructions to never resort to "mere officialism or bounce" to gain the day, but instead use "Courtesy" that "has a wonderful effect."[54] Just as his stories narrativize the rules and procedures of the institution, so too does Payne himself enact the kind of Inspector constructed by the NSPCC's training and rhetoric.

By presenting cases and training as a series of personal encounters between individuals, however, Payne essentially makes invisible the NSPCC as institution. That is, the workings of the NSPCC's authority, and even the workings of the law, are largely absent from this memoir, and absent even in Payne's meetings with parents and children. As a result, Payne's text demonstrates the ways in which the workings of an institution can be obscured by the construction of "personal" relationships between parent and inspector. Rather than striking fear into a parent's heart with its name, as it had desired in the 1890s, the NSPCC in Payne's text instead seeks to be seen simply as a friend of the family—a friend that can punish, certainly, but only when persuasion and respect fail to meet with the proper response. Such a stance is indicative, I would argue, of the greatly altered position of the NSPCC and of the project of child protection in the twentieth century. While in its early days, the London SPCC had represented itself as a fairly radical organization, one that had to combat ignorance, mistrust, and even the laws of England so as to bring justice to the suffering child, by the time of Payne's memoir, the institution and the work that it performed had become somewhat naturalized. That is, even though the reader can certainly question the extent to which families actually welcomed or appreciated the work of the Inspector, it can at least be said that by the twentieth century, institutional involvement in family life had become a given.

But what of the abused child in Payne's text? Throughout this study, I have examined the suffering, endangered, and abused child in many manifestations, as either victim or threat, innocent or knowing, salvageable or irretrievably damaged. I have argued throughout that the rise to dominance of conceptions of

---

51   NSPCC, *Inspector's Directory*, 9–10.
52   Ibid., 8.
53   Payne, *The Cruelty Man*, 32–56.
54   NSPCC, *Inspector's Directory*, 12.

the child as innocent, dependent, and at risk of violence led, perhaps inevitably, to the emergence of child protection at the end of the nineteenth century. This construction of the child is still very much present in Payne's early twentieth century text, and though his child characters are not as silent as they were in the case studies printed in *The Child's Guardian*, they are, nevertheless, still important primarily for the ways in which they can be read by the adults around them, and for the effect they have upon that adult audience. The meaning of the abused child is always the same: it always asks for help, for justice, and for the intervention of the inspector and of the law. In his story of "The Cottage at the End," for example, Payne writes of Nellie, who gazes at him "with a curious yearning expression on her face, as though half terrified at what was to come, and yet in some vague way knowing instinctively that it was for her good."[55] While the "as though" qualifies Payne's ability to truly know what goes on in this girl's mind, yet he is able to read her gaze as fully welcoming and sanctioning his authority within her home. And in the story of "Alfred—the Unwanted," Payne decides to trust the foreman of the jury, Mr. Cramp, despite the fact that he "is an old friend of the prisoner" because "Mr. Cramp had an honest English face. He would see the child and hear the evidence. No honourable man could resist the mute appeal in that youngster's eyes."[56] Here again, Alfred's eyes are eminently transparent, and eminently true. They ask for justice, and no one who looks into them, even one biased against the message within them, can be mistaken as to the meaning of their gaze.

If the abused child's eyes speak louder than words, so too does the abused child's body. In one of the most disturbing narratives in the text, "A Babe in the Wood," Payne tells of a seven-year-old girl who loses her feet and legs to gangrene as a result of sleeping outside, with her mother, in the cold and frost. The story tells of the child's deposition, which begins "I am seven years old, and I see my mamma in the room sitting near the bed," and describes how the mother and the child had been "For some time past … tramping along the road," and staying "all night in the open."[57] It is evident from the deposition that the mother had never left the child's side, and that she had tried, by taking the child to a public-house and by covering the child with bags, to keep the child as warm as possible. The mother, however, unlike most parents with whom Payne interacts in the memoir, is never given any voice; instead, Payne asks the reader to "Think of it just a moment":

> The mother who had brought her into being had refused the shelter of her own home, the good advice of many friends, and had thrown up farm work, where she might have earned at least an honest living for herself and her child, to wilfully waste her life in wantonness and sin, and to drag this poor little mite from place to place, to suffer hunger and almost perish with cold.[58]

---

[55]   Payne, *The Cruelty Man*, 19.
[56]   Ibid., 42.
[57]   Ibid., 54–5.
[58]   Ibid., 56.

While these details purport to explain (or at least prove) the mother's cruelty, they fail to do so. Unlike his other narratives, this particular story leaves out a great deal, relying more on rhetoric, implication, and invective to make its case. It is the child's maimed body that provides the necessary evidence, that speaks most loudly to the mother's "willful" neglect and cruelty.

But if the child has failed to meet with the proper protection from her mother, she does, particularly after the loss of her legs, meet with it from everyone else. Payne proclaims "it was my privilege to carry this little rescued darling to safety and shelter," a privilege others seem to want to share with him: "On the way to the train one could see the tears start from women's eyes, as they caught a glimpse of little Amy; strong men wished her 'God-speed' in thick voices as they pressed pennies or chocolates into her tiny hands." Amy's rescue by an institution, to an institution—in which "kind hearts would soon take the place of a mother to her," and after which "she would be placed in some situation in life such as her deformed condition would allow"[59]—seems merely a natural extension of the concern her body elicits from all adults. Everyone who sees Amy wants to protect her, but the "privilege" of doing so is entrusted, in the end, to the Inspector.

The Inspector's privileged role in caring for the abused child is what makes me grant this figure such prominence at the end of a project that has focused almost exclusively on the endangered and abused child. The work of the NSPCC in conceptualizing the abused child at the end of the nineteenth century has had lasting impact on how a suffering child is perceived, and on what that suffering might mean. But it has also had lasting impact on the action we all believe should be taken on behalf of that child. In the end, we all now see a child's suffering through the eyes of the Inspector, wondering what has caused that suffering, who is to blame, and what can be done. But most importantly, we wonder who we can call, recognizing that the "privilege" of ameliorating that suffering is not in our hands. The story of the abused child today is that of trusting the institutions we have put in place to take care of that child, instead of asking what it is that suffering child might mean outside the parameters of those institutions.

---

[59]   Ibid.

Bibliography

"£17 7s. 0d.: Bonuses on Neglect." *The Child's Guardian* 4.8 (August 1890): 88.

Armstrong, Nancy. *Desire and Domestic Fiction: A Political History of the Novel.* New York and Oxford: Oxford University Press, 1987.

Assael, Brenda. *The Circus and Victorian Society.* Charlottesville and London: University of Virginia Press, 2005.

Bannerjee, Jacqueline. *Through the Northern Gate: Childhood and Growing Up in British Fiction, 1719–1901.* New York: Peter Lang, 1996.

Barlee, Ellen. *Pantomime Waifs, or, a Plea for our City Children.* London: S. W. Partridge & Co., 1884.

Behlmer, George K. *Child Abuse and Moral Reform in England, 1870–1908.* Stanford: Stanford University Press, 1982.

——. *Friends of the Family: The English Home and its Guardians, 1850–1940.* Stanford: Stanford University Press, 1998.

Berry, Laura. *The Child, the State, and the Victorian Novel.* Charlottesville: University of Virginia Press, 1999.

Betensky, Carolyn. "Knowing Too Much and Never Enough: Knowledge and Moral Capital in Frances Trollope's *Life and Adventures of Michael Armstrong, the Factory Boy.*" *Novel* 36.2 (Fall 2002): 61–78.

Blake, William. "Holy Thursday." In *From Instruction to Delight: An Anthology of Children's Literature to 1850*, edited by Patricia Demers, 278. Don Mills, Ontario: Oxford University Press, 2004.

——. "Spring." In *From Instruction to Delight: An Anthology of Children's Literature to 1850*, edited by Patricia Demers, 277–8. Don Mills, Ontario: Oxford University Press, 2004.

Böker, Uwe. "Childhood and Juvenile Delinquency in Eighteenth-Century *Newgate Calendars.*" In *Fashioning Childhood in the Eighteenth Century: Age and Identity*, edited by Anja Müller, 135–44. Burlington, VT: Ashgate, 2006.

Bolton, Mary. "A Branch to Be Copied." *The Children's League of Pity Paper* 6.1 (August 1898): 11–12.

——. "Living Pictures." *The Children's League of Pity Paper* 2.10 (May 1895): 82–3.

Bowen, John. "Performing Business, Training Ghosts: Transcoding *Nickleby.*" *ELH* 63.1 (1996): 153–75.

"Boy Murderers." *The Child's Guardian* 9.10 (October 1895): 134.

British Parliamentary Papers. Industrial Revolution: Children's Employment. Report from the Select Committee on the "Bill to Regulate the Labour of Children in the Mills and Factories of the United Kingdom." Volume XV – Sess. 1831–1832. Shannon, Ireland: Irish University Press, 1968.

Brown, Penny. *The Captured World: The Child and Childhood in Nineteenth-Century Women's Writing*. New York: Harvester Wheatsheaf, 1993.

Burdett-Coutts, Angela. "Our Object." *The Child's Guardian* 1.1 (January 1887): 5.

Carlyle, Thomas. *Past and Present*. London: J. M. Dent & Sons, 1960.

Carpenter, Mary. *Juvenile Delinquents: Their Condition and Treatment*. Patterson Smith: Montclair, 1970.

——. *Reformatory Schools for the Children of the Perishing and Dangerous Classes*. New York: Augustus M. Kelley Publishers, 1969.

Cobbe, Frances Power. "Wife-Torture in England." In *Criminals, Idiots, Women, and Minors: Victorian Writing by Women on Women*, edited by Susan Hamilton, 111–46. Peterborough: Broadview, 2004.

Coleridge, Samuel Taylor. "To a Young Ass: Its Mother being tethered near it." In *Awe for the Tiger, Love for the Lamb: A Chronicle of Sensibility to Animals*, edited by Rod Preece, 187–8. Vancouver: UBC Press, 2002.

Collins, Wilkie. *Armadale*. New York: Peter Fenelon Collier, n.d.

——. *Hide and Seek*. Oxford: Oxford University Press, 1993.

Cunningham, Hugh. *Children and Childhood in Western Society since 1500*. Harlow, Essex: Pearson Education Limited, 1995.

——. *The Children of the Poor: Representations of Childhood since the Seventeenth Century*. Oxford: Blackwell, 1991.

——. "The Employment and Unemployment of Children in England, c. 1680–1851." *Past and Present: A Journal of Historical Studies* 126 (February 1990): 115–50.

Cutt, Margaret Nancy. *Ministering Angels: A Study of Nineteenth-Century Evangelical Writing for Children*. Wormley, England: Five Owls Press, 1979.

Dailey, Abram. "The Conflict Between Parental Authority and the Society for the Prevention of Cruelty to Children." *Medico-Legal Journal* 10 (1892): 376–85.

Davidoff, Leonore and Catherine Hall. *Family Fortunes: Men and Women of the English middle class, 1780–1850*. London: Hutchinson, 1996.

Davin, Anna. *Growing up Poor: Home, School and Street in London, 1870–1914*. London: Rivers Oram Press, 1996.

Dean, Richard. *An Essay on the Future Life of Brutes*. In *Awe for the Tiger, Love for the Lamb: A Chronicle of Sensibility to Animals*, edited by Rod Preece, 156–7. Vancouver: UBC Press, 2002.

DeMause, Lloyd. *The History of Childhood*. New York: The Psychohistory Press, 1974.

Demers, Patricia Demers. "Puritan 'Hell-Fire': Warnings and Warmth." In *From Instruction to Delight: An Anthology of Children's Literature to 1850*, edited by Patricia Demers, 45–8. Don Mills, Ontario: Oxford University Press, 2004.

Dickens, Charles. *Barnaby Rudge*. London: The Waverly Book Company, n.d.

——. *Dombey and Son*. Harmondsworth, Middlesex: Penguin Books, 1970.

——. *Hard Times*. Peterborough: Broadview Press, 1996.

——. *Oliver Twist*. London: Penguin Books, 2002.

——. *The Life and Adventures of Nicholas Nickleby*. Hertfordshire: Wordsworth Editions Limited, 2000.

——. *The Mystery of Edwin Drood*. New York: Pantheon Books, 1980.

Donzelot, Jacques. *The Policing of Families*. Translated by Robert Hurley. London: Hutchinson, 1979.

Driver, Felix. "Moral Geographies: Social Science and the Urban Environment in Mid-Nineteenth Century England." *Transactions of the Institute of British Geographers* 13.3 (1988): 275–87.

Duckworth, Jeannie. *Fagin's Children: Criminal Children in Victorian England*. London and New York: Hambledon and London, 2002.

Dzelzainis, Ella. "Charlotte Elizabeth Tonna, Pre-Millenarianism, and the Formation of Gender Ideology in the Ten Hours Campaign." *Victorian Literature and Culture* 30.1 (2003): 181–91.

Eliot, George. "The Natural History of German Life." In *Essays of George Eliot*, edited by Thomas Pinney, 266–99. London: Routledge and Kegan Paul, 1963.

Elliot, Dorice Williams. "Servants and Hands: Representing the Working Classes in Victorian Factory Novels," *Victorian Literature and Culture* 28.2 (2000): 377–90.

Ferguson, Moira. *Animal Advocacy and Englishwomen, 1780–1900: Patriots, Nation, and Empire*. Ann Arbor: The University of Michigan Press, 1998.

Fielding, Henry. "Covent Garden." In *Awe for the Tiger, Love for the Lamb: A Chronicle of Sensibility to Animals*, edited by Rod Preece, 134–5. Vancouver: UBC Press, 2002.

Fletcher, Andrew. "The Life and Times of Benjamin Waugh" (NSPCC, 1994).

Foucault, Michel. *Discipline and Punish: The Birth of the Prison*. Translated by Alan Sheridan. New York: Vintage Books, 1979.

Frankel, Oz. *States of Inquiry: Social Investigations and Print Culture in Nineteenth-Century Britain and the United States*. Baltimore: Johns Hopkins University Press, 2006.

Hall, William Clarke. *The Law Relating to Children*. London: Stevens and Sons, Limited, 1905.

——. *The Queen's Reign for Children*. London: T. Fisher Unwin, 1897.

Hammerton, James A. *Cruelty and Companionship: Conflict in Nineteenth-Century Married Life*. New York: Routledge, 1992.

Harrison, Brian. "State Intervention and Moral Reform." In *Pressure from Without in Victorian England*, edited by Patricia Hollis, 289–322. London: Edward Arnold, 1974.

Hendrick, Harry. *Child Welfare: Historical Dimensions, Contemporary Debate*. Bristol: The Policy Press, 2003.

Herbert, Christopher. *Culture and Anomie: Ethnographic Imagination in the Nineteenth Century*. Chicago: University of Chicago Press, 1991.

Horsley, Victor. "The Morality of Vivisection." In *Animal Welfare and Anti-Vivisection 1870–1918: Nineteenth-Century Women's Mission, Volume Three: Pro-Vivisection*, edited by Susan Hamilton, 237–44. London: Routledge, 2004.

"Insurance and Suffocation in Liverpool." *The Child's Guardian* 2.22 (October 1888): 93.

Jackson, Louise. *Child Sexual Abuse in Victorian England.* London and New York: Routledge, 2000.

Jarvie, Paul A. "'Ready to Trample on All Human Law': Financial Capitalism in the Fiction of Charles Dickens." PhD diss., Tufts University, 2004.

Kant, Immanuel. "Duties Towards Animals and Spirits." In *Awe for the Tiger, Love for the Lamb: A Chronicle of Sensibility to Animals*, edited by Rod Preece, 173–4. Vancouver: UBC Press, 2002.

Kaplan, Deborah. "The Woman Worker in Charlotte Elizabeth Tonna's Fiction," *Mosaic* 18.2 (Spring 1985): 51–63.

Kay, James Phillips. *The Moral and Physical Condition of the Working Classes, Employed in the Cotton Manufacture in Manchester.* London: James Ridgway, 1832.

Kincaid, James R. *Child-Loving: The Erotic Child and Victorian Culture.* New York: Routledge, 1992.

King, Peter. "The Rise of Juvenile Delinquency in England 1780–1840: Changing Patterns of Perception and Prosecution." *Past and Present* 160 (August 1998): 116–66.

Koven, Seth. *Slumming: Sexual and Social Politics in Victorian London.* Princeton: Princeton University Press, 2004.

Laqueur, Thomas. "Bodies, Details, and the Humanitarian Narrative." In *The New Cultural History*, edited by Lynn Hunt, 176–204. Berkeley: University of California Press, 1989.

Leps, Marie-Christine. *Apprehending the Criminal: The Production of Deviance in Nineteenth-Century Discourse.* Durham and London: Duke University Press, 1992.

Mahood, Linda. *Policing Gender, Class, and Family: Britain, 1850–1940.* London: UCL Press Limited, 1995.

Malton, Nicholas. "The Story of Mary Ellen and the Founding of the New York Society for the Prevention of Cruelty to Children." http://firststop/archive/Mary.Ellen.htm.

Manning, Henry Edward and Benjamin Waugh, "The Child of the English Savage." *Contemporary Review* 49 (May 1886): 687–700.

Mayhew, Henry. *London Labour and the London Poor.* London: Penguin, 1985.

Miller, D. A. *The Novel and the Police.* Berkeley: University of California Press, 1988.

Morgentaler, Goldie. *Dickens and Heredity: When Like Begets Like.* London: Macmillan, 2000.

Murdoch, Lydia. *Imagined Orphans: Poor Families, Child Welfare, and Contested Citizenship in London.* New Brunswick, New Jersey, and London, Rutgers University Press, 2006.

"Neglect and Blindness—A Father and His Daughter Convicted." *The Child's Guardian* 7.7 (July 1893): 93.

Norton, Caroline. *A Voice from the Factories*. Oxford and New York: Woodstock Books, 1994.

NSPCC, *A History of the NSPCC: Protecting Children from Cruelty since 1884*. 2000.

——. "Courts and Children's Cases." *The Child's Guardian* 9.5 (May 1895): 64–5.

——. *Inspector's Directory*. London. National Society for the Prevention of Cruelty to Children, 1901.

——. "Links Between the NSPCC and the RSPCA." http://firststop/archive/RSPCA/RSPCA.htm.

——. "Our National Scheme." *The Child's Guardian* 6.1 (January 1892): 6.

——. "Quarterly Return of the Society's Cases." *The Child's Guardian* 5.11 (November 1891): 116.

——. "Sir Charles Warren on Our Society." *The Child's Guardian* 1.3 (March 1887): 20.

——. "The 'Morning Advertiser' On Our New Bill." *The Child's Guardian*, 2.19 (July 1888): 58.

——. "The National Society's Position in Liverpool." *The Child's Guardian* 10.3 (March 1896): 35.

——. "The System of Dealing with the Suffering Child: The 'Local' versus the 'National.'" *The Child's Guardian* 10.8 (August 1896): 109-110.

Payne, Walter. *The Cruelty Man: Actual Experiences of an Inspector of the N.S.P.C.C. Graphically Told by Himself*. London: NSPCC, 1912.

Pearson, Susan J. "'The Rights of the Defenseless': Animals, Children, and Sentimental Liberalism in Nineteenth-Century America." PhD diss., University of North Carolina, 2004.

Perkins, David. *Romanticism and Animal Rights*. Cambridge: Cambridge University Press, 2003.

Plotz, Judith. *Romanticism and the Vocation of Childhood*. New York: Palgrave, 2001.

Pollock, Linda. *Forgotten Children: Parent-child relations from 1500 to 1900*. Cambridge: Cambridge University Press, 1983.

Poovey, Mary. *Making a Social Body: British Cultural Formation, 1830–1864*. Chicago: University of Chicago Press, 1995.

Pope, Alexander Pope. "On Cruelty to the Brute Creation." In *Awe for the Tiger, Love for the Lamb: A Chronicle of Sensibility to Animals*, edited by Rod Preece, 128–30. Vancouver: UBC Press, 2002.

Prochaska, Frank. "Mary Carpenter." *Oxford Dictionary of National Biography*. http://www.oxforddnb.com/view/article/4733?docPos=1 (accessed June 2007).

Radbill, Samuel X. "A History of Child Abuse and Infanticide." In *The Battered Child*, edited by Ray E. Helfer and C. Henry Kempe, 3–17. Chicago: The University of Chicago Press, 1968.

Robson, Catherine. *Men in Wonderland: The Lost Girlhood of Victorian Gentlemen*. Princeton: Princeton University Press, 2001.

Rodensky, Lisa. *The Crime in Mind: Criminal Responsibility and the Victorian Novel*. Oxford: Oxford University Press, 2003.

Rose, Lionel. *The Erosion of Childhood: Child Oppression in Britain 1860–1918*. London and New York: Routledge, 1991.

Ross, Ellen. *Love and Toil: Motherhood in Outcast London, 1870–1918*. Oxford: Oxford University Press, 1993.

Rousseau, Jean-Jacques. *Emile, or, On Education*. London: Everyman's Library, 1974.

Ruffer, M. Armand. "The Morality of Vivisection." In *Animal Welfare and Anti-Vivisection 1870–1918: Nineteenth-Century Women's Mission, Volume Three: Pro-Vivisection*, edited by Susan Hamilton, 245–50. London: Routledge, 2004.

Schlicke, Paul. *Dickens and Popular Entertainment*. London: Allen & Unwin, 1985.

Sewell, Anne. *Black Beauty*. London: Jarrold & Sons, 1877.

Shore, Heather. *Artful Dodgers: Youth and Crime in Early Nineteenth-Century London*. Woodbridge: The Royal Historical Society, 1999.

Shuttleworth, Sally. "Victorian Childhood," Roundtable: Victorian Children and Childhood, *Journal of Victorian Culture* (Spring 2004): 107.

Smith, Lindsay Smith. "The Shoe-Black to the Crossing Sweeper: Victorian Street Arabs and Photography," *Textual Practice* 10.1 (1996): 29–55

Smith, Sheila M. "Blue Books and Victorian Novelists." *Review of English Studies: A Quarterly Journal of English Literature and the English Language* 21.81 (February 1970): 23–40.

Springhall, John. *Coming of Age: Adolescence in Britain, 1860–1960*. Dublin: Gill and Macmillan, 1986.

Stead, W. T. "The Maiden Tribute of Modern Babylon." Study Pack: The W. T. Stead Resource Site. http://www.attackingthedevil.co.uk (accessed November 2006).

Steedman, Carolyn. *Strange Dislocations: Childhood and the Idea of Human Interiority, 1780–1930*. London: Virago, 1995.

——. "The Watercress Seller" in *Reading the Past: Literature and History*, edited by Tamsin Spargo, 18–25. Basingstoke, England: Palgrave, 2000.

Stone, Lawrence. *The Family, Sex and Marriage in England, 1500–1800*. Middlesex, England: Penguin Books, 1979.

Surridge, Lisa. *Bleak Houses: Marital Violence in Victorian Fiction*. Athens, Ohio: Ohio University Press, 2005.

Toise, David W. "'As Good as Nowhere': Dickens' *Dombey and Son*, the Contingency of Value, and Theories of Domesticity." *Criticism* 41. 3 (Summer 1999): 323–48.

Tonna, Charlotte Elizabeth. *Helen Fleetwood*. London: R. B. Steeley and W. Burnside, 1841.

Trollope, Frances. *The Life and Adventures of Michael Armstrong, the Factory Boy*. London: Henry Colburn, 1840.

Turner, James. *Reckoning with the Beast: Animals, Pain, and Humanity in the Victorian Mind*. Baltimore: Johns Hopkins University Press, 1980.

Vickery, Amanda. *The Gentleman's Daughter: Women's Lives in Georgian England.* New Haven & London: Yale University Press, 1998.

Walkowitz, Judith R. *City of Dreadful Delight: Narratives of Sexual Danger in Late-Victorian London.* Chicago: University of Chicago Press, 1992.

Walton, Mrs. O. F. *A Peep Behind the Scenes.* Fairfield, IN: 1ˢᵗ World Library–Literary Society, 2005.

Waugh, Benjamin. "An Invalid Child Acrobat," *The Child's Guardian* 3.31 (July 1889): 113–14.

——. "A Righteous Call to a Universally Neglected Duty." *The Child's Guardian* 1.5 (May 1887): 34.

——. "Baby-Farming." *Contemporary Review* 57 (May 1890): 700–14.

——. "Cannibalism in England." *The Child's Guardian* 5.2 (February 1891): 9–10.

——. "Changed Children." *The Child's Guardian* 6.9 (September 1892): 118.

——. "Child Forgiveness." *The Child's Guardian* 2.14 (February 1888): 15.

——. "Child-Life Insurance." *Contemporary Review* 58 (July 1890): 40–63.

——. "Children and Street Begging." *The Child's Guardian* 5.12 (December 1891): 130.

——. "Children as Articles of Commerce." *The Child's Guardian* 4.10 (October 1890): 122.

——. "Cruelty to the High Born." *The Child's Guardian* 3.25 (January 1889): 131.

——. "Cui Bono?" *The Child's Guardian* 1.9 (September 1887): 66–8.

——. "Doing Children to Death for Money." *The Child's Guardian* 4.8 (August 1890): 85.

——. "Emancipation—Child and Parent; or, Can Bad Homes be Reformed?" *The Child's Guardian* 10.3 (March 1896): 33.

——. "Introduction." In *The Queen's Reign for Children*, by William Clarke Hall, v–xiv. London: T. Fisher Unwin, 1897.

——. "No Cruelty Here." *The Child's Guardian* 2.13 (January 1888): 4.

——. "Notes." *The Child's Guardian* 1.2 (February 1887): 14.

——. "Notes." *The Child's Guardian* 2.23 (November 1888): 107.

——. "Notes." *The Child's Guardian* 2.24 (December 1888): 119.

——. "Notes." *The Child's Guardian* 3.26 (February 1889): 25–6.

——. "Notes." *The Child's Guardian* 3.29 (May 1889): 83–4.

——. "Notes." *The Child's Guardian* 3.31 (July 1889): 124.

——. "Notes." *The Child's Guardian* 3.36 (December 1889): 224.

——. "Notes." *The Child's Guardian* 4.4 (April 1890): 43.

——. "Notes," *The Child's Guardian* 4.8 (August 1890): 91.

——. "Notes." *The Child's Guardian* 6.11 (November 1892): 136.

——. "Notes." *The Child's Guardian* 7.10 (October 1893): 134.

——. "Notes." *The Child's Guardian* 7.11 (November 1893): 149.

——. "Notes." *The Child's Guardian* 7.12 (December 1893): 165–6.

——. "Notes." *The Child's Guardian* 8.5 (May 1894): 66.

——. "Notes." *The Child's Guardian* 11.11 (October 1897): 130.

——. "Notes." *The Child's Guardian* 12.11 (November 1898): 130.

——. "Our New Year." *The Child's Guardian* 2, no. 1 (January 1888): 1–2.

——. "Police and Ill-Used Children." *The Child's Guardian* 3.28 (April 1889): 53–4.

——. "Prevention of Cruelty to Children." *The Child's Guardian* 3.32 (August 1889): 133–4.

——. "Prevention of Cruelty to Children." *Dublin Review* 110 (January 1892): 140–51.

——. "Punishments." *The Child's Guardian* 6.7 (July 1892): 94.

——. "Rod-pain as Educator." *The Child's Guardian* 10.10 (October 1896): 134.

——. "School Teachers and the Society." *The Child's Guardian* 7.2 (February 1893): 16.

——. "Some Conditions of Child Life in England." London: National Society for the Prevention of Cruelty to Children, 1889: 1–14.

——. "Street Children." *Contemporary Review* 53 (June 1888): 825–35.

——. "The Dawn of Justice to Little Children." *The Child's Guardian* 3.25 (January 1889): 125.

——. "The Morals of the Young – A New Departure." *The Child's Guardian* 7.10 (October 1893): 134.

——. "The Rights of the Working Man." *The Child's Guardian* 4.8 (July 1890): 81.

——. "The Story of the Shrewsbury Case." *The Child's Guardian* 1.2 (February 1887), 9–10.

——. Untitled editorial. *The Child's Guardian* 1, no. 1 (January 1887):1–2.

Wiener, Joel H. "Introduction." In *Papers for the Millions: The New Journalism in Britain, 1850s to 1914*, edited by Joel H. Wiener, xi–xix. New York: Greenwood Press, 1988.

Wiener, Martin. *Men of Blood: Violence, Manliness and Criminal Justice in Victorian England*. Cambridge: Cambridge University Press, 2004.

Wolff, Larry. "'The Boys are Pickpockets, and the Girl is a Prostitute': Gender and Juvenile Criminality in Early Victorian England from *Oliver Twist* to *London Labour*." *New Literary History* 27.2 (1996): 227–49.

Wollstonecraft, Mary. *Original Stories from Real Life*. Otley: Woodstock Books, 2001.

Wood, J. Carter. "A Useful Savagery: The Invention of Violence in Nineteenth-Century England." *Journal of Victorian Culture* 9.1 (Spring 2004): 22–42.

Woolf, Virginia. "Modern Fiction." In *The Common Reader*, 150–158. New York: Harcourt, 1925.

——. "Mr. Bennett and Mrs. Brown." In *Collected Essays: Volume 1*. New York: Harcourt, 1925.

Zelizer, Viviana A. *Pricing the Priceless Child: The Changing Social Value of Children*. Princeton: Princeton University Press, 1985.

Index